THE 'BAD' GIRL'S GUIDE TO ~~GOOD~~ Better

THE 'BAD' GIRL'S GUIDE TO ~~GOOD~~ *Better*

A stealth-help guide to getting your act together

CASEY BEROS

murdoch books
Sydney | London

Published in 2021 by Murdoch Books, an imprint of Allen & Unwin

Copyright © Casey Beros

All rights reserved. No part of this book may be reproduced or transmitted in any form or by any means, electronic or mechanical, including photocopying, recording or by any information storage and retrieval system, without prior permission in writing from the publisher. The Australian *Copyright Act 1968* (the Act) allows a maximum of one chapter or 10 per cent of this book, whichever is the greater, to be photocopied by any educational institution for its educational purposes provided that the educational institution (or body that administers it) has given a remuneration notice to the Copyright Agency (Australia) under the Act.

Murdoch Books Australia
83 Alexander Street, Crows Nest NSW 2065
Phone: +61 (0)2 8425 0100
murdochbooks.com.au
info@murdochbooks.com.au

Murdoch Books UK
Ormond House, 26–27 Boswell Street, London WC1N 3JZ
Phone: +44 (0) 20 8785 5995
murdochbooks.co.uk
info@murdochbooks.co.uk

A catalogue record for this book is available from the National Library of Australia

A catalogue record for this book is available from the British Library

ISBN 978 1 92235 120 3 Australia
ISBN 978 1 91166 805 3 UK

Cover and text design by Emily O'Neill
Typeset by Midland Typesetters, Australia
Printed and bound in Australia by Griffin Press

The content presented in this book is meant for inspiration and informational purposes only. The author and publisher claim no responsibility to any person or entity for any liability, loss or damage caused or alleged to be caused directly or indirectly as a result of the use, application, or interpretation of the material in this book.

10 9 8 7 6 5 4 3 2 1

The paper in this book is FSC® certified. FSC® promotes environmentally responsible, socially beneficial and economically viable management of the world's forests.

For Lala

Learn from the mistakes of others.
You can't live long enough to make them all yourself.
— **Eleanor Roosevelt**

CONTENTS

Introduction:	Harnessing Your (B)advantage	1
Lesson 1:	Make Peace with Your Past *You are not your mistakes*	7
Lesson 2:	Forgive Your Parents *They did their best*	18
Lesson 3:	Stop Worrying *No one knows WTF they're doing*	27
Lesson 4:	Get a Grip on Your Emotional Intelligence *You are in charge here*	49
Lesson 5:	Be Your Own BFF *Stop being such a c*nt to yourself*	61
Lesson 6:	Be Kind to Your Body *It's the only one you've got*	80
Lesson 7:	Rein in the Drinking *Alcohol makes you do stupid things*	97
Lesson 8:	Get Smart About Money *The best kind of freedom is financial*	111
Lesson 9:	Being Good in Bed Is Easy *But loving sex is hard*	132
Lesson 10:	Let Go of the Idea of 'the One' *Embrace all of your 'ones' instead*	150
Lesson 11:	Friends Are Like Wine *They make everything feel better*	164

Lesson 12:	Know That Things Will Go Wrong	
	Embracing the darkness of the bad times	174
Lesson 13:	What You Need to Know About (Professional) Success	
	Someone has to win, so it may as well be you	203
Lesson 14:	Get Good at Conflict	
	How to have tough conversations	234
Lesson 15:	Forget Fame	
	Being 'average' is more than okay	244
Lesson 16:	Spend Your Life with Someone Kind	
	It's the best decision you'll ever make	257
Conclusion:	Build a Life You'll Be Proud Of	269

Acknowledgements	273
Support services	277
Good things to get your eyes and ears around	279
Bibliography	283
Index	287

Introduction
Harnessing Your (B)advantage

Hands up if you've ever done something you're not proud of, hurt someone you cared about, made a mistake, kept a secret or just plain fucked up—and it made you feel bad about yourself. If I had five hands, they would all be in the air right now. Me—and most people I know. And possibly you too.

For the longest time I thought I was the only one grappling with my 'bad' side. Good me valued kindness, trust and respect, yet bad me gossiped, slept with (all of) the wrong people and put others down under the guise of humour. The truth is, though, that we all act in ways that aren't aligned with our values sometimes. Good people do bad things every day for a whole range of reasons. Sometimes the environment is bad, or the rules are bad—or we simply make a bad judgement call. We cheat, lie and steal. We hurt the people closest to us and complete strangers alike. But we don't do it because we're awful—we do it because we're human.

It could be driven by lust, hunger, fury, boredom or because we just need a break from all of the thinking and striving and being and doing. Sometimes it's because we need to push the boundaries, test our values and see what else is out there so we can stop asking, 'Is this it?' A bit of bad is what breaks rules and makes new ones, and drives scientific progress, economic advancement and social change. Just ask Frida Kahlo, Amelia Earhart, Ruth Bader Ginsburg, Coco Chanel, Malala Yousafzai or Elizabeth Taylor—I mean, Liz was married eight times to seven men, because why the fuck not.

But here's the thing: the only person who gets to decide what is 'good' or 'bad' for you, is you. You decide if 'good' and 'bad' even exist, and if they do, how you define them. That definition will depend on many things—your culture, religion or spirituality, the state of the society into which you were born and how you were raised, as well as your influences and friends—and your take on it will change over time. The last thing this book is about is telling you not to be rebellious, empowered and independent—I literally live for that shit. Instead, my aim is to help you question some of the more self-destructive patterns that might be holding you back, while still celebrating everything that is perfectly imperfect about you.

Here's why … When I was growing up I felt like everyone else had it together, that I was the only one flailing around like an idiot. I was desperate to arrive at true adulthood: that magical place where you can afford Aesop hand soap and where you look, feel and behave better than ever because you know all the things. The place where life looks like you thought it would. But now I know that we're all just doing our best to survive, while wondering if there's some magical life secret we haven't been let in on. If only we could get our hands on it, surely it would throw open the door to our wildest dreams, truest love, most mind-blowing success and ultimate self-love, right? But we can't crack the code. And that, my friend, is because 'the code' is bullshit—it doesn't exist.

The truth is, you will never have it all together. Not after you read this book, or any book. We can pay every life/business/wellness coach, have shares in the self-help genre and stuff 57 steps into our morning routine, but we still won't be able to figure everything out. And we're not supposed to, because once we do, the game is over. That said, there comes a moment in everyone's life when they decide it's time to get their shit together. We get sick of being broke, lonely and mistaken for a doormat. We have enough of waking up hungover, wriggling out from under Tom/Tim/Tammy's arm before slipping out the door, and spending our rent money on shots. We recognise that the only person who is going to build us an amazing life, is us.

If you've really lived your life so far, there will have been times when you've failed, faltered and fucked things up. This book is about helping you make peace with the parts of yourself you would prefer the world didn't see—the bits that make you terrified you'll be 'found out'. Found out for not being good enough at your job, or for not being a good enough friend/daughter/person. The bits that make you feel like you're 'bad'. Before anyone chases me out of town with a pitchfork, know this: I'm not talking about what society once deemed 'bad'. I don't care how many people you sleep with, whether you eat Dexamphetamines (that's speed, for kids) for breakfast or if you rock up to family Christmas so hungover you have to spend the entire day lying down (no idea who did that,

BTW). I'm talking about the sort of behaviour that makes you feel shitty about yourself.

You see, I've made a lot of mistakes. Some I made a few times just to make sure I'd really clocked them. And for the longest time they all contributed to a huge amount of shame that coloured my perception of who I was. It felt like I was wearing a thick winter jacket in a swimming pool, and no matter how hard I tried, I could barely keep my head above water. I based how I felt about myself on what I believed other people thought of me, outsourcing something that should—and can—only come from within. I was forever hunting for validation from external sources—relationships, professional success, praise from my boss and even 'likes'—in an effort to overcome who I used to be and run as fast as possible in the direction of who I wanted to become.

But no matter what I do, I can't erase who I was. The bad bits are a part of me, just as much as the good and the great bits. They need to coexist, and in fact, rather than beat myself up, I look back and see how far I've come. I don't shy away from the bad bits, I embrace them, celebrate them even. So, if you've ever failed, fucked up or felt bad about yourself, this book is for you. You are not broken, and you deserve every happiness and success, no matter where you've come from.

A teacher once told me I ask too many questions. I asked how she defined 'too many' and then turned it into my career. In all my questions I've found some answers, and I'm sharing them with you so you don't have to look as hard for them as I had to. What I've learned is that, while no one has it 100 per cent together 100 per cent of the time, there are a few tricks that make navigating life a little easier. As such, I've broken this book into sixteen lessons

I wish I'd learned sooner. It is by no means an exhaustive summary, but we will cover the themes that have surfaced again and again in my life, in my work and in the world around me. And if you take them on board, I suspect you'll be about 10,652 steps ahead of where I was when I was younger. So, you're basically already killing it.

If you think I'm going to get all self-help-y on you, know this: I don't blame you for wanting professional success without giving up Netflix, for wishing you could feel awesome in a bikini without giving up dessert and for wanting all the opportunities without really having to put yourself out there. I'm grateful as hell but living is hard, and 'doing the work' is not the path of least resistance. Most of us are inherently lazy despite the 4000 things on our to-do list, and if I'm honest, half of me wants to hustle to build an amazing life and the other half just wants to binge-watch other people living theirs.

But you deserve whatever you want out of life, and this book is about helping you get it (and making sure you have a bloody good time along the way). As for all those things you wish you hadn't done? You're about to learn how to use them to your (b)advantage.

See this book as a giant glass of wine that soothes your soul, makes you giggle and maybe alters your perspective on the most important relationship in life: the one with yourself. Because life is a shitload easier when you have your own back. I've designed it to be read cover to cover, but also so you can double back to the chapter you need at any moment in time. Not everything will be for everyone, but I encourage you to try the concepts on—take them for a walk around the block and see how they feel.

You ready? Line 'em up and let's get this party started.

PS: This book covers challenging topics such as sexual assault, abortion, mental illness and suicide. I'll give you a heads-up at the beginning of those chapters in case you want to skip ahead.

PPS: Before we get started, I want to acknowledge the privileged position from which I wrote this book. I am a cisgender, heterosexual white woman, living in one of the most developed countries on the planet. I have a family who loves me, a healthy body and mind* and enough money to afford a mortgage (lucky me), child care and occasionally something from Target. I recognise the limitations of this lens and apologise for any unintentional bias in the text. Also, while I refer to 'he' and 'she' throughout, please know that no matter what body you came in, who you identify as or which pronouns you use, everyone is welcome here.

---

* debatable

Lesson 1
Make Peace With Your Past

You are not your mistakes

I believe firmly in reinvention, which is lucky because when I was younger I was a fucking nightmare. Now I understand that we are supposed to go through renovations, upgrades and even the occasional backward slide in life. But at a micro level, we forget that we're allowed to choose who we want to be, every single day. Okay, so you can't choose to be Beyoncé, but you can choose to be a boss. You can't choose to be Michelle Obama, but you can choose to be informed. And you can't choose to be Oprah, but you can choose to be inspirational.

You can also choose to be a psychopath like my alter ego, Lola. She's still in there, though she's pretty much retired now. But before she hung up her glittery high tops, anything could happen on her watch. She could be fun and cool and sexy, but she could also be tipsy and dangerous and annoying. Casey got invited to parties, but sometimes Lola would tackle, bind and gag her before throwing her in the trunk of a car and turning up in her place, cackling like Harley Quinn.

Many years ago, when I was in my early twenties, I went to a party, where a much older man (who, side note, was a family friend whose kids were my mates) tried to kiss me. I felt cornered, awkward and dirty. What is it with men (especially of the rich, powerful variety) thinking they can take whatever they want, especially from young girls? I escaped to the beach with a handful of friends, ready to blast that experience right out of my psyche the only way I knew how. I hadn't clocked that we were jumping on a friend's boat (the rich kid's version of jumping on the bus) and getting out of there altogether, but I no longer cared—anywhere was better than there.

We motored across to a secluded bay where we knew we wouldn't cause too much of a ruckus to nearby boats and houses with our music and skulduggery (I say that like I had any sway in where we went or any idea what was going on). After we moored I went to open a beer off the table on the back of the boat—putting the lip of the cap on the edge of the table and then banging the top of the beer to get the lid off. The owner of the boat saw what I was about to do and understandably told me off. He'd been kind enough to take me on his (lovely and probably very expensive) boat and here I was using it as a giant bottle opener.

I felt my cheeks go hot and prickly and I wanted to evaporate, but instead I chose the next best option, which was to strip and swim. I'm not sure what my plan was—to swim to shore and then get a cab home, I suppose … sopping wet, in my undies, with no phone and no money. The trouble with my genius plan was that we were moored in a bay at the bottom of a cliff, so there was no 'shore'.

Now, your girl can swim (school swim champ seven years in a row, thank you very much) but even at 5 per cent brain capacity I knew I was in no position to make it further than a few protest laps around the boat. I had no choice but to come back to the vessel with my wet tail between my legs. Face, meet palm.

Older me knows that what happened with Creepy McCreep wasn't my fault. And, while I take full responsibility for acting like a twit afterward, I want to acknowledge that good people don't usually act badly for no reason. There's often hurt, shame, fear—something—driving them. It's not a get-out-of-jail-free card, but it's reality. This was far from the worst thing I've done (it's more embarrassing than anything else) but luckily for me, I subscribe wholeheartedly to the notion that reinvention is your right. So, the only way for me from there, was up. Then down, backward, forward, backward, more backward, around the corner, up a little bit and then down again. But, over time, loosely trending up.

We all carry around secrets and experiences that bring with them an epidemic of shame—an insidious disease that rots our self-worth, self-esteem and self-compassion from the inside out. It makes you believe that the 'real' you is faulty, so you keep it hidden away with your secrets and create a new persona so you can keep existing. The shame is always there, but you figure if you bury it deep enough and make up for it in other areas of your life, it'll cancel out—but it never quite does. The only way to truly move forward is to make peace with the past; to acknowledge and accept that every living thing casts a shadow, and you don't get the light without the darkness. Also known as easier said than done.

You've probably heard of shame researcher and Oprah favourite Brené Brown. If you haven't, YouTube her TED talks and

Netflix special immediately. Brené is an old-school bad girl. I know this because she gave up drinking 25 years ago, and usually that's something only people who've done some bad shit do. Instead, she has poured the past couple of decades into researching shame and its capacity to derail us. She says shame makes you feel that you as a human entity are awful and beyond repair—unworthy of love, success or connection. It's the thing that tells you you're not good enough, that knows your secrets and threatens to expose them. It's dangerous and damaging, and, Brown says, linked to addiction, depression, violence, aggression, bullying, suicide and eating disorders.

But we are so much more than the secrets we keep

You know how squirrels carry nuts around in their cheeks? They gobble them up and then use their little cheeks as storage until they get home or to the squirrel markets or wherever. I used to do that with secrets. My friends and I had a joke where I would pretend to pop nuts into my mouth and then blow my cheeks out to symbolise my squirrelling away whatever naughty things I had recently done. We would all laugh, but deep down I knew those secrets were significantly affecting my happiness— I felt like I was drowning in them. And I thought I was all alone.

I lived in near-constant fear of being found out, of the subsequent rejection that would inevitably come when people learned who I 'really' was because of the mistakes I'd made. Rather than feel guilty that I *did* something bad, I thought I *was* bad, also known as textbook shame. Now I know that everyone has secrets. You, me, Oprah, your boss, your mum, my mum—everyone. In fact, 97 per cent of us will have at least one big secret at any time, and the average person has thirteen—five of which they have never told anyone.

The secret life of us

We carry our secrets around in emotional backpacks that weigh us down, big time. But we keep them for good reasons—usually because we're trying to protect ourselves or people we care about. So, we wrap up our secrets and lock them away before swallowing the key, hoping no one finds them. However, because of the potential threat they represent (by way of rejection, hurt feelings or social suicide), our brain hunts them down frequently, making sure they're still where we left them and that no one has found them. It's like holding on to something valuable: it burns a hole in your pocket until you can get rid of it. But secrets stay with us—sometimes forever.

The study of secrecy is evolving, but it appears that there's a reason holding on to them feels crappy—secrets can hurt our health, damage our relationships and make us depressed and anxious. A group of researchers at Columbia University has studied secrecy in depth and found that the poison isn't the act of hiding the secret, but rather how frequently we think about it. You know, when you're doing the dishes and your mind flicks over to that thing you feel awful about, for no reason. When you're driving home from the shops and all of a sudden you're thinking about that thing you should have said but didn't. Or when you're in a work meeting and can't for the life of you focus on what's being said because you're thinking about that time you stole silkworms when you were in Year Two.

Adult secrets probably carry more weight than stuffing a few silkworms up your sleeve and making a run for it (I'd like to take this opportunity to formally apologise to Mr Schmidt and also the worms), but whether it's sexual or emotional infidelity, driving your car after too many mojitos or pilfering toilet paper from work—everyone is hiding something. We're quick to judge ourselves (and others) but forget that fucking things up is just part of being human. It's not an invitation to go rogue and hurt people, but it's an important reminder that we're all in the same, screwed-up boat.

Getting a grip on your 'bad'

Once the damage is done, we don't have control over what we did or what other people might think of it—we only have control over how we allow it to make us feel about ourselves, and our capacity to make amends where we can. And if it plagues us (as negative thoughts have the tendency to do) we can start to think of our secrets as an undercover report card—one that reflects the 'real' us that we have to keep hidden from the world.

German philosopher Friedrich Nietzsche espoused that there is no such thing as right and wrong, that we should make our own rules. I disagree—there are some things that are absolutely wrong: acts of terrorism, taking a life, hurting a child. But sometimes we judge our behaviours too harshly and punish ourselves unfairly for them because we are following other people's rules rather than our own. Knowing that almost everyone is carrying secrets around should bring us some comfort. We just have to learn to live with them better.

How to coexist with the skeletons in your closet

Regrets? I have a few (dozen). But given I can't go back and change things, I will have to settle for learning to forgive myself for, or at least coexist with, my mistakes. After all, they've made me who I am today—just as yours have. To make peace with our past we need to learn to put our secrets to bed, even (and especially) if the person we are now doesn't agree with what we did back then. You're probably no stranger to your brain acting like a homing pigeon to unresolved personal issues, distracting you from the present and transporting you to either a past mistake or its future ramifications. This can be incredibly damaging to our sense of self, because feeling like we're hiding something and living in fear of people's judgement is, quite frankly, exhausting.

'You have to disassociate yourself because you can't control other people's perception of you,' sexologist and relationship expert Dr Nikki Goldstein tells me. 'If you kept a secret because you didn't want to hurt somebody, then you need to find a way to make peace with that secret. And if something does get out and you're dealing with people judging you for that, then you have no control over that situation and nor is it your place to change their judgement.

'Infidelity happens, shit happens, people fuck up, they don't always do morally what is the right thing, and that is the society we live in. Those people that are judging you are not perfect and will have done something in their own life. That's kind of one of the realities of the #grownupworld.'

These words are like gospel to me, yet it took me many (many) years to learn them, and I still sometimes forget. What I do know is that the sooner you can learn to do this next bit, the better off you'll be.

Chuck it in the fuck-it bucket and move on

Imagine you're a small child who's just done a poo on the floor. You know defecating on the new plush pile is bad but holy hell you needed to go and you just couldn't get your tiny legs to the potty in time. You're in big trouble, Mum is upset and Dad sticks you in the naughty corner. You cry like a banshee but you do your time, then you move on. You don't wallow in your shame around being a human Mr Whippy—you just huff and puff for a few minutes and then get on with it.

As adults, we tend to punish ourselves harder. Delve into your secret chamber and fish something out for me. Maybe you fell over and landed on the wrong penis. Perhaps you never had a conversation you needed to have and then it was too late. Or maybe you didn't treat someone fairly, and you know they deserved better. Now, let's practise letting it go. Trust me when I say I know this is easier said than done. I still grapple with the idea of what people think of me for the dumb things I've done. While the person who made those decisions is completely different to the woman I am today, modern-day me still has to clean up my worst self's mess—even if it's just in my head.

I believe there are eight vital steps to moving past something you feel bad about.

1. **Stop judging yourself so harshly.**

    Are you human? If you answered 'yes', then welcome to the world's least exclusive club—the people-who-fuck-things-up-occasionally club. In here, you'll find pretty much everyone you've ever met, so you're in good company.

2. **Separate what you've done from who you are.**

    Believe it or not, these two things are not the same. Who you are is your spirit, your resilience, your generosity—it can't be taken away. What you've done is transient, like the clothes you wear. That was then and this is now.

3. **Ask yourself: Is the punishment worth the crime?**

    In other words, do you think you've maybe tortured yourself enough? I'm going to guess you probably have, in which case, it's time to let yourself off the hook.

4. **Find the positive.**

    Maybe you learned something. Maybe it brought you empathy and understanding for other people who make mistakes, making you an excellent agony aunt for the fallen. Either way, there's probably a silver lining if you look hard enough.

5. **Rewrite the script.**

    Embrace the fact that you have the opportunity to change how you feel about your mistake moving forward. Just because you've spent a long time feeling a certain way about something (or talking to yourself in a certain way about it) doesn't mean you don't get to change.

6. **Apologise.**

    First, apologise to yourself for doing something that has since caused you distress. You didn't know then what you know now, and that's worth acknowledging. Then, apologise to whomever you affected, even if it's just putting it out to the universe rather than to them directly (because I know firsthand that some secrets have the capacity to blow up people's lives). Say it out loud, write it down—just get it out of your head and your heart.

7. **Lighten the load.**

    Talking it out with a professional or a trusted confidant who will listen and love you anyway is vital—because shame can't survive empathy. Just know that sharing might also make you feel vulnerable and exposed, so choose the right person to share with. Then feel the weight lift off your shoulders.

8. **Break the habit.**

    When the memory pops up again (and it will), acknowledge you can still feel bad about it, but remind yourself that you've done your time and that the only person you're still hurting by holding on to it, is you.

Just quietly, I think people who say they have 'no regrets' are liars. Everyone I know has regrets, even if they don't lose sleep over them. What I want you to remember, though, is that you are not your mistakes. They are just things you've done, nestled in among all of the good things and the amazing things, the silly things and the dumb things. They are part of what make you who you are, and you learn more from them than you'll ever learn from the things you get right.

Bad-to-better takeaways

- Be okay with those skeletons in your closet—literally everyone has them, so you are far from alone. Think of them as really skinny mates who taught you something.
- The best thing about coming from a baseline of bad is that the only way to go is up.

- If you're still agonising over things you've done 'wrong'—chuck it in the fuck-it bucket and move on. You've done your time.
- You get to choose who you want to be, every single day. Today, I'm choosing to be someone who doesn't wear pants, and that's okay.

Lesson 2
Forgive Your Parents
They did their best

Regardless of whether you had a run-of-the-mill upbringing, an amazing one, or one you'd rather leave in the dust, it has had a hand in making you into the person you are today. You know, like whether you're a dancing-on-the-tables kinda gal or the one quietly enjoying a Chablis in the corner. In order to make peace with the past and move forward we need to have a firm grasp of where we've come from, so we can keep the bits that help us and get over the bits that don't. But before we delve into your background, I should probably share a glimpse into mine.

Disclaimer: I'm not a fan of blaming parents for screwing up their kids. I adore my parents and have an excellent relationship with both of them. I'm grateful for their time and energy in raising me and for a long time have seen them for what they are: human beings who are strong and smart and kind but also flawed and just doing their best. You should forgive yours, too—just so you're not a hypocrite when you unintentionally but inevitably do the same thing to your own kids one day.

Welcome to the big 'bad' world

My mum is one of those people who says giving birth is orgasmic, which may go some way to explaining why I never felt compelled to squeeze a human out of my vagina (I've had two, and they both came out the sunroof). I know that when she met my dad they loved each other, purely based on how much they dislike each other now, but they broke up when I was really young, so I don't have memories of them together.

Even though they despised each other, I had two parents who adored me, which is more than a lot of people can say. I shuttled back and forth between two homes, two beds, two rooms, and two sets of rules, values and beliefs. At Dad's I had a menagerie of animals to keep me company: a cat called Chookie, several budgerigars (which I would breed and sell to pet shops with healthy entrepreneurial spirit), some quails and what started as two but ended up as eight rabbits (before Dad released them into the wild because they were multiplying exponentially, single-handedly starting a local rabbit infestation). My pride and joy, though, was a labrador named Commond. Yes—like 'common' with a 'd'. 'Cool name!' no one says. The jury is still out on where this came from. I'm certain I named him Commond because I'd just got my first bank account with what I was convinced was the Common-d-wealth Bank and was adamant my dog be named after my new-found interest in finance. Dad says it's because I was obsessed with the TV show *Full House* and they had a dog called 'Comet'—but try telling that to a six-year-old.

Life with Dad was full of wonder. He took delight in teaching me things, using letterboxes to help me learn to count and spreading out hundreds of toothpicks attached to tiny Australian flags on our kitchen table, grouping them in different variations to teach me multiplication. I didn't care that he couldn't get me to school on time (or some days, at all). He made me feel smart and encouraged my rampant curiosity. He spoke to me like I was a grown-up, and we would spend hours talking about the world and reading grown-up books. He would roll around in sarongs, sending my female teachers and the school mums into a frenzy, and getting into trouble with one or more of them, more than once.

I can only imagine how hard co-parenting was pre- FaceTime, WhatsApp or any form of social media. If Mum wanted to talk to me she had to ring on the landline (that's a 'house phone' if you were born after the year 2000) and hope we were home. Dad's house was an eclectic, bohemian mix of interesting folk. The neighbourhood kid-gang and I would 'hit the town' with no shoes and barely enough street smarts to cross the road, but they were different times—when you could ride your bike in the street and disappear for hours as long as you were home by dark.

There was a bit of a choose-your-own-adventure vibe at Mum's too, with her working a lot. She had to—she had two kids to provide for so just rolled up her sleeves and got on with it. Mum has always had an inspirational work ethic. She has gumption, even in the moments when life has dealt her a less than stellar hand. My sister (same mum, different dad), who is fourteen years older than me, was already trying to navigate the rocky road that is teenage-dom and find her way in the world, and couldn't go anywhere without toddler-me. I would tag along to her boyfriend's house (whose family I loved), but while my sister had pretty good taste in men, it wasn't necessarily genetic.

One especially weird douche canoe my mum went out with was good for one thing, though. He promised me a pony, and after he and Mum broke up before I got the chance to secure my steed, I told Mum that 'a promise was a promise' and asked her to drive my nine-year-old arse to his house. I knocked on his door and politely demanded he come good on his promise of said pony. And to his credit, he did. A month or so later, 'Misty' would be mine. She was a white part-Arabian part-lunatic that tried to buck me off every 30 seconds, and I loved her. Moral of the story? You don't ask, you don't get.

It's worth noting here that Mum is an OG bad girl, which in my study population of one proves it's genetic. Kicked out of her private girls' school for failing the kneel-to-see-if-your-skirt-touches-the-floor test enforced by the nuns (naughty), she got married and had a baby at seventeen (naughtier) before getting divorced and travelling the world as a model in her heyday of the 1970s and 1980s (where, I imagine, she was inconceivably naughty). She didn't even know she was pregnant with me until she was six months along, and I'm pretty sure the only prenatal vitamins she had taken until that point didn't come from the pharmacy. She wonders where I get it from, yet it is literally in my genes.

The world taught Mum that her greatest asset was how she looked, something she (unconsciously) passed on to me. I think many parents take delight in their kids' beauty and youth, which can sexualise them in a way I don't think is intentional, but for me it felt like the idea was something to aspire to, and so I enjoyed the attention of people commenting on my physicality even though I didn't really understand the implications. My body and behaviour wanted to grow up faster than my brain was capable of safely managing, and, looking back, no one was ready to catch me when I inevitably fell. More on that later.

Getting a grip on what makes you, you

It's undeniable that our genes and environment have an impact on our sense of self, so it is worth knowing a bit about yours and considering how they might have affected you up to this point. You had no jurisdiction over your environment in your early life, and the make-up of your genes will help explain some of those traits over which you have no control, like your less-than-ideal hairline or that ridiculous snort you do when you laugh too hard. It's easy to think that these early determinants will dictate whether your developing brain becomes a strong foundation for lifelong learning, good behaviour and thriving health, or a puddle of mush that's destined for smoking bongs and a lifelong relationship with Centrelink. But the good news is you have *way* more control over that than you think you might.

You'll be familiar with the fact that we are born with genes that predispose us to particular conditions (such as BRCA genes giving us a higher risk of breast or ovarian cancer, as well as our eye colour, blood type and height). But you might be surprised to learn that they also play a role in our behaviours including important stuff like how good we are at learning. We used to think our genes were our destiny, but now we know that because of something called 'epigenetics' many genes can be switched on or off and turned up or down (kind of like the volume on your car radio) through experiences, particularly during our developmental years. While our DNA is fixed (like the text of this book), epigenetics is like taking a highlighter and marking a section on it. It's not easy to do, but change is possible—and for many of us, that's good news.

You are basically a pizza

Your genes are the dough, your environment is how that dough was raised and your experiences are the toppings. Let me explain.

If you think of yourself as a lump of dough (not because you had too much fun at that music festival, though that is probably an issue and the reason you can no longer remember the upper end of your 7x tables) ready to be shaped and baked, your genes are the ingredients that went into it: the flour, water, eggs, yeast and salt. Those could be carefully selected organic, biodynamic, grown-on-the-Peruvian-hillside ingredients from Wholefoods, or one of those frozen numbers that was almost out of date and on special.

Then, it's all about your environment. If your parents or carers roll and knead the dough well, cover it and let it rise somewhere warm before spinning it out like Luigi, that's good. If they scrunch it up twice with dirty hands and drop it on the floor before throwing it uncovered into the fridge, it's not going to make-a the good pizz-a. Bear with me, because this pizza analogy is almost over and it's making me hungry, so I'll need to take a snack break soon. Your experiences are like toppings. Just like bad toppings such as anchovies and chicken can ruin a pizza, bad experiences can ruin your day, your week or in extreme cases, your life. If, however, you lovingly top it with fresh basil and mozzarella (grossly underestimated pizza champions) or good, rich, loving experiences, you've got a pretty epic pizza/life on your hands, even if you started with shitty dough. Now, if you're thinking, 'Well, my genes are average, my environment was a generous 5/10 and my experiences have probably done more harm than good'—you're not ruined. You just need new and better toppings. To get there, though, we need to take a look at your pizza.

Consider the three strongest qualities for each of your parents, things like whether they're stubborn or clever or averse to affection. If you don't know your parents and can't find out, go you—you have mystery genes and there's every chance your parents are famous genius billionaires, which will only serve you well. Instead, grab a journal, the notes section of your phone or the back of a Coles receipt and write down three traits that have been with you ever since you can remember; there's a good chance they came from your parents.

Next, let's talk about your environment. Ask yourself these questions.
1. What was home like for you when you were growing up?
2. Were there any important life events that happened either to you or around you, especially in your early life? What impact did they have?

Now, let's top that bad boy. Think about the most influential experiences in your life to date, things that shaped the way you view the world. They can be good or bad, like losing your job (or getting one), grieving a friend, your parents splitting up, having a baby, meeting the love of your life or breaking free from a shitty relationship. These have a profound impact on who we are and who we'll become.

What does this all mean?

In essence, you are programmed to behave the way you do as a result of your genes, environment and experiences. But now we know what we're working with, we can make a plan for moving forward. And don't forget—it's those exact genes and experiences that have made you who you are, and who you are is pretty special.

Think about it. Even though there are almost 7.8 billion of us and counting, it's kind of remarkable that you're here. On the day you were conceived, unless you were made in a test tube (which is its own kind of magic) your parents boned (sorry, gross but true). Millions of sperm fought each other off like they were on *The Bachelorette* to get inside that egg. There was a bloody good chance you wouldn't make it, but you did. And since then a million things could have cut your time here short, but they didn't. Your unique combination of DNA made only one version of you in the whole wide world, which makes you just as precious as someone who boasts a million Insta followers, or someone who plays to sold-out stadiums around the world. As valuable as someone who saves lives for a living, or someone in charge of running a country. As worthy as someone who carries water for miles for her family to drink, or someone who sifts through rubbish to earn a living. And as delicate as the newborn baby seeing the world for the first time, or the beloved grandmother taking her last breath.

When you were a child you had literally no control over your experiences. But now … you is grown! Which means you have the best chance you've ever had to treat yourself in ways that make you feel like a legend, regardless of what's happened up until now.

Put it all on black

The chances of you dying one day are 100 per cent; we've all gotta go sometime. But even if we live to be 100, life is unfairly short. So, until Elon Musk builds us a Tesla Time Capsule (copyright) that can stop the clock or buy us extra time, we have to make the most of what we have. Do you want the good news or the bad news? Bad news first? Good choice. The bad news is that what's done is done. And the good news? What's done is *done*. We're not kids anymore, and we're finished looking back. It's time to look forward, baby. Next, I'm going to share with you one of the most powerful lessons I have (ever) learned.

Bad-to-better takeaways

- The name of the dog on *Full House* was 'Comet'—not 'Commond'.
- Stop blaming your parents, they did their best. And if their best sucked, then good news—you're in charge now.
- You don't ask, you don't get—even when it comes to ponies.
- You have more control over how your pizza/life turns out than you might think. Just don't put anchovies on it, you sicko.

Lesson 3
Stop Worrying
No one knows WTF they're doing

Warning: This chapter deals with mental health and suicide. If you need to, please skip ahead.

Bringing your unique brand of magic to the world would be much easier if you had a linear trajectory upward from birth toward your best life. But in reality, that line looks like a toddler took a texta and drew all over the walls; there's ups and downs and squiggles and a big smear of what looks like shit but you can't be sure.

So, it's comforting to know that one of the greatest universal truths I have ever learned is this: *No one knows what the fuck they're doing.* Sure, we get better at our jobs, start to understand what works for us (sleep—yes, turquoise—no) and develop a stronger grasp of adult-y things such as politics, finance and current affairs, but most of us still don't really *know*. That influencer who appears to have your dream life? No idea. Your friend who is 'killing it'? Not a clue. Our leaders and bosses? Taking their best, educated guess. We're all just winging it.

This can be a scary premise; like, *But wait, I thought there were adults somewhere who were in charge of everything?!* But it can also be overwhelmingly empowering, because we're all in the same boat trying to operate a navigation system that's seemingly in another language and upside down. Take my friend Dr Nikki Stamp, for example. She's a cardiothoracic surgeon, which means she spends her days operating on one of the most vital organs we have. People's lives are in her hands, and for that privilege (and responsibility) she has undertaken years of training. She's a bloody good surgeon in one of the toughest professional fields there is, so give her a heart and a scalpel and she absolutely knows what she's doing—but that's not the case across every area of her life.

'I used to see getting divorced as a total failure,' she tells me. 'Because to me, a successful life included getting and staying married. But we need to take that corporate mentality away from our personal lives. When it comes to success, it's not that black and white. I don't see my divorce as a failure anymore; in fact, I won—it's a big success.'

I ask Nikki whether, given how accomplished she is, there are parts of life she does badly. 'The thing I'm not good at is taking care of myself. I put all my effort into taking care of other people and don't give myself the same attention and that means I get tired, sick, hurt and sad. It's to my detriment.'

I've heard Nikki say this a number of times over the years, so I ask why she hasn't changed it, given she's able to identify and articulate the issue. And her answer reinforces the fact that there's a gap between knowing what we need to do and actually doing it, even for really smart people.

'I think the barrier is that I'm never going to be perfect at it, so I might as well not do it,' she says. 'But it's impossible to be good at everything, so I need to learn to be good enough—to be okay with being imperfect.'

To look at Nikki's life from the outside, you would assume there's not a thing in the world that could ruffle her feathers. And yet, when it comes to what worries her on a daily basis, here's what she tells me: 'Making the wrong decisions and not being able to control my life and the outcomes of those choices—that stresses me out. Failing worries me a lot, but other people's perception of me as a failure worries me the most.'

Hold up. Let's just do a quick stocktake on Nikki. She's one of only thirteen female cardiothoracic surgeons in Australia. She's written three books, been on countless TV shows, has a highly successful podcast and tens of thousands of followers on social media. Oh, and—the best bit—she's nice. Even though I know we're all the same when it comes to having (sometimes irrational) worries, Nikki's answer still floors me, and reminds me that no matter how mature or successful or accomplished we get, there's something that unites us all.

Our brain is designed to seek out threat

Me: 'What if something happens to the girls?'

Him: 'Nothing is going to happen to the girls.'

Me, up one octave: 'You don't know that! You can't control the future!'

Him: 'That's true. But we're doing everything in our power to keep them healthy and safe.'

Me again, up two octaves: 'But don't you think X, Y and Z [insert at least three working examples here to prove point] were doing exactly that? And look what happened to them!'

Him (losing hope of winning this argument and also in humanity): 'You're right, bad things happen and we will deal with them if they ever happen to us. Now, go to sleep.'

My husband and I are very different people. I'm go-go-go, he's whoa-whoa-whoa. I'm a jet fighter pilot doing spins and backflips, he's steadily getting an A380 in the air and putting it on cruise control. I'm not saying he has it all worked out, but he knows what's important in life and doesn't sweat the small stuff, he just gets on with it, day to day, in the most peaceful and beautiful way. My brain, on the other hand, is like a dog chasing cars down the street. Each car is a worry: some I catch, others are too fast for me but I have a red-hot go at running them down anyway just to check. It operates on a worry-about-everything-now-so-you're-not-caught-unawares policy, which is: A) futile, and B) bloody exhausting.

Of course it's normal to feel concerned about certain things: the wellbeing of our loved ones or not having enough money to pay our bills, for example. Cerebrally we know that worrying about things beyond our control is a waste of time and emotional energy, but it doesn't stop us, and there's a good reason why. But before I tell you why this happens and what to do about it, let me tell you …

What not to do

Before I learned to manage my anxiety, I made *all* the mistakes. A trigger for me is social settings, because I get nervous around big groups of people even if I know them well. On days I would have to attend a wedding or party, I would be so beside myself with nerves you'd think I was about to address the nation. I hid it well, but I couldn't eat or concentrate, I just needed to get to the event so I could have a few drinks to calm myself down. There's no salve like the world's most efficient relaxant/depressant, which, for an anxious person on an empty stomach, is a recipe for fucking disaster.

By the time my brain caught up with my mouth, it was like I'd passed GO, collected $200, turned into the human version of soup and replaced my formerly knotted self with someone far too loose for anyone's good. If neuroscientists had cracked my head open they would have seen a rat lying at the bottom of one of those wheels eating peanut butter. Relieved to be rid of my usual angst, I would swing too far the other way.

'It comes down to how we're wired, which is for survival,' clinical psychologist and anxiety expert Dr Jodie Lowinger explains. 'Even though our context and technology have evolved, our brain, which is of course incredible in so many ways, is still primed to focus on threats to help keep us alive.'

Lowinger is talking about what's called the negativity bias. Meaning, the brain seeks out things that give us fear and anxiety so we can stay safe. If we still lived on the land, where real and lethal threats constantly abound, we would need to have our wits about us. But even though we're no longer in the wild, our brain can't tell the difference between real threats and the ones in our head. It considers your fear of, say, being talked about negatively at a party or wedding to be on a par with a lion chasing you down the street. While there's no big cat in sight, hormones such as adrenaline and cortisol kick in, and you pull on your activewear and get ready to *run*. This fight-or-flight response (you know, the one that makes you feel like you've drunk ten cups of coffee and are going to shit your pants) *could* save you from that pesky lion but it could also strike when you're perfectly safe, because of a fear that is either completely outside your control, or you might have made up altogether.

When you have an unending supply of worry

When I was younger I used to get this sense of impending doom and gloom. Everything would go quiet, as if I were watching a scary movie and the bad guy was about to appear. It took me a long time to understand that that feeling was anxiety, and while it's not necessarily 'normal' to experience it like that, it's oh-so-common. In fact, according to Beyond Blue, anxiety is the most common mental illness is Australia, affecting one in three women (and one in five men) in their lifetime. It affects plenty of kids, too. In young women it's actually thought to be much worse, with 64 per cent of women aged eighteen to 35 feeling nervous, anxious or on edge nearly every day or at least weekly according to the 2019 Jean Hailes Women's Health Survey.

There are a couple of things that make you more vulnerable to anxiety. One is genetics, so if you have anxious family members, you're more likely to be anxious too. The other is going through a traumatic event. It doesn't need to be exposure to violence, sexual abuse or losing someone you love—it could be the memory of being ridiculed during 'show and tell' or being bullied by your boss. Regardless of the source, this trauma essentially puts your fight-or-flight response on speed dial. And as we all know, life has no shortage of trauma. Which means we have to learn to live with a never-ending supply of potential worry.

Seeing the 'good' in anxiety

My anxiety has driven plenty of genuinely terrible behaviour in my lifetime. But aside from turning me into a turbo bad girl, now that I've learned to harness it, I can see some of the gifts it has delivered too. One of the things that makes me anxious is the fear that people will discover that I'm not very clever/lovable/good at what I do. I'm terrified of being 'exposed', which means I want to do every task to the best of my ability, to knock it out of the park and be praised accordingly regardless of whether it's a project at work or cooking dinner for friends. This can absolutely work in my favour, helping me turn out high-quality work in my job or making a difficult process easier for my family. But it can work against me too, paralysing my progress or delaying me from having a go until I miss the boat altogether.

Lowinger says you don't have to be shaking in a corner to have anxiety, and that some of the faces of the condition might surprise you.

'Often the people I work with are high performers, phenomenal individuals—athletes, Olympians, CEOs, leading actors and singers,' she explains. 'You would think they'd be as confident as can be, but they are experiencing anxiety at all levels of severity under the surface.'

Like them, rather than fight it, we can learn to use it to our advantage.

'I think of it as a superpower,' says Lowinger. 'Let's leverage and respect the energy that comes from this deep passion, deep feelings, deep-thinking mind and recognise that yes, that can trigger emotional pain and suffering or fear and avoidance, but we can still recognise the qualities that underpin this and engage in strategies to stand up to the challenges.'

To harness it, there's one thing we need to get under control.

The worry bully

Lowinger introduces me to the concept of the worry bully, and let me tell you, the guy (or girl) sounds like a dick. We all have one—they're the thing that prevents us from going to that party or throwing our hat in the ring for that work promotion, out of fear of rejection or—heaven forbid—what people will think. And when we let the worry bully boss us around, we hold back and miss out on valuable lessons in resilience and having a go.

I am terrified of going to parties because I never have the right thing to wear or say and I feel like people are judging me, even if that couldn't be further from the truth. But these thoughts are my version of a sabre-toothed tiger. They make me notice the people sitting in the corner whispering, because it aligns to my perceived threat; I think they're talking about me even though that's unlikely to be the case. Most people are so caught up in their own world they barely think about anyone other than themselves, but—just like so many things in life—the truth is that I will never know. And is there any point in worrying about things entirely outside of our control? No!

Uncertainty is uncomfortable

Wouldn't it be awesome if you could be sure that all those amazing plans you make in life would go off without a hitch? That when you walk out the door in the morning, you're 100 per cent guaranteed to return that night? There are thousands of moments in each and every day where you don't have certainty. You don't know what's about to happen in that meeting, or whether your boyfriend is asking to catch up because he wants to see you, propose to you or ditch you. Sure, there are likely outcomes, but you don't know which is going to play out until it happens. Just ask anyone who's been blindsided by anything, ever.

Most of the time we just go about our day, though, hoping things will work out in our favour. We trust in the universe and believe—to some extent—it has our back. When you're sitting at the lights in your car and the light turns green, you don't creep out looking left and right. You just go, trusting that the people on the other side will obey the traffic rules and allow you safe passage. You don't let fear or uncertainty stop you getting from A to B—you have shit to do! And yet, many of us are terrified of flying. That big-arse plane is really heavy and high up and what if we fly into a pack of birds?! Let's look at the stats of driving versus flying. According to the Australian Bureau of Statistics, in 2019 in Australia, 1195 people died in car accidents. Want to know how many died from air travel? Thirty-five.

So, we are selectively biased with our worries, sometimes in ways that don't make sense. But because we'll never have certainty over, well, pretty much anything, we need to learn to coexist with that discomfort. And to do that, we need to have a chat with our worry bully.

Wrangling your worry bully

Getting your worries out of your head and onto paper is a simple but effective short cut to perspective. With this in mind, I want you to write down your most pressing worries, the ones that trouble you regularly or keep you up at night. Next to each one, write as a percentage how much of it is within your control. Don't overthink it, it's just a guestimate. Once you've done that, for each worry, list the aspects that are *out* of your control followed by what (if anything) is *within* it. I've done three of my (privileged) worries as examples to get you started—but everyone's worries are unique to them.

MY WORRY	% WITHIN MY CONTROL	WHAT I *CANNOT* CONTROL	WHAT I *CAN* CONTROL
Getting older/time 'running out'	0%	The tick-tock of the clock	Ageing well through regular exercise, a healthy diet and staying connected
Something awful happening to me or the people I love	50%	Natural disasters, the existence of predators, disease	Staying vigilant and keeping us all as safe and healthy as I can
Losing my job	50%	The economy shitting itself, my employer going into voluntary administration, my job being taken over by robots	Doing my job as well as I can, asking for areas to improve, upskilling with training and education

Now that you have shone a light on your biggest worries, you can see them for what they are—troublesome thoughts, even if the concerns are valid—and come up with positive ways to take away some of their power and momentum. Disclaimer:

36 THE 'BAD' GIRL'S GUIDE TO ~~GOOD~~ BETTER

Some worries are, of course, genuinely concerning. Maybe you're worried about your cancer returning, your partner hitting you again or not having enough money to cover next week's rent. I'm not suggesting you can rationalise issues like this away, but we spend a lot of time worrying about things that are out of our control and simply aren't worth worrying about, and *that* is what I'm trying to help you overcome. Life is hard enough without that shit.

Let's go worst-case scenario

Ask yourself this: What would you do if your worries materialised? Don't spend hours dwelling, but it's worth scoping out so you can see that, if it ever eventuates, you *will* cope. Many have gone before you in experiencing your exact worst-case scenario: losing their job or business, getting a life-changing diagnosis or losing a loved one. If it occurs, life will move on whether you want it to or not, and you will move forward just as they did. But you'll be one step ahead because you'll have a bit of a plan.

But what if the worst-case scenario is the genuine pits? Like, you *do* lose a loved one? As much as it sucks, the reality is that you would survive. You would be heartbroken, yes. Angry, probably. Devastated, for sure. But you would survive, even if there were moments in which you weren't sure you wanted to.

Be aware that your negative thoughts are pretty much on autopilot

We've all had the experience of driving somewhere familiar and then realising we've arrived at our destination without even really thinking about it. That is your brain on autopilot. But it doesn't just do it to nip to the shops for milk, it does it with your thoughts, too. Dr Sarah McKay is an Oxford-educated neuroscientist and author of *The Women's Brain Book*, and she tells me that thoughts become so ingrained they happen automatically.

'Worrying is basically just thinking the same thought in your imagination over and over again, you're almost practising a scenario,' she explains. 'The more you do it the easier it becomes, so then you just keep doing it until it becomes automatic and you do it without even having to try, which is a terrible state of affairs if it's a damaging or negative thought pattern. It's almost biologically embedded in you if you've been working away at it for long enough.'

If this feels familiar, you're not alone. And if you've got a PhD in talking smack about yourself, you're not alone there either. So, can we change it—even if we've been doing it forever? McKay says the brain is most plastic and open to learning new skills when we're younger, and though it gets harder to change the older we get, it's (very) possible.

'Emotion regulation and cognitive control, self-regulation to modify behaviour in response to certain situations, being flexible and resilient—they are very higher-order cognitive skills,' she explains. 'But not everyone learns them well enough in their teenage years, so you have to pick up the slack when you're older.'

Good shout, McKay. Here's how.

Living with that worrywart brain of yours

While we might not all experience an anxiety disorder, no one is immune to worry—especially if you've done things that make you feel shitty about yourself. To manage it, I like to think of the four As of Anxiety (or worry).

AWARENESS

We can only change what we're aware of, and that awareness in itself is one of the most powerful strategies for positive change. Feeling worried or anxious is a cerebral experience but you feel it in your body, so pay attention to the sweaty palms, nervous tummy and down-the-rabbit-hole feeling you get when a worry carries you away. If you can notice it and take a moment to assess it, you'll buy yourself some time to identify why you might be worrying, and then you can work out what to do with it.

ACCEPTANCE

Accept that feeling worried or anxious is okay, that you're human and that's what your brain is built to do to keep you safe. Make friends with the uncertainties of life, they're the same for all of us.

ASK

Should I be worried about this? Do I have any control over the outcome? Will worrying about it help or change anything? If the answer is no, simply acknowledge it like you would bumping into your friend's creepy cousin: with a wave from a distance. Then let it go.

ALTERNATIVE

One of the greatest aspects of life is that we almost always have a choice. So, you can choose to do what you usually do, or you can try something different, such as the following.

- **Allocate a designated worry time.** 'I'm going to let myself worry about this for the next five minutes, or for 30 minutes when I go for my walk this afternoon.' When the troublesome thought pops back up (as it will), remind yourself that you've worried about that already and it's time to move on. If the thought persists, set another designated worry time.

- **Be proactive.** If there's something you *can* do about the worry, do it. Make the call, book the appointment, have the conversation—taking action will make you feel like you've had a positive impact on something that's troubling you.
- **Find a healthy distraction.** You can't outrun your worries, but training your mind to focus on something else can help quieten them. Meditate, focus on your breath, learn a new dance move, do a puzzle or play a board game—give your brain a break by giving it something else to follow.

Remember, this stuff takes practice. You've spent years embedding old patterns, so you've got to invest some time to create new ones.

Let's work through a few common worries like the adults we are and make a pact to let them go.

Stupid shit to stop worrying about (from a stupidly privileged perspective)

WHAT OTHER PEOPLE THINK

Aside from acting like an arsehole (which I've done but don't condone) you have very little control over other people's opinions of you. Sure, it's nice to be liked, but the world is big and the number of people whose perception of you matters should be very, very small. You won't be everyone's glass of Shiraz, so try to only care about the opinions of people who count.

NOT HAVING A THIGH GAP

I'm all 'yaaaaas' when queen Bey lovingly flaunts her curves and yet when it comes to myself I still secretly want to be about as curvy as a nine-year-old boy. As I get older, though, I'm so very grateful for my body. My legs (of which I have two that diligently and loyally carry me around) are perfect for me. My tummy has given me two beautiful children and may even give me a third (jury's still out on that one). My boobs are heading south for a hacky-sack convention but they were exquisite in my younger years, and they're bloody sensational now. They've fed two human beings, and that is no mean feat. But *you* don't have to have a baby to appreciate your body, you can skip ahead and do it now because you are smart and you know that your self-worth does *not* correlate with the size of your pants.

WHOSE FAULT SOMETHING IS

We *love* playing the blame game. Because, responsibility! Fingers! Pointing! We need a scapegoat so we know whose fault it is that you and your sister aren't talking, who fucked up the presentation at work or who did/didn't remember to pick up little Billy from school. Of course, there are certain times it's important to know the answer to this, such as in the court of law, otherwise honestly—it's inconsequential. Let it go and move on.

PEOPLE NOT SHARING YOUR OPINION

There's a halfway house we're conditioned to feel very uncomfortable in when it comes to opinions: the right to agree to disagree. And that's unfortunate, because life would be so much easier if we didn't waste energy having to prove we're right all the time. Just because someone holds a different opinion to you doesn't negate yours, so don't agonise over it if someone doesn't agree with you.

YOUR PARTNER BEING UNFAITHFUL

There is no amount of worrying that is going to stop your partner from cheating on you if that's what they want to do. Yes, pay them attention and 'work on the relationship' if you're committed to it. Yes, make sure you both get laid frequently, but do it because it feels good to connect with your partner, not to stop them looking elsewhere. Worrying about and fighting with your partner over what they were doing from 12.13 a.m. to 12.39 a.m. when their 'phone died' and they seemingly forgot your number is futile. You either trust them or you don't.

WHY YOU DIDN'T GROW UP TO BE BLAKE LIVELY

This one fucks me off no end. To be hot, rich and famous is one thing, but to also be seemingly nice, funny and married to Ryan Reynolds is just plain greedy. It's an unfair fact of life that some people get really, really lucky—and that's not to take anything away from how talented they are or how hard they've worked, but there is also an element of luck required. Right time, right place, right zeitgeist shit, you know? Buy a Lotto ticket, cross your fingers and just *do your best with what you've got*. Only one person gets to be her, and it's her, so focus on being the best version of yourself instead.

AND WHILE WE'RE ON IT, NOT GROWING UP TO BE 'WHATEVER YOU WANT'

The mum in me hates myself for writing this. But, while we're closer than ever before to gender equality and less discrimination based on race or ability, the reality is that there are some things you probably can't be. Here are a few things I will never be: a pop star (I can barely hold a tune), an Olympic snowboarder (I'm allergic to the cold) or a lawyer (I don't even understand the Ts and Cs on my phone plan). I'm not saying don't shoot for the stars—please do—but also be realistic and flexible enough to allow your dream to take on a different shape to what you originally thought it might. Your life will be better for it, promise.

While the brain is one of the most perfectly designed organs we have, the user's manual is as flawed as we are. I spent many years operating on a 'do now, think later' basis (and you can guess how well that worked out), so I know firsthand that those unhealthy mental habits are difficult to break. Sure, no one knows WTF they're doing, but that doesn't mean we can't upgrade that operating system a little bit so we can still live a kick-arse life. And in the next chapter, we'll start to learn how.

Before we get there, though, how do you know if your worry is something to worry about?

Did you know that, according to Australian statistics, if you're aged between fifteen and 44 and a woman, you're most likely to die from (in order of frequency) suicide, 'accidental poisoning' (that's poisoning yourself with drugs, prescription meds or too much vodka) or in a car accident. Just to make sure you clocked that—the *number one* reason women (and men, while we're at it) between the age of fifteen and 44 in Australia die is by choice. Not cancer, not car accidents—suicide. Even more troubling is the fact that of the more than 3000 Australians who died by suicide in 2017, many more attempted it—65,000 people, in fact.

Now, these stats aren't new. We hear them a lot, then tuck them neatly into a 'best not to think about' drawer and close it—out of sight, out of mind. But I don't know anyone who hasn't been affected by suicide, and I can't bear to think of how many people are walking around in so much psychological pain that they think the only answer is to not be here. You don't need to be suicidal to understand what it's like to live with mental illness, though. One in five of us will experience a mental illness (most commonly an anxiety, depressive or substance-use disorder) in any given year, and almost half of us will experience one in our lifetime—but more than half of those won't get help or treatment.

Whether it's because we're getting better at talking about it or diagnosing it more, or it's simply getting worse, rates of mental illness seem to be increasing, and the world is going through some really fucked-up shit, so we're all feeling a bit crappy. So, how do you identify in yourself whether that feeling is just a normal response to your environment or whether you need to do something about it?

'If it's something that is persistent and impacting everyday life, you need to go and talk to someone,' explains GP Dr Preeya Alexander. 'It doesn't necessarily mean you're going to be medicated or referred off anywhere, it's just someone to go, "Okay, let's keep an eye on this, let's make sure it doesn't get worse and implement some easy lifestyle changes as a first step," perhaps. If you're not feeling like your sleep is being affected, your mood is okay and you're still getting joy out of life, you can probably have a crack at managing it.'

She prescribes the following simple but effective measures for herself and all of her patients.

- **Exercise**

    A brisk walk for 30 minutes, three times a week, where you get a bit huffy and puffy. 'Regular exercise is basically how I manage my own stress levels and anxiety, and just an hour of exercise a week has been shown in studies to help prevent depression. Exercise is a beautiful way to mitigate stress and anxiety because it burns off cortisol, the hormone that makes you feel anxious and stressed.'

- **Meditate**

    Alexander says to start low and build up: 'Three times a week for five minutes is a great place to begin … Try apps like Headspace, Calm, Smiling Mind—there's a five-minute one on there called "Body scan" I get people to start with.'

- **Cut (or reduce) caffeine and booze**

    Alexander cuts booze when she's feeling anxious, and recommends her patients do the same. And, 'no more than one coffee per day if you're struggling with stress or anxiety, and nothing after 2 p.m. if night-time sleep (or lack of it) is an issue,' she says.

- **Know your triggers**

    'Actively go through your triggers and see what you can perhaps modify. One of mine when I'm feeling anxious is to stop reading the news.'

WHAT ABOUT MEDICATION?

Medication may, to some, seem like a quick and easy fix when it comes to depression and anxiety. We've long heard about a 'chemical imbalance', and given we take medication for so many other things (headache, blood pressure, contraception), why wouldn't we pop a pill when it comes to our mental health? Like the conditions themselves, the answer, Alexander says, is complex.

'I think there are still a lot of people who are reluctant to take medications despite it being warranted; fear of being a failure, stigma and fear of addiction are often factors I encounter in the clinic,' she explains. 'For mild and moderate depression, psychology and lifestyle options are shown in studies to be superior to medication alone in managing symptoms. But if you step into the kind of moderate to severe category, we know that medication is superior to the other stuff. Even in severe circumstances, medication still needs to be used in conjunction with the lifestyle interventions but we know that certainly medication can play a very important role.'

This is an approach Preeya knows inside out professionally, but has experienced personally, too.

'I had to take antidepressants when I struggled with generalised anxiety disorder over ten years ago,' she says. 'Among psychology and exercise and all the other stuff, it's probably what stopped me from potentially getting worse or even ending my life. Medication worked really well for me, among the other measures, and it's worked for many of my patients, but people kind of go, "I don't want to cop out, I want to be able to do it on my own." And I say to people, we can't all do it on our own all the time. Sometimes we've got to quieten the brain down or give it a bit of a kickstart so that the psychology, exercise, meditation, caffeine reduction (and all the other good stuff) can come in and do its job. You've got to use all the tools available to you.'

PLEASE KNOW YOU ARE NOT ALONE

Even if, for any reason, life sucks now—it gets better. And there is so much help available to bridge the gap between now and then. I know how confronting it can be to get that help, and I want to remind you that an easy and logical place to start is your GP. They can monitor you and put you on a mental-health care plan to subsidise sessions with a psychologist. It's unlikely to be free (I'm on one and I still find it expensive) but a good psychologist is worth their weight in gold. GPs can suggest psychologists they work closely with, which is great, but if you see a psych who doesn't hit the mark for you, see someone else. Keep going until you find someone you click with.

Lifeline has 24/7 counselling available on 13 11 14, as does Beyond Blue on 1300 22 46 36, or you can chat to them online at www.beyondblue.org.au/get-support/get-immediate-support—I've also put a list of resources at the back of this book.

Bad-to-better takeaways

- Worries are designed to keep us safe and our brains are designed to hunt them, but that doesn't mean they get to rule your life.
- Get your worries out of your head and onto paper to work out whether they're justified or futile—that will inform how much oxygen you give them.
- Be okay with uncertainty—you literally have no choice.

- Remember the four As of Anxiety: Awareness, Acceptance, Ask, Alternative.
- You've spent many years embedding old patterns and it will take some practice to lay down new, better ones. Be patient.

Lesson 4
Get a Grip on Your Emotional Intelligence

You are in charge here

When I was in Year Six I got a ringworm on my neck. I was putting in some time on the parallel bars one recess when our school chaplain approached and asked me about it. There were other kids within earshot and the last thing I wanted was my tiny comrades thinking I was some worm-riddled street kid, so, panicking, I did what any self-respecting tween would do: I lied. 'Oh it's a hickey, from my boyfriend,' I said casually, as if recounting what I'd had for breakfast. I was in deep but I tried to coax myself through it: *Stay cool. You've got this. No one will know you sleep with your dog and that your sheets probably haven't been washed in a month.*

I'm not sure what part of telling our school's religious figurehead I had a love bite from a dude at age eleven I thought was a good idea, but I got hauled into the principal's office for being a saucy little minx and had to admit to making the whole thing up.

The worm was out of the bag and I was mortified. Not just about being a breeding ground for fungal infections, but about concocting such a stupid lie rather than just telling the truth. Looking back I can see that my mouth had simply bypassed my brain, but at the time I was not only embarrassed, I was ashamed. And shame is a bitch to deal with, even when you're eleven.

This gross and seemingly irrelevant story is not a cautionary tale against lying, but an illustration of the truth that our emotions play a huge role in our behaviours and decisions. I wanted to avoid feeling embarrassed, so I lied. I could lie to you now and tell you I've left my scumbag liar ways in the past, but I still lie all the time. I lie to my boss about having capacity to take on extra work; 'No problem!' I lie to myself about that extra serve of dinner not *really* making a difference; 'I'll start eating well again tomorrow.' I lie to my kids about the dummy fairy, the Easter Bunny and Santa Claus, and a large part of my younger years were spent living by the motto, 'Deny, deny, deny.' But there's an emotional trade-off for not being honest, even if it's only with yourself.

Making adult friends with your emotions, 101

It's easy to assume that by the time you're an adult, you've got a Master's degree in emotional intelligence. I mean, you've got this far in life, right? Once we leave the nest, we figure the parenting job is as done as it's going to get and we leap out into the world, hoping for the best. No one tells us that it's now our job to parent ourselves. It's up to us to make ourselves do the things we need to do (and the things we don't want to do) so we can be who we want to be. And it's a lifelong job, one that starts as soon as we can grasp the concept and ends only at our final breath. And there's no fucking star chart for adulting.

If you've seen the kids' movie *Inside Out* (if you haven't, add it to your list and thank me later), you'll have been treated to a simple but powerful lesson in emotions and how they are designed to coexist within us. While some are more likeable than others, they are all equally important.

'There are some misconceptions about how we should feel good all the time, how if we don't feel good then there is something seriously wrong,' says Dr Tim Sharp, one of Australia's foremost positive psychologists also known as Dr Happy. 'But the reality is the so-called negative emotions—so, things like sadness, grief, anxiety, anger and frustration—are not only common and normal, but they serve a purpose. They're a call to action to take a productive course that will remedy some aspect of your life.'

Now, this is truly excellent advice from Dr Sharp, but the trouble is that when we feel these negative emotions we tend to act like we're in *Jumanji*, swatting at them like they're a swarm of bees as we scream-run away. Confronting our feelings isn't fun, so instead of sitting with them, digesting them and deciding on the best and least destructive course of action, we look for something to distract us from their discomfort; such as booze, drugs, sex, food or social media. Sound familiar?

Bumping up your emotional literacy

Just like using stupid words such as 'pee pee' and 'twinkle' to describe genitals when we are kids, many of us are averse to naming our emotions as adults. When was the last time you sat down and thought to yourself, *Wow, I feel really angry/sad/disappointed*? We feel these things frequently, but we don't truly acknowledge them or bring them out into the light where we can see them. Being more aware of our emotions starts with becoming genuinely familiar with them.

'Expand on the vocabulary you use to label your emotions,' offers neuroscientist Dr Sarah McKay. 'It's a bit like taking a thesaurus to your feelings. Improved "emotional granularity" teaches you to recognise your emotions and, in turn, regulate them.'

In other words, pay attention to your emotions and call them out. Say, 'I'm feeling [insert emotion] today,' even if it's just to yourself. Once you've named it, you'll be better placed to know what to do with it.

Remember, too, that emotions can be tricky little fuckers. Close your eyes and think of a time you were nervous. Remember how that felt? Now think of a time you were excited. They feel similar because the physical symptoms are almost exactly the same, the difference is simply context and interpretation. Dr Sharp explains: 'If you look at someone who is experiencing intense fear and anxiety, and hook them up to a whole lot of physiological measures—their heart rate, blood pressure, breathing, amount of sweat—and then you hook someone up who is maybe on a rollercoaster ride or watching a movie and excited in a positive way, they'd be almost exactly the same.

'If we think the symptoms are an indication something terrible is going to happen, then we start to experience more of the fear and anxiety. If we think that, "This is just what my body is doing and it's normal under these circumstances because I'm having a great time," then we can actually feel good about it.'

If Oprah were here (and of course she is because god is everywhere), she would call this an 'aha' moment. Too often we diagnose our feelings quickly based on the most utilised neural pathways in our brain. It's kind of like always driving the same way home—we like our regular route, even if it's not necessarily the best one. But, just like in the car, emotionally we tend to go on autopilot as we navigate the streets of life. The only way to change this is to actively decide to take a different route once we turn the key.

In the moment, it is difficult to diagnose whether that fear you are feeling means, *I've got to get out of here*, or, *This is an uncomfortably exciting opportunity for growth*, but we forget that we almost always have the option of pausing to consider it. The good news is that getting a better handle on our emotions (also known as emotional intelligence) is a skill we can hone like any other, even much later in life. To do so, we need to understand how the brain deals with emotions.

Bad neuroscience

Part of my bad-girl routine was to try to act like I had zero fucks to give, which is ironic, because in reality I had them coming out of my ears. I'd take my big, bad bravado out on the town for a night and spend the whole next day physically and emotionally paying for it. 'Who needs a boyfriend?' I'd surmise over *another* bottle of wine while secretly wishing he would text. 'Snore,' I'd lament with an eye roll to the group of perfectly nice girls in the corner, just because they didn't want to drink shots like water and see the sun come up. I thought that if I could crack the jokes and act tough and void of emotion, then the world wouldn't be able to come after me. But it always did, largely because I wasn't acting in a way that was aligned with my values. And that always bites you on the arse.

Now I know I'm as emotional as they come, and whether you realise it yet or not, you are too. We used to think emotions were pre-wired into our brains, kind of like buttons on a talking doll. We knew there were hormones involved and that we felt angry when someone pushed our angry button, and happy when someone pushed our … you get the picture. This classical view of emotions is, however, outdated; we are starting to understand that rather than emotions happening to us, we create them, using various 'ingredients' that are processed by the brain to construct feelings in the moment—such as sensations in our body, where we are and who we're with, our memories and experiences and the words we've learned over time to describe how we are feeling.

Part of the challenge in truly understanding emotions is that, while science is largely across what's going on in your brain when it's controlling your heart rate or when you see a colour for example, we know much less about the brain's illusive cousin—the mind. We can't scan or measure it; instead we have to rely on self-reported data—what people tell scientists.

'But it's relying on humans explaining what they're thinking and feeling,' McKay explains. 'It's not necessarily a reliable source of data; you've got a human's mind talking about the human mind, and the human mind isn't always necessarily correct, or accurate.'

We tend to use the terms interchangeably, but there's a big difference between the 'brain' and the 'mind'. I'm pretty simple, so I like to think about it like this: Your brain is kind of like a car—it's mechanical. Without you having to tell it what to do it moves your body, regulates your vitals and keeps your organs chugging along. Your mind is the driver: it operates via the thoughts you think, such as, 'I'll text Sarah,' 'Time to leave for work,' and, 'I want pasta.' Both the brain and the mind play a role in emotions—the brain triggering the hormones that create the symptoms that play out in our body, and the mind experiencing them in our head by way of feelings.

Someone smarter than me who can explain this better is Dr Lisa Feldman Barrett. She's a Professor of Psychology at Northeastern University in Boston, and she says emotions are guesses or predictions that our brains constantly construct in the moment, linking sensations in our body to what's going on around us in the world.

'Your brain doesn't react to the world—using past experience, your brain predicts and constructs your experience of it,' she explains in her TED talk titled 'You Aren't at the Mercy of Your Emotions—Your Brain Creates Them'. 'When you're born, you can make feelings like calmness, agitation, excitement, comfort, discomfort—but these simple feelings are not emotions, they're summaries of what's going on inside your body like a barometer, and they're with you all the time.'

She goes on to say that billions of neurons work together in our brains to tell us how to feel about a churning stomach, for example, directing us to take an action or make a decision.

This means that emotions that seem to happen *to* you, are actually made *by* you. And it's great news, because it means you can be the architect of your experience rather than at the mercy of it.

Who's driving this thing, anyway?

Have you ever done something that made you think: *Holy mother of god, why the fuck did I do that?!* It makes you want to punch yourself in the face, which you don't do, but it also begs a very important question, which starts with 'w' and ends with 'hy'.

Consider this:
- We know we shouldn't eat the whole block of chocolate. But we do.
- We know we should pull on our sneakers and go for a walk. But we don't.
- We know we shouldn't flirt with that person who is out of bounds. But we do.
- We know we should get a jump on that upcoming report. But we don't.

You might have heard of the concept of our two brains—the thinking (analytical) brain and the feeling (emotional) brain. Our thinking brain's job is to crunch numbers and calculate risk, but our feeling brain tells us to get the fuck out of there if we see a pointy grey fin pop out of the water when we're swimming at the beach.

If they were in a car together, it's easy to assume our thinking brain would be driving; she sounds like just the responsible brain for the job. My feeling brain is more likely to be drinking a roadie and deep in a D&M than reading the map. But Feelings McGee is actually the one behind the wheel, which is why most of the time we don't make the wrong decision because we don't know better—we do it because in the moment, that's what we feel like doing. And that means we need to learn to trick the system (or at least question it a bit).

Upgrading your emotional intelligence

We forget that just because we've been operating one way for a long time, it doesn't mean we don't have the power to take a different tack moving forward, and our brain is designed to facilitate that change. Dr Sarah McKay says our plastic brains continue to change throughout our lives, not maturing until much later in life than we originally thought—well into our twenties and even thirties. In a sense, it doesn't finish developing until we die.

In *The Women's Brain Book*, she writes, 'Every experience we have—from reading the words of this book, to entering puberty, to interacting with co-workers, to running a race, to loving a child—shapes our brains. Trillions of connections are continually flourishing or being pruned back, forming and re-forming, moulding and refining to fit our environment.'

In an ideal world, we would all grow up in a loving family environment with parents who gently guide us through the emotional clusterfuck that is growing into an adult. But for many, that's not the case. As such, there are plenty of fully-fledged 'grown-ups' walking around who still have no clue how to deal with their emotions, much less how to teach their kids. But if you feel like you're starting off at a disadvantage, don't dismay. You can rewrite the ending by being responsible for your emotions rather than held hostage by them.

To do that, though, you're going to need a few tools.

Introducing ... Your emotional toolkit

Like lasagne, there are some things in life you just need. And a kick-arse emotional toolkit is one of them. Here's what needs to go in it.

IDENTIFICATION AND PERSPECTIVE

As soon as you feel sensations in your body, take a big, deep breath and buy yourself some time. I'll often find myself ranting to someone or ploughing through a tub of ice cream without stopping to ask what it actually is I'm feeling. Sometimes I'm disappointed, vulnerable or anxious about a looming deadline, but all I feel is crap. Being self-aware enough to take a minute to identify why invites some breathing room to then do something productive about it, which might in fact be downloading to a trusted pal or getting stuck into a sweet treat (YOLO), but it might also be going for a walk to clear your head or writing it down (by hand is best). Put your coach's cap on and ask: 'Okay [YOUR NAME], you're feeling [INSERT EMOTION] and I understand why. Let's sit with it for a sec, and now—what's the best next move?'

AWARENESS OF THE NEGATIVITY BIAS

Your brain is playing a constant video game where the objective is to survive. So-called negative emotions such as stress, worry, fear and anger are like those guys in camo that keep jumping out from behind corners, but instead of trying to shoot you in the face they're actually warning you, teaching you and shepherding you in a new direction. It's counterintuitive, but your brain is always going to prioritise negativity over warm and fuzzy feelings such as happiness or satisfaction to make sure that if there's danger around (even just made-up danger in your head), you stay safe.

You've no doubt caught yourself in a moment—maybe you just got a promotion at work or realised that you've fallen in love, or you got a puppy or had a baby—and you felt so happy you thought you might burst. But a few seconds in, the grim reaper of thoughts interrupts your love-fest and you are confronted with the fear of something awful happening. When something means a lot to you, it's natural to fear it being taken away. Try to stay in the moment, remind yourself you have no control over the future and worrying about what might happen isn't going to have any bearing on whether or not it does. So, you might as well enjoy feeling good.

KNOWING THAT EVERYTHING IS TEMPORARY

All feelings, good and bad, are temporary. They come and go and come back and go again. While we would love to hold on to the good ones and banish the bad, that's not how we are designed. A DJ can't play the same song over and over again, he needs a mix of slow jams and bangers to take people on a journey, and feelings are the same. Acknowledging their fleeting nature can help you bear some of their discomfort.

MOVEMENT

Emotions are just energy, and energy can be transformed. You naturally do this every day, transforming anger at the jerk who cut you off in traffic into a honked horn and a flip of the bird so you can make like *Frozen* and Let It Go. Imagine if you held on to that shit all day! But you can also transform energy by moving. You don't need to get to a gym class or run around the block, just pop on some music and dance it out for a song, take some deep breaths while doing a few sun salutations if that's your thing, or do ten star jumps—whatever floats your boat, just move. Then see how you feel.

CONNECTION

We know reaching out is key when we're feeling flat. Finding a trusted ear to share your feelings with is like divvying up the emotional load. It'll make you feel less alone, less awful and more able to face the feeling head-on. Share with the right people, though; you don't want sympathy, ridicule or someone who turns the attention back to them, you just need someone to let you download without judgement and love you anyway.

As kids, we outsource all of our needs to other people. But as we grow up, we start to understand that we need to rely on others less and ourselves more—not because we don't need connection, but because at the end of the day we are the only ones in charge of our happiness. Which is why in the next chapter I'm going to introduce you to the most important person you'll ever meet.

Bad-to-better takeaways

- Wash your sheets, FFS. Ringworms are gross.
- We don't make bad decisions because we don't know better; rather, we make them because our feelings override our logic.
- We're not designed to feel good all the time—remember: a mix of slow jams and bangers.
- Emotions aren't like preset radio stations—we make them, which means we have considerable control over them.
- You already have the tools and skills to deal with whatever life has to throw at you—make sure you remember them in the moment.

Lesson 5
Be Your Own BFF

Stop being such a c*nt to yourself

Despite growing up with a family who loved me, plenty of friends and being generally well liked, it took more than 30 years for me to be able to say I like myself. In fact, for most of my life I didn't even think that was possible, let alone something to strive for. But the happiest and most successful people I know genuinely like themselves. Sure, they fuck things up every now and again, and they don't always feel at their absolute best, but in general they are very comfortable with who they are. They're not narcissistic, but they know that, over literally anyone else in the world, they need to have their own back.

But few of us graduate to adulthood with such a robust sense of self, and it means we're operating without a vital piece of software, or at a minimum, one that's glitchy and frequently dropping out. So, if your relationship with yourself is more like that of an annoying family member you can't get rid of, we need to do something about it, pronto.

How to like yourself

If you truly know your value (like, deep in your bones), it is highly likely you will navigate the world with more ease. You will be clear on what you stand for and firm on what you will put up with (as well as what you won't). You will go after the promotion, kick the deadbeat to the kerb and speak up when you see something that isn't right, because you have faith in yourself and the universe around you. But trying to operate with low self-worth is like walking around naked. You feel exposed, vulnerable and like you're in a very poor position to negotiate. You're just praying someone hands you a fucking coat.

So, the question is: Do you feel worthy? Worthy of being spoken nicely to? Worthy of respect from your boss and colleagues? Worthy of being loved by great friends, nice partners and even bitchy aunts?

If you asked me out loud, I would outwardly agree that yes, I am worthy of all those things. But my actions have often spoken differently. I stayed in relationships with people who didn't deserve me, in jobs where I wasn't valued and around people who, evidently, didn't love me at all. I was waiting for them to 'get it', hoping that if I hung around long enough they would see my value and shower me with the sort of love and affection (or remuneration, promotion or friendship) I deserved. But in sticking around and staying quiet, I validated their poor valuation of me, and reinforced my own poor valuation of myself.

When you think poorly of yourself, you treat yourself poorly in response. Why would you take care of something you don't value? Think about how you treat your old, shitty jumper compared to a brand new one. SJ (shitty jumper) gets used as a giant bib, then scrunched into a ball and thrown in the corner in the hope that it will eventually make its way into the washing machine.

NJ (new jumper) gets admired in the mirror, dabbed when splashed and lovingly handwashed in organic soap before being swaddled like a newborn baby and lovingly put to bed in its cot/shelf. For many years, I treated myself like SJ. These days? I won't lie, I still have SJ tendencies, especially in the self-care department. But more and more, I try to treat myself like NJ.

How we treat ourselves directly correlates with our self-worth. But self-worth is often misguidedly based on achievement, putting how worthy we feel in the hands of our ability and performance, especially when compared to others. It's self-evaluated and therefore skewed by what we deem to be valuable, and we use these tainted yardsticks to measure not just ourselves, but others too, on things such as appearance, material or financial worth, who we know, what we do and what we achieve.

Of course doing well feels good, but if our self-worth cup is filled only by our wins, then any failure or even moments in neutral can take away from it. You nail your solo of 'Three Blind Mice' at the Kindy concert—fill the cup a bit. You graduate from high school or get your first job—top it up again. A university degree, TAFE certificate or trade adds a little more, as does getting married or earning your first paycheque. But when you crash and burn in that meeting or don't get the promotion, it spills. When you break up with who you thought was your forever person, you knock it over. You frantically try to scoop the liquid back up with your hands, but it's gone, and—along with your cup—you're left feeling empty.

I'm not saying people with a good sense of self don't feel deflated when crappy things happen. But they know they aren't measured by their successes or shortcomings; they are more than them. And they are valuable whether they're kicking goals or kicking the kerb, whether they're coupled or singled, and whether they're twenty or 80.

Ideally, we would measure our worth on more wholesome things—how kind we are, or how much we contribute to the lives of people less fortunate than us. But given that's not usually the case, you're going to need to identify what's really important to you, so you know where to focus your energy. An easy way to tap into who you want to be, is to ask what you want written on your headstone, because that's not morbid at all. Here's what I want written on mine:

Here lies Casey Beros. Great friend, amazing mum and kick-arse dance-floor buddy. She always made you feel like you mattered.

Write yours down and stick it on your fridge.

Being reminded of what makes you feel worthy gives you more chance of behaving in a way that's aligned with it, and that feels good.

Ramping up your self-esteem

We know that self-esteem is important but we sometimes forget that it's about so much more than whether we like what we see in the mirror. Self-esteem is our opinion of ourselves, the lens through which we think, feel and act. People with healthy self-esteem can take risks and give things their all, because although failure might upset them, it doesn't diminish them. They don't rely on status or income, or crutches like alcohol, drugs or sex to pump up their tyres. They just go about the business of treating themselves (and others) with respect.

It's worth working on because healthy self-esteem is protective of your physical and mental health, and poor self-esteem is associated with a range of issues from depression, anxiety and eating disorders to violence and substance abuse.

So, how do you fake it till you make it?

Model the masters

We all know someone with a strong self of self; that person who seems to move through life easily navigating obstacles as they come up, enjoying the fruits of their labours and relishing their relationships. They seem content, but perhaps until now you've never really thought about why.

A group of Swiss and American researchers have looked at how self-esteem develops over our lifetime and tested its influence over how satisfied we are in our lives. They found we tend to like ourselves more as we get older; self-esteem increases from being fairly low in adolescence (shocker) to better in middle adulthood, reaching a peak at around age 50 before decreasing again in old age. But interestingly, self-esteem is the cause rather than the consequence, meaning it has a determining effect on our experiences rather than our experiences (successes and failures, for example) bolstering or battering our self-esteem. In other words, it's the chicken, not the egg.

Sure, you can spend the next few decades slowly piecing yours together, or you can cut the queue and model the masters. Here's how people with healthy self-esteem tend to operate.

- They're modest but not too self-deprecating. They know their worth and their value.
- They speak the truth without fear of rejection.
- They don't take on other people's shit or use theirs against anyone else.

- They dig deep on their emotions, knowing the role they play in how they're feeling.
- They steer clear of knee-jerk reactions.
- They tread their own path and don't need people to hold their hand.
- They respect and appreciate others, and encourage them to be their best.
- They do what they say and say what they do. Why wouldn't they?
- They don't let the past define them.

Okay, so building healthy self-esteem isn't as simple as reading a list of attributes and trying to emulate them, but to drive home why this is important, let's take a look at a few quick fun facts.

- When you die, you're probably going out on your own.
- Some research suggests you lose half your network every seven years, which means friends you thought you'd have forever may just become a flash in your feed rather than BFFs.
- If you get married, there's a solid chance it'll end in divorce.

As such, the most important relationship you will ever have is with yourself. Which is why hating or even disliking yourself is a terrible idea. You will never have a tougher critic but you'll also never have a better champion, and you get to start playing that role for yourself today. Not so you can feel good about taking selfies and posting them online (though that might be a side effect), but so you can cultivate the life you deserve.

A big dollop of adult-y perspective

I look at my daughters, who in my eyes are perfect in every way, and I rack my brain trying to work out how and where our relationship with ourselves starts to go wrong. My girls move around so freely, like their little systems haven't yet downloaded the apps (both literally and figuratively) that allow us to judge, compare and criticise ourselves. They're not choosing not to agonise, they don't know how to. And yet, somewhere along the way we learn. Instead of seeing ourselves through other people's eyes, we squint at our reflection through our own. And we would be doing ourselves a favour to take the filters off every now and again.

Here's you: *I hate my legs.*

Here's a double-leg amputee: *Fuck yeah! You have legs!*

Here's you: *These wrinkles can fuck right off.*

Here's Holly Butcher, who died at 27 from Ewing's Sarcoma: *I always imagined myself growing old, wrinkled and grey—most likely caused by the beautiful family (lots of kiddies) I planned on building with the love of my life. I want that so bad it hurts.*

Here's you: *I can't afford to take that trip, my life sucks.*

Here's your counterpart from a housing-commission block in middle Australia: *Imagine ever going on an airplane …*

If you don't have your head inserted firmly in your own arse, you might take a quick bath in this perspective and feel thankfulness and even a sense of shame for not being more #grateful. I'm good at this; my compassion and perspective switch is off the charts—all it takes is one sad news story and I'm preaching about how lucky we are like a giant four-leaf clover. For a moment, the 'fog' will lift. But days, hours or even minutes later, it settles back in. Sound familiar? We've borrowed perspective that didn't belong to us and eventually it wears off. So, how do we apply it in a way that sticks?

Self-compassion in a nutshell

Champagne moments come and go, but we have far more days where life involves simply existing; the hanging of washing, the rushed commute to work, the coffee spilled on your shirt. There will also be days where we feel like everything is too hard, or when things really go wrong, and it's on those days in particular that we need to practise self-compassion, or treat ourselves with the same kindness we would treat a dear friend. Here's how.

1. **Don't judge yourself too harshly.**

    If a friend told you they'd fucked up a presentation at work, would you come down on them, or reassure them they would do better next time? If your mum put on a couple of kilos, would you tell her she needed to get it together? No. Extend the same kindness to yourself.

2. **Remember that no one is perfect.**

    There will always be parts of ourselves we don't like, and we're going to get things wrong, often. All of us—even the people with seemingly 'perfect' lives. Promise.

3. **Practise modern mindfulness.**

    Without being too woo-woo, this is simply about not trying to psychologically escape the moments that feel icky. Try to be truly in the moment, whether it's good, bad or mundane.

Basically, if it's not how you would treat your best friend, don't do it to yourself. In other, more swear-y, words, stop being such a c*nt to yourself.

Be your own BFF, but be your own BB too

Bowerbirds have one of the coolest courting practices of all time. The male builds a bower (which is like a hut) and then decorates it by collecting things such as sticks, leaves, pieces of plastic and flowers. But it's not a nest, it's a shopfront, designed to catch the attention of passing females, who judge his fitness for mateship according to his ability to construct this bower. It's basically *The Block* crossed with *The Bachelor*, for birds.

What I love about this concept is that it's kind of like us: we carefully construct ourselves with our experiences, mistakes, successes, education and character. Not necessarily so we can attract a mate, but so we can build a bower (and a life) we are proud of. Bits of your bower might fall down sometimes, and this is when many people give up. But not you. You're playing the long game—and you know that building something amazing takes time.

If you're clever, though, you'll actively pour time and energy into things that build your self-worth and make you like yourself more. Things like these.

DOING GOOD

Happier people give more, and giving makes people happier. This could be donating money or time to a charity or buying a stranger a coffee, but it could also be making a meal for a friend who's going through a rough time. Make it less about you and reap the benefits.

EXERCISE

The evidence for exercise is irrefutable. It doesn't just make those jeans feel amazing over your arse, it is an effective and vital tool in the prevention of chronic diseases such as heart disease, diabetes, cancer, high blood pressure, obesity and osteoporosis, and can help ward off depression. Exercise activates your body's natural pharmacy of endorphins that make you feel good—like ecstasy but not made in a toilet. Win!

SCALING BACK ON THE 'STUFF'

Do you like who you are without all the trimmings in your life? Or do you play the 'I'll be happy when' game—'I'll be happy when I get that promotion/apartment/jacket.' I'm not here to lecture you on consumerism, but if you find yourself getting a little dopamine hit when you buy something new, maybe try channelling that energy elsewhere for a while and see how you feel. You need to like yourself when you're dressed to the nines *and* when you're in old, stained trackies on the couch.

REMOVING THE THINGS THAT MAKE YOU NOT LIKE YOURSELF

If you act like a twit when you've had a few Chardonnays, curb the drinking for a bit. If you feel guilty when you eat a block of chocolate, stop buying it. If you've got a friend who makes you feel bad about yourself, give them a wide berth for a while. And if social media makes you feel 'less than', take a break. We sometimes forget we have choices.

SPENDING TIME WITH THE PEOPLE WHO ALLOW YOU TO BE 100 PER CENT YOURSELF

You know, the people who don't care what you wear, or that you'd rather watch that daggy rom-com (again) over the doco for smart people. The ones with whom you can exhale. Those people are like human gold, hold on to them.

AVOIDING COMPARISONS

We have to buck the trend of needing to feel better than others in order to feel good about ourselves (comparing down) and giving ourselves a hard time when someone else is 'doing better' than we are (comparing up). While feeling like the grass is greener on the other side is really normal, this is *your* story, not theirs. So, the only person you should compare yourself against is you.

EMBRACING GRATITUDE

Researchers from the University of California, Berkeley say focusing on what you have rather than what you don't is one of the best ways to upgrade your happiness. Write it down, talk it through with someone or just think about it, but getting in the habit of coming up with three things you are grateful for when you wake up and doing it again just before you go to sleep at night is a game-changer. If you do nothing else, add that to your daily routine. It takes 30 seconds and delivers big benefits.

GETTING A FEW RUNS ON THE BOARD

Making good choices is addictive, whether it's choosing the nutritious meal, the sweet guy or pulling on your sneakers for a walk. Like building a muscle, it's time to get good at making good choices. And that takes practice.

CLEANING UP YOUR ACT

When your world is cluttered, your headspace is too. There's no need to origami your undies, but you want your space to be clear, calm and collected—just like you. So, the pile of clothes on the chair, the cupboard of overflowing beauty products in the bathroom, and that mountain of stuff you've been meaning to go through for four (six, okay nine) months? Clean that shit up. When you successfully accomplish a task (even one as trivial as tidying your room), you feel more effective as a human being—competent, autonomous and ready to take on the world. Building a little of that into every day will make you feel like a superhero. The way we apply ourselves to these simple tasks spills into other areas in our lives and makes us better adults—and being more adult-y feels good.

EDUCATING YOURSELF

Having faith in your ability feels good too, and educating yourself builds knowledge and capacity to better operate in the world. It could be related to your profession, but it could also be learning how to cook or dance or speak a different language. See the space outside your comfort zone as your favourite place to play—it's there that you create new reasons to believe in yourself.

BEING A SPECTATOR

Sadly, we don't get to choose our thoughts. I wish we could, because I think some really fucked-up things sometimes that would probably get me chased out of town by an angry mob. But given we have little control over them, when it comes to your thoughts you want to be sitting in the stands rather than on the field. Blocking and defending the silly or nasty ones is kind of futile; it takes less energy to calmly observe the thoughts getting tossed around like a footy.

Once you've ramped up the behaviours that make you like yourself and scaled back on the ones that don't, the next step is learning to trust yourself and your judgement again.

How to trust your gut

Part of the problem with 'bad' behaviour is that it interferes with your ability to trust your own gut. Intuition doesn't come naturally to many people (myself included) but it is a worthwhile skill to master. My gut, however, is like a tour guide doing the morning shift after a night on the crack pipe. It speaks a curious mix of Swahili and whale and, as such, I have no idea what it's saying. Ever. Which makes people's advice when facing big decisions ultra-annoying: 'What does your gut say?'

My gut belongs in an asylum for incoherent guts, okay, Brenda? I don't know what the fuck it's saying.

I've lost count of the number of situations I've been in where my gut screamed at me that something wasn't right. But instead of tuning in, I convinced myself I was feeling that way for some other reason, so I could tune it out. Let me give you an example. When I was eighteen I nannied in Italy for a European summer, before heading to London to party like it was 2002 (which it was). A girlfriend and I went out one night to the local pub, where we drank pints of snakebite (beer with red cordial in it, kind of like cellulite in a glass) and played pool. Toward the end of the night the managers asked if we wanted to stay and kick on. My gut said no but my head said YOLO. We cranked up the music to dance and as the girl behind the bar lined up shots for us over and over again, the guys suggested we head upstairs to the private accommodation. As we started to say no, I glanced at the shots on the bar. They looked the same, all clear liquid, but two (ours) had no bubbles and the rest (theirs) did. All of a sudden, I sobered up.

I looked at my friend, then at the front door, which had been locked. The guys (of which there were three, so we were outnumbered) were getting progressively pushier about taking us upstairs. We knew we had to get out of there and fast. As one of the men attempted to physically steer me toward the stairs, I shoved him away, grabbed my bag and my friend's hand and bolted for the door. I could hear them yelling behind me as I unlocked and threw open the door to the freezing London night. Luckily a friend lived about five doors down, and we ran as fast as we could toward his house with the guys trailing us, where we slipped down the side and banged on the back door until we woke him up and he let us in. We were safe, but that night could have ended oh so differently.

If you have trouble reading your gut, you might find it difficult to make decisions, but you might have also lost faith in its (and therefore your) ability to steer you right. The good news is that if you're not born speaking fluent gut, you can learn, and you're probably already more attuned to it than you think. It's the 'ick' you feel when someone you don't like goes to kiss you, the 'not quite right' you feel when something someone said keeps popping up; all those moments you feel uncomfortable but aren't sure why.

Smart, hardworking people (like you and me) tend to favour reason over intuition, and while there's a time and place for reason, in a world where finding a mate is as easy as swiping right, and applying for a job is as simple as the click of a finger, it's probably worth honing our gut-reading skills.

Get out of your head and into your body

Turning to your body sounds obvious, but how do you know if those butterflies are your gut talking to you or just gurgles from those chickpeas you had for lunch? And those butt tingles, are they 'a sign' or have you just got pins and needles from sitting down for too long?

Over on her blog, entrepreneur and self-help guru Marie Forleo says thinking about everything we do (and every choice we make) will feel either expansive or contractive.

If something feels *expansive*, you'll get a feeling of everything opening up. Your shoulders and chest roll back and up, you feel excited and like you're in forward motion.

If something feels *contractive*, it will feel like dread. You will naturally pull in and shrivel up. When that happens, 'Stay away, honey, do not go near that thing with a ten-foot pole!' Forleo warns.

Let's say you're weighing up staying in your current job versus jumping ship to a new one. Close your eyes and think about one of the options (say, staying in your current job), then ask yourself whether it feels expansive or contractive. Then, think about the other option (landing a new job or starting that dream project) and ask yourself the same.

If you're still unsure, recruit your mates. Forleo goes on to say when people start to talk about their ideas, their body doesn't lie. When they talk about something they shouldn't do, 'they actually start to look dead, they get pasty, they start to look depressed'. And when people talk about something they *should* do? 'Even though it scares the crap out of them, they light up like a fucking Christmas tree.'

So, gather the people whose opinions you value the most, break out the popcorn and let them enjoy the show.

How to make better decisions

I am naturally terrible at making decisions. I'm a total over-analyser and often incapable of making the most banal choices. On those days when I have to make seven million decisions and I get decision-making fatigue, I tell my husband he's going to need to call the shots on the home front for a bit while I lie on the floor and pray someone else comes to adult for the day.

But regardless of whether you have kids, we all have to make lots of decisions in life. Thousands of them a day. Some are rapid and inconsequential—which coffee shop to go to—but others are more serious—whether to rent or buy a home, or whether to stay in the job you know inside out or go for something out of your comfort zone. Those big decisions can drag on for months or years, keeping you in a sort of limbo (and boring the shit out of the poor souls who have to listen to you weigh things up again and again).

Like many other things in life, decision-making is a skill. One of the things I do to try to get better at it, is start with the ones that don't really matter—like what to have for lunch. Don't agonise, just choose. Whether you have the pasta or the salmon doesn't *really* matter in the grand scheme of things. Okay, so you probably shouldn't choose the pasta every day, but you can today. And if you get order envy? Get the salmon next time. Swiftly choose what to wear, which way to go and whether to walk or drive. Give yourself a little fist bump when you make a quick and clear decision, even if it's just fish or carbs.

Bigger decisions will require a little more heavy lifting. Aside from Forleo's gut-tuning strategy, I'm still a fan of a good old pros-and-cons list. Before you get there, though, work out your non-negotiables. To use the job example from above, maybe it's flexible working hours or a boss who will also act as a mentor. If it's where to live, maybe proximity to your family or a good friend is important, or having a balcony or flatmates who aren't murderers. From there you can easily identify if you are considering something that—given your non-negotiables—simply isn't going to work.

When it's time to do up your list, really draw it out, take it as far as you can go. Then you need some outside perspective. Sometimes we get so ingrained in the back and forth of a decision that we get too close to it. Someone objective can ask questions you may not have thought of and pose other ways to consider your decision. I always find that the best advice comes from people a little further ahead of you in life. Remember, though, that while you might engage people for their opinion, you don't need anyone else's approval—only you truly know what is right for you. Bear in mind, too, that sometimes you are choosing between two quite crappy choices, and your job is to work out which will be the least shit.

Imagine you were coaching a good friend through a tough choice. What would you say? Consider this too: What if there is no 'right' or 'wrong' choice, but rather, simply choices A and B with different outcomes?

Be a decision gymnast

You might have heard the expression 'best-laid plans'. The planner in me wants to rage against that machine, but I also know that incessant planning is simply trying to control the uncontrollable—because it frequently leaves my husband in need of a lie down and a head massage. So, plan away, I say, but be flexible. Things almost never work out exactly the way we think they will (for better or worse), which makes everything that little bit more exciting. And remember that most things are temporary anyway, so you can choose one way today and a different way tomorrow, next week or in a year from now. Except tattoos, those are permanent, and no, a Japanese symbol on your lower back is not a good idea. Trust me.

Your roadmap

One of the challenges in building a life you love is that there's no operating manual. So, it's good to have a tool that allows you to make decisions about where to spend your time and energy. A good question to ask yourself is how you want to *feel* in each area of your life, and these answers will help form your roadmap. You might pick one word (or more) and you will have different words for each area.

Here's what my roadmap looks like.

In my *work* I want to feel: expanded, capable and inspired.

In my *relationships* I want to feel: trusted, unconditionally loved and completely myself.

In my *home* I want to feel: safe, warm and relaxed.

In my *body* I want to feel: strong, flexible and vibrant.

In my *finances* I want to feel: independent, secure and comfortable.

Write yours down and pop them somewhere you can see them. Whenever decisions crop up, given you have already identified how you want to feel, you can ask yourself questions to uncover whether doing that thing will make you feel the way you want to.

- Will taking that job make me feel more _____?
- Is this relationship allowing me to be _____?
- Will eating that make me feel _____?

If you are guided by how you want to feel (rather than what your head thinks you should do), it is harder to fuck up your decisions—which is a win for the ~~good~~ better guys. Remember, *you* are the best BFF you'll ever have, so stop fucking yourself over. Your life will improve immeasurably as soon as you can get on your own side.

Bad-to-better takeaways

- Learn to speak fluent gut—even if until this point it has been about as reliable as the battery on your phone.
- Refuse to attach value—how much you like yourself—to things that don't matter. Do more of the things that make you like yourself and less of the things that don't.
- Ask yourself: Does this feel expansive or contractive? Your body won't lie.
- Start acting like someone with strong self-esteem. Flex that muscle—it might just stick.
- Making decisions is hard. Approach them through the lens of how you want to feel and then try not to sweat them. Fist bump.

Lesson 6
Be Kind to Your Body

It's the only one you've got

Warning: This chapter deals with eating disorders. If you need to, please skip ahead.

Most women I know have a complicated relationship with their body, especially when they're young. Instead of seeing ourselves in all our glory, all we see are flaws we become desperate to fix. If we're lucky we grow out of it, but if we're not we can live the rest of our lives in an abusive relationship with the only vessel we've got. And that's a battle I'm no longer up for.

When I was fifteen, I woke up on the floor of the shower one day, the water still running and my head throbbing. I got up and turned off the tap, then cautiously stepped onto the bathmat and grabbed a towel without looking in the mirror. I hated the mirror.

'What was that thump?' Mum said as I made my way back down the hall to my room.

'Uh, I think I passed out in the shower,' I said sheepishly.

'Something's not right with you, we're going to the doctor.'

I didn't fight her. There *was* something wrong with me. For months I had been limiting what I ate and exercising whenever I could, and I had dropped weight quickly. People had started to notice. My dad confronted me about it, and the school counsellor got involved after concerned friends went to her for advice. I had been 'eating lunch' in the library in an attempt to hide my behaviour, and my friends had long grown tired of me calling (this was back in the days where people called each other and held actual conversations) to ask what they had eaten that day so I could do a quick stocktake against my own intake.

I must have been in need of attention, because I was desperate for Mum to notice, to worry about me. So, I trundled off to the doctor in my tracksuit in the height of summer, where the doctor took one look at me and told me to get on the scales. The number read 53 kilograms. It's worth noting here that I am no slip of a thing. I'm tall, athletic and curvy. If it helps paint a picture, one of my best guy friends nicknamed me Bif. Bif The Bouncer. For context, these days I weigh at least 20 kilograms more than that (I think, I rarely weigh myself), so dipping into the low 50s was bloody slim for me. Even so, Mum's reaction wasn't what I'd hoped for.

'Oh, she's *fine*,' she assured the doctor, and before I knew it we were on our merry way. Except I wasn't merry, I was fucking hungry. And Mum had just shut it down faster than I could burn off a rice cracker. In her defence, Mum's view of body image and what was 'normal' when it comes to weight had been skewed by decades working in the fashion industry. For her, being slim was just part of the job. But I found it harder, and before I knew it, starving myself was a part of my life.

Eating disorders are incredibly serious—they are notoriously difficult to treat and are usually nothing to do with the way someone looks, even if that's how it starts. Luckily, my love for pies eventually won out and I slowly recovered, but the disordered-eating mindset stayed with me for years, and my weight went up and down like a yoyo. On weekends I would eat nothing but fun and during the week I would ransack my own cupboard like a pirate. Bowl of muesli? Give me two. Pizza for lunch? Won't say no. Thai takeaway that could literally feed a family of four? Let me at it.

Food gave me comfort. It was the boyfriend I was sorely missing, the best friend who never left and the family I needed when things were tough. These days I eat pretty well, treat myself often, move my body frequently and feel fairly good when I look in the mirror, regardless of whether my weight is up or down. But boy was it a journey to get there.

Cleaning up your relationship with food

The desire to be slimmer starts when we are a lot younger than you might think. In one study, published in the *British Journal of Health Psychology*, more than half of girls aged six to eight said their ideal weight was lower than their actual weight. And you know where that comes from, don't you? Daughters of dieting mothers are twice as likely to already have thoughts about dieting than those whose mothers don't diet.

Given we will eat (at least) three times a day, every day, for the rest of our lives, it is worth putting in the work to have a healthy relationship with food. Unlike an addiction to, say, meth, food doesn't lend itself to abstinence—you can't just go cold turkey. It has taken me a long time to learn to eat to live, rather than live to eat, and there are plenty of people who never get there. Don't get me wrong, I still love food. I cook all the time, plan what I'm going to eat hours (sometimes days) in advance and often eat more than I should. But I've lost that insatiable hunger (which was never actually for food) and largely stopped compulsive eating for the sake of it.

For the past fifteen years I have interviewed leading experts in health and wellbeing, and a cornerstone of many of those conversations has been nutrition. After all, what we put in our mouth is one of the most tangible levers we have to affect our health, and we have multiple opportunities a day to do it.

As consumers we are forever hearing about the latest diet plan, 'breakthroughs' and 'weight-loss wonder foods', but the messages that have come through to me over the years have remained largely consistent. I am summarising them here for you so you don't have to dick around with the latest 'silver bullet', usually aimed at women who want to lose 'five pounds by Friday' so they can go to that wedding/conference/party and feel like a superbabe. Don't think I am immune to those messages, I like 'hope' as much as the next person (and I'm also partial to looking hot as revenge).

But the sad truth is that we can't eat everything we want all the time and look the way we'd like to. Of course, there are exceptions to this rule.

- If all you want to eat is beautiful fresh wholefoods, limited portion sizes and occasional treats.
- If you're one of those rare unicorns who really can eat whatever you want and still look like you run marathons for fun.

Otherwise, we are going to have to employ some semblance of healthy eating, most of the time, if we want to feel good.

The skinny on being skinny

Kate Moss said, 'Nothing tastes as good as skinny feels.' But I disagree. What about Cheezels? Those little orange wheels of crunchy crack are fucking delicious. How about a fresh, creamy piece of cheesecake? I would rather literally deposit those calories onto my arse than say no to cake at a party. And don't even get me started on potatoes.

I know women who eat like birds because being a size six is genuinely important them. They get pleasure from their ability to control what they eat, and sadly I also know we still live in a society that reveres them for being tiny. But I also know that life is too short to say no to the ice cream. To not have the burger. To go without pasta. And to enjoy all of them without feeling crap about it. Sure, I don't want to die from heart disease or cancer because I behaved like one of those people on *My 600 lb Life* (YouTube it immediately), and we know that carrying extra weight is a risk factor in those chronic conditions as well as others such as dementia and diabetes, which I also wouldn't mind avoiding. But there has to be a more measured approach, one that allows the good stuff without us blowing out and being at risk of the bad stuff, and it's one the evidence and experts support.

The pretty-good-most-of-the-time approach

Think about your body in terms of gravity and physics. There's a good reason why we feel better when we're lighter and stronger: we find it easier to move. It's the same reason most athletes train the way they do—lean muscle (with the exception of sports that require brute strength) is almost always our optimum state. But there's more to it than the size of our jeans. We are biologically wired to stay alive, and carrying too much weight is counterintuitive to that. And yet, there's no denying we are getting fatter and sicker. The Department of Health tells us that two-thirds of Australian adults are overweight or obese, as are a quarter of our kids.

No matter what beauty ideal you subscribe to, eating well has universally positive results of feeling good. And those results create a loop of behavioural success: you will exercise because it feels good to move, you will make healthier food choices because you like how it makes you feel and you will treat yourself occasionally, with less guilt, because you deserve it. And doing all of that, in theory, should reward you with better health and wellbeing.

On the other hand, we have all drowned our sorrows in double serves of dinner, ice cream 'just because' and way too many calories, figuring we'll subscribe to the notion of 'fuck it' now and then get back on track later. The pleasure centres in our brain light up like we won the jackpot on the slots as we gulp down our prize and our feelings along with it. Then, enter a tidal wave of guilt, stage left. You're not going to exercise now, why would you? It's not going to make a difference anyway, right? You may as well stay here and make that chocolate pudding that's been in your cupboard since 1994 and then eat it because you need to get all of the bad food out of the house before you start your new life on Monday. The life over which you have total control. The one where you wake up every morning at five to exercise, meditate and drink warm lemon water as if it were the last liquid on Earth.

You can see, touch and taste how good you're going to look, and, more importantly, how great you're going to feel. You play scenes in your head of collecting compliments over coffee before bumping into your ex at the local cafe, where you'll order a salad (naturally). They will be overwhelmed by how amazing you look and you'll bless them with a smile and bid them good day before skipping down the street to 'Walking On Sunshine' like you're in a Kate Hudson movie.

Monday comes and you are *ready*. You treated the weekend like a Sizzler buffet because you wanted to send off your old self in style. The fridge is full of kale that you'll eat so quickly it definitely won't wilt like a bag of dicks in the sun, spinach that will form the basis of your morning smug smoothie and enough lean protein to start a boutique butchery. You set your alarm, get up and work out, drink your smoothie and *by god you are killing it*. You jet through your Monday meetings, smash your salad at lunch and round out the day settling into your white fish and veggies with a side of power. You swear you feel lighter already.

Tuesday comes and you're still in control. You're hungry as fuck but also like, 'I've got this.' Then, you start slipping. You don't say no to the muffin in the meeting, but you only have half, so *that's okay, right?!* You pick up your soup for lunch and the guy behind the counter asks if you want a bread roll and you're, like, *Okay, Steve, today I will because it's cold and I'm tired and it's just one fucking bread roll.* That night on the way home you feel a bit crap but you're not sure why. You do a quick stocktake of all the things you hate about your life right now. Your job sucks, you're lonely and why hasn't Tiffany called in so long? Selfish bitch. You drive past the bottle shop and think about how nice a glass of red would be. 'No,' you reason. 'I'm not drinking until the weekend.' Within minutes you have rivalled Daniel Ricciardo with a perfect U-turn and you're in the Shiraz section. You're barely through your front door before you pour a (big) glass, but red wine has antioxidants anyway, so #healthy.

I don't need to tell you how the rest of this night goes, nor the rest of the week. I know. You know. I know that you know. You know that I know that you know. And besides, we'll just start again on Monday, right?

Food is the most readily available vice/reward we have. It's cheaper than a bag of coke, better for you than a bag of meth and more satisfying than a bottle of vodka. And we use it constantly to celebrate, commiserate and compensate. It's powerful, much more so than the tool with which we try to control it.

The trouble with motivation

Like fossil fuels, motivation is a finite resource. We can't rely on it to sustain any long-term behaviour because humans simply aren't designed that way. Have you ever ridden a mechanical bull? You know, the ones you see in American movies where some impossibly beautiful woman walks into a bar, spots the bull, 'Wild Thang' starts playing and she throws a leg over like that bull was the last D on Earth? She starts off okay, but very quickly she loses her grip. She holds on for dear life, but there comes a point where she just has to let go and pray she lands in a way that doesn't break any bones or flash onlookers her lady parts. That's what dieting is like.

We need to make friends with a long-term approach, but before we can do that, we must identify what is driving our desire to lose weight in the first place. For you, is it any of the following?

- Your health? Have you spoken to a doctor and after a few simple checks decided it's in your best interest to lose weight?
- The media and social media feeding you unattainable images that you are (unfairly) comparing yourself to?
- To get back at an ex who should know what they're missing?
- Because you think if you were slimmer, you'd be happier?

Knowing the answer is important, because we still tend to peg our happiness on achieving some future goal, particularly around the way we look. So, how do we balance wanting to be our best selves with enjoying all the wonderful consumables the world has to offer? It starts with making a change, but it's not in your body, it's in your head.

'We've got to cut through the nonsense and really see food as having a positive role in our lives—not as the enemy,' explains dietitian and nutrition scientist Dr Joanna McMillan. 'It greatly concerns me when I speak to young women who tell me about how depressed they are when they follow their Instagram feed and everything is about the bikini body instead of it actually being about enjoyment, pleasure of food, the way you feel and health from the inside out. We have to lose the singular definition of what we define as being beautiful. What is a beautiful body? It's a healthy, beautiful body.'

The lowdown

Too often I allow outside influences to determine how I nourish myself. It's been a long day, I'll have a wine. (Most days are long days.) It's cold, let's just order Chinese. (There are two seasons, every year, which are frequently cold.) I'm stressed, here's a chocolate survival reward. (I am perpetually stressed.) Before I know it, it hasn't just been a 'bad' food day, it's been a bad week, month and year. I can no longer avoid the fact that my pants have been getting tighter (Jeez, these must've shrunk in the wash) and I catch a glimpse of a similar-looking but heavier woman in the mirror. These days I don't freak out, yoyo-diet and punish myself. Instead, I tell myself that I'm loved and worthy anyway, but that it's time to pull my head in.

With all the experts I have spoken to in my work as a health journalist, there are some common themes that come out in their advice. I have broken them down into five DOs and five DON'Ts, honestly because I'm a bit OCD so everything has to be balanced, and ten feels like as good a number as any. Let's start with the DON'Ts, because I like bad news first (and besides, this is actually good news … promise).

DON'T DIET

Truth: Many 'diets' will allow you to lose weight. It's simple maths; if you decrease calories by restricting your food intake to the point where you expend more energy than you ingest, you will probably lose weight. But most of the time you will put it back on, and then some. Every single expert I have ever interviewed agrees on one thing: for sustainable weight loss and prolonged weight control, a long-term approach is the only approach. The motivation required for a 'diet' simply won't go the distance.

DON'T FALL FOR FADS

I know. The Kardashian on the cover of *Who* used it to 'drop 30lb in 4 days' but that doesn't mean it's going to work for you. You know why? Because she has trainers and chefs and make-up artists and personal spray tanners and nipple tuckers and all the help required to justify that magazine paying her a zillion dollars for the story. It's her livelihood, and real life just doesn't work like that. Have you ever thought, *I'll just use this diet to lose the weight and then I'll be the healthy person I've always wanted to be.* Me too. A hundred times. But we both know that as soon as we start to relax the restriction, the weight slowly creeps back on, and we're back to being miserable about it.

The stuff that works is boring and doesn't sell magazines, but the science is clear: move your body. Eat well most of the time with lots of wholefoods such as grains and vegetables and lean proteins. Treat yourself occasionally. Drink water and limit soft drink and booze (sorry). And probably, eat a little less than you would like to. I get it, the diet that promises you will look like J-Lo in two weeks is tempting. We start strong, but a few hours in we're already compiling a mental list of all the things we are going to devour as soon as this diet hell camp is over.

So, how do we switch the temptation off? We can't, and that's why we've got to get a bit more critical about the entire system.

'The weight-loss industry is designed to set us up to fail,' says integrative psychologist Leanne Hall. 'It's like the gambling industry: you're never going to win when you play the card machines, that's how they make their money—you lose. The weight-loss industry is no different. So, every program that comes out, they set you up to fail because then they can, you know, kind of move to something else and continually get people's money.'

When I heard Hall say this, it was like a light turned on. *Of course* those industries don't want us to win, because as soon as we do, they lose their market. People don't open a coffee shop with the intent of serving people once, they do it with the hope people will come back again and again, daily even. Now, I don't know about you, but I like my money in my pocket, and I certainly don't want to throw it down the toilet on things that don't work.

DON'T BULLY YOURSELF

There will always be gear changes in life. Sometimes your relationship is thriving, sometimes you swear your partner is deliberately blinking loudly just to piss you off. Sometimes you're slaying it at work, sometimes you're crying in the toilets wondering what the hell you're doing with your life. Likewise, when it comes to your body and your relationship with yourself, there will be ups, downs and everything in between. Hall says it's just not possible to love ourselves unconditionally, but rather it's about learning to say we are good enough the way we are.

'We are going to have times when we just don't love ourselves—that's part of our human condition,' she explains. 'We're frail, we're flawed, and by saying, "You know what, I'm not perfect, I don't really like myself that much today, I'm a bit unhappy with how I've done this that and the other, but I'm actually good enough the way I am"—it's less of a drastic shift.'

Case in point: Beyoncé. The closest thing we have to a living god does not appear to give a flying fuck if she's lighter, heavier or anything in between, she wears no pants regardless and slays. Whenever I'm a bit heavier, I try to channel Yoncé. I wear pants, though, because not wearing pants in public just makes you look unhinged (which is probably fair, but unnecessary for people to know).

DON'T SCOFF TOO MUCH PROCESSED CRAP

I know, preparing fresh food is harder than picking something up. You have to shop for it, sometimes wash it and then cook it,

FFS. But the more processed things are, the more crap they have in them, and the more crap you eat, the worse you feel. Now, I love a cheeseburger as much as the next guy, but the majority of what I eat is home-cooked using wholefoods and fresh produce. It's a simple rule that serves me well. If you're already yelling, 'But I don't have time!' I hear you. Make double so you don't have to cook as often, do a 'dinner swap' with a friend once a week and get familiar with your freezer.

DON'T SCRIMP ON VEGGIES

You can shoot up scotch fillet for all I care, but if there's one tip the science backs again and again, it's ramping up our vegetable intake. Veggies are basically a dietary hero. Aw. I just imagined their skins as little superhero outfits ... *cuuuuuuute*. Sorry, I got sidetracked. Anyhoo, they're chock full of nutrients, readily available and versatile enough to do almost anything with. I'm not talking about making cauliflower into rice; let cauliflower be cauliflower and just eat the bloody rice (not too much, though; fluffy white rice in particular is like a line of coke for your blood sugar). Eat all the veggies: starchy ones such as potato, sweet potato and corn, and green leafy ones such as spinach, rocket and broccoli. Make them the hero of every meal and reduce your meat intake by trying proteins like tofu, nuts or legumes such as chickpeas instead. If you're a meat junkie, cut down by having meat at lunch *or* dinner rather than both, and maybe a smaller serve. Your health will thank you for it, as will the environment.

And now, to all the stuff you should do. Or don't, but definitely consider doing.

DO EXERCISE

Every time I don't feel good mentally, I clock that I haven't exercised for a few days. Even if it's the last thing I feel like doing I force myself out for a walk, and the impact of the movement and fresh air is almost immediate, as those lovely endorphins flood my system and come to the rescue. I'm a different person and a much better one to be around afterwards, which is why carving out time to exercise is, I believe, the ultimate act of self-care. And it's not just me who says so—even a small amount of exercise is scientifically proven to be an excellent antidepressant, and in some cases studies have shown that it's as effective as medication.

Exercise is not only good for weight control and to keep your bones and heart healthy, it also fosters social connection if you go for a walk with a friend or join a team sport. So, it's good for your arse, but it's even better for your head and your health. You don't have to hit the gym—incidental exercise such as taking the stairs instead of the lift, or walking instead of driving, all helps too. Simply aim to move, in some way, most days.

The Australian Government's Department of Health recommends 150–300 minutes a week of moderate activity (that's 30–60 minutes, five days a week, where you are moving but can still hold a conversation—such as brisk walking) or 75–150 minutes a week of harder exercise (that's 15–30 minutes, five days a week, where you struggle to chitty chat). Also make sure you do weight-bearing exercise twice a week for healthy bones and to strengthen your muscles—that's anything where you're working against gravity, such as walking, jogging, tennis or dancing. Do whatever you have to do to find the time, and remember—something is always better than nothing. If you have ten minutes to walk around the block three times, do that.

DO MAKE FRIENDS WITH HUNGER

We're all scared of being hungry. We often eat because the clock tells us to or simply because food is in front of us. Well before those hunger cues kick in we have helped ourselves to another 'snack' (often enough to be considered an entire meal) to 'tide us over' because our last meal was at least an hour ago and damn it we're peckish. It's time to get back in touch with our hunger cues and eat smaller portions, and only when we are hungry. (Side note: I *suck* at this. More often the reason I go back for seconds is not because I'm hungry but because I want to taste the flavours again.) The only way to get around this is mindful eating: take your time, savour the meal and have a break when you're done to assess if you're still really hungry. Also known as waa fucking waa waa waa.

My dear friend and leading dietitian Jaime Rose Chambers says it's important to give the body a break from food by practising some semblance of intermittent fasting.

'There are a couple of different methods, I refer to them as "part-day" fasting, where you fast for a number of hours as many days as you like, and "full-day" fasting, where you choose one or several days of the week where you have limited calories,' she explains to me. If that's not for you, she says you can simply look to extend the overnight fast. 'I encourage people to think about it as simply eating breakfast as late as you possibly can in the morning and then having an early dinner at say five or six at night. It's popular because it's easy, and the evidence is starting to show it delivers significant health benefits.'

DO PRACTISE SELF-COMPASSION

If you have been looking for a silver bullet when it comes to your body, self-compassion is it. We speak to ourselves in ways we would never—like, in a million years—speak to someone we love (*Good one, dickhead*, is a frequent favourite of mine). Let it be known: there will be times you'll fall 'off the wagon' and punch through a packet of Tim Tams because you had a shitty day at work. Be kind to yourself anyway. There will be times you'll stand next to someone gorgeous and feel less than. Kill yourself with kindness then. Honestly, does the fact you ate the cake when you said you wouldn't eat the cake matter in the scheme of things? Enjoy it and move on.

DO DRINK A SHIT TON OF WATER

Do you ever get to the afternoon and realise you are thirstier than a thousand suns? When you're dehydrated you can feel fuzzy in the head, and we often mistake this thirst for hunger. Being hydrated makes you feel better; you're more alert and your systems function better, probably because water is super good for your cells and helps your body flush waste. The best trick I ever learned (and then forgot, but now I'm remembering, so thank you) is to keep a full bottle of water on your bathroom sink. Fill it up at night before you go to bed and when you wake up in the morning, down the thing. It's a 10/10 start to the day, promise.

DO CLOCK HOW GOOD IT FEELS TO MAKE HEALTHY CHOICES

If you have spent a long time in a difficult relationship with food, you might feel a little gun shy from battling 'the beast' every day. Life is too short to be tortured by something so delicious, but a healthier approach is not a click-your-fingers solution. To get out of the

I'll-start-again-on-Monday cycle, we need to think of every meal as an opportunity to make a healthy choice. That's not to eat perfectly, but to see food as fuel to nourish yourself and the people you care about.

Here are some easy, healthy choices.

- **Slightly less:** Is the parmigiana at the pub huge? Share it with a friend.
- **Slightly more:** A side of anything green.
- **On the side:** Dressings and sauces.
- **Either or:** Bread *or* dessert for example, not both every time.
- **Go 'whole':** Fibre-rich and kind to your blood sugar, go for brown rice over white, wholegrain bread and whole fruits and veggies.

And then, every now and again, you should fuck it all off and really let loose with a blowout. Buy the Cheezels, finish the cheesecake, grab the tub of ice cream—whatever you want. Because life is for living, and scrapping 'the rules' is a psychological holiday we all deserve every now and again.

Bad-to-better takeaways

- Eat the cake, FFS! Life is too short not to.
- Don't 'start again on Monday'—view every meal as a chance to eat pretty well, most of the time. A long-term approach is the only approach.
- Motivation is a finite resource and there is a 100 per cent chance you will fall off the wagon. Be okay with that.
- Remember: slightly less, slightly more, on the side, either or.
- Every now and again, orchestrate a blowout and have whatever you want. Twice.

Lesson 7
Rein In the Drinking

Alcohol makes you do stupid things

When I was younger I was quite good at holding my liquor. I was never the drunk girl at the party, rather the girl 'keeping up' with the guys. As I got older (and became a better human being) I would take care of the drunk girl, making sure she was safe and not being stuffed with unwanted dicks while she wasn't looking (which makes me furious that I ever lived in a time when we had to, and to some extent still do). But while my increase in age correlated with an improvement in responsibility for others, for some unknown and wildly unfair reason, I got worse at taking care of myself. Maybe it was hormonal, or maybe it was the damage I had done to my poor liver over time, but I would have one or two glasses of wine and be seriously tipsy. So, I would take myself home to sip chamomile tea in bed. Just joking—I would stay out and force myself to drink more wines/vodkas/beers than I could count, just like the good old days, and then enter what can only be termed 'the dark side'.

Have you ever seen those stories on the news where people take a sleeping tablet and then drive their car/eat their fridge/take off all their clothes and do a lap around the block? That's the dark side. Your body is largely functional; dancing, walking, talking (piffle) and making decisions on behalf of your brain, which has protected itself by entering some sort of short-term coma, presumably so it doesn't have to witness all the stupid shit you're about to do.

It turns out that allowing your body to call the shots while its captain is in sleep mode is a terrible idea. Decisions are a job best left to your brain, which was built to handle such affairs. But given the chance, my body would go on a bonanza, thrilled to have been put in charge for even a few hours. It's like letting your two-year-old decide what to buy from the supermarket: you need muesli and milk but end up with Froot Loops and Coca-Cola.

My alter ego, Lola, is usually reserved for hens nights and the like, where she can get appropriately inappropriately wild. But she occasionally makes an appearance at events from which she has been well and truly blacklisted, such as work functions and my wedding night. I rounded out the 'best day of my life' by complaining that I didn't want the party to end (story of my life), with a bottle of red wine in hand (the glass was getting in the way) and thinking it was a genuinely good idea to invite people back to our beautiful and very expensive wedding suite for an after-party.

'I have the rest of my *life* to spend with him, let's just all stay together!' said the dark side.

'No,' said my responsible and loving new husband, eager to act like normal people and spend our first night together, alone, as husband and wife.

But let's get back to the part where I'm a super-reformed and responsible adult now. The mum who definitely did not go to a hens party, enter the dark side, then come home and wake up naked in bed with her mother-in-law. Interesting! No time to unpack that. What I can tell you is that every single time I have made a bad decision, where I have put myself or someone else in danger, I have been under the influence.

Like the time I spewed (vodka cranberry) on a rock star's (white) carpet

When I was in my early twenties I spent a few months in the US. My then-love had ditched me in Europe to head back to Australia and I took a leap of faith to fulfil my dream of spending some time in 'Merica. One of Mum's friends kindly let me stay with her and showed me around, giving me a glimpse into LA life most people could only dream of. When she asked if I wanted to go to a party at the Playboy mansion, my answer was a *Hell yes!* (followed by a *Holy shit!* because parties are my anxiety kryptonite).

I gave my name and entered the gates, the grounds sprawling open in front of me. The mansion sat supervising the action with a big marquee, the pool and infamous grotto, the famous 'painted ladies' and lots of people standing around ogling them. I was there with Mum's aforementioned friend, a woman by the name of Cheryl Rixon, a former Penthouse Pet of the Year as well as a model/actress/jewellery designer, her entrepreneur husband and their niece who was around the same age as me. I hung at the bar taking it all in, chatting to disgruntled ex-playmates who hadn't cut the mustard as girlfriends but still wanted to be associated with the brand.

I'm a terrible feminist for being a bit enamoured with *Playboy*. Looking at the pictures over the years, I always thought the women looked powerful and in control. They seemed bulletproof in terms of their confidence and self-esteem, though I suspect that wasn't always the case. Rixon was one of them and had always spoken of her *Penthouse* days with such fondness, managing to carve out an amazing career, with nudity just one string to her very impressive bow. Of course, many women have used getting their kit off to their advantage, earning great money and building lives they love by using brands such as *Playboy* and *Penthouse* as a platform to bigger and better things.

But the women I saw there that night seemed young, nervous and vulnerable. They were all gorgeous, like big versions of those little girls you see in beauty pageants (which is its own brand of fucked up); spray tanned within an inch of their lives, fake boobs without exception, big hair (up top only) and more make-up than I would wear in a year. The body paint really is exquisite, and the female form is a beautiful thing, but these girls looked like they had come off a conveyor belt—they could have been the same person. Behind their heavily shadowed eyes struggling to blink under the weight of their false eyelashes, I could see the painful reality of standing nude at a party, praying that someone 'important' (namely Hugh Hefner, a man who was at that stage in his eighties) would notice them.

I only processed this in the years following my time there. On that night, however, I had one goal and one goal only: fun. 'Hef' gave us a wave from the window (I mean he was 80 FFS, I'm pretty sure he was upstairs doing crosswords and sucking on Werther's Originals), and as the night came to a close, we heard a familiar accent coming from a group of guys about to jump into a limo.

They asked if we wanted a ride to an after-party, which we politely declined. *Jokes!* In the limo I asked what they did, which was met with a laugh and a response I'm sure they had rolled out a million times. 'We play music,' they said. I would have asked more dumb questions and probably told them about my own experience of playing the kazoo in Year Four, but luckily my friend knew exactly who they were and whispered in my ear that they were, in fact, one of Australia's most iconic bands ever. We went to the W hotel in Beverly Hills, where my naïve little mind was blown by the fact that not only did the hotel seem to know we were coming (not that hard to arrange, really, given mobile phones existed) but that they had a private section just for us with bottles of Grey Goose and every kind of mixer and garnish you can imagine. Like those Pick & Mix lolly stations at the corner deli but for alcoholics. By this stage I had managed to placate my social anxiety with enough vodka to anaesthetise a small pony, which allowed my pickled brain to think it was a good idea to get stuck in anyway.

Unsurprisingly, this is where things start to get hazy. I remember getting bored in the private section (what an arsehole) and nipping out every so often to find new people to chat to in the peasants'/public section of the bar. I remember my friend hooking up with one of the guys and I remember it being time to go. I couldn't tell you where we went or how we got there (a vehicle, presumably) but my next memory is of being in a lovely apartment, where I noticed there were only four of us left: me, my friend and two of the guys. Given my friend and one of the guys had already hooked up, it wasn't a stretch to assume the same might be expected of me. As much as I love their music and respect the guys (and was enjoying their company), there was no way the other one was sticking his guitar in my amp.

I decided the safest thing to do given how intoxicated I was, was take myself off to bed. I can only imagine how I got to a bedroom—a cross between doing 'the grapevine' down the hallway and feeling my way for a door like I was playing Pin the Tail on the Donkey—but I found an empty room that had two single beds in it and no stuff, so I knew I wasn't stealing someone's sleeping space (courteous, even while operating at negative brain capacity). I closed the door and realised I'd hit the jackpot: it locked, which meant I could barricade myself inside and not have to sleep with one eye open. Win!

Proud of my efforts, I tucked myself into one of the beds with all my clothes on and settled in for the night. If you've ever been to bed with too much liquor in your system, you'll know what it's like to wake up with the spins. It's like your brain is on a roller-coaster but your body is in a coma. The only way to get rid of the spins is time, but getting whatever it is out of your system is often a natural reaction to your poor, inebriated carcass attempting to get off the ride and back to the land of the steady. And that's exactly what my body did, emptying the contents of my stomach onto the poor (white) carpet beside me, which had been quietly minding its own business, doing its job of covering the floor.

In the darkness I figured I could scoop the offending liquid under the bed with my hand and it would be like nothing ever happened. Defeated, I surrendered to sleep/unconsciousness, and woke in the morning with a still-locked door, gratitude to my organs for not shutting down overnight, and a purple patch that resembled what I imagine it would look like if Dorothy the

Dinosaur had drunk, well, 100 vodka cranberries and then melted into a puddle. It wasn't healthy, it wasn't responsible and it sure as shit wasn't cute.

Reinventing your relationship with booze

If you really think about it, the fact that we drink alcohol the way we do is quite bizarre. Imagine calling a friend and saying, 'Hey Barbara, wanna come sit somewhere and smash ten lemonades with me?' before adding, 'The lemonade has a toxin in it that'll slow your reflexes and make you a bit confused and clumsy!' Barbs is a hard no at this stage, and by the time you add that tomorrow she'll wake up feeling like someone unplugged her blood supply, she'll be telling you to fuck right off with your lemonades.

Even though we know more than we ever have about the harm associated with drinking alcohol, it remains a potent and damaging crutch of developed society. It causes more harm than any other drug, and yet, it is expected. Welcomed. Encouraged.

If I didn't love a glass of wine so much, I would clip drinking for sure. I am a more productive and clear-headed—not to mention nicer—person when I don't drink. These days I no longer pillage my parents' coin jar to get my hands on a six-pack so I can overdose in a field, but I am absolutely reliant on a wine or two to soothe my soul after a rough day or week. Or a good one. Or a mediocre one. While I might have left the days of getting totalled behind me, I still use alcohol for relaxation, celebration (like to celebrate it being Wednesday, for example) and commiseration when something goes wrong. Most of us do. And that's fine, right?

What the experts and evidence say

The National Health and Medical Research Council does important research about our health and then tells us (as well as health professionals and governments) what to do with it.

Here's what their guidelines around alcohol say for healthy men and women: To reduce the risk of harm from alcohol-related disease or injury, drink no more than ten standard drinks per week and no more than four standard drinks on any one day (for context, that's no more than sharing a bottle of wine at dinner).

To tackle the issues around our binge-drinking culture, it's important to look at why we start drinking in the first place. When we're younger, I believe there are a couple of reasons. One is to fit in, another is because it makes us feel good, retarding the parts of our brain that can inhibit us when we're sober. We feel like we're a more open, friendly and relaxed version of ourselves when we have a couple of drinks, and we relish the 'extra' personality and enhanced connection we get when we let down our guard. It can be a salve to ease the burden of busy lives and a way to mark the end of a day or week; it's a full stop, a way of punctuating the distinction between week and weekend, or work and home.

According to the Australian Institute of Health and Welfare, one in six of us drinks at levels that place us at lifetime risk of alcohol-related disease or injury. One in four consumes enough booze to put us at risk of harm on a single occasion at least monthly. And one in seven of us has put away eleven or more standard drinks at least once in the last year. That might sound like a lot, but in my twenties, that would have been me most nights of most weekends.

I figure I'm better off now given that, while I'm a more frequent drinker, I rein it in after a glass or two (or three occasionally). But that jump from two to three has a big impact; for both men and women, the lifetime risk of death from alcohol-related disease more than triples when we increase our consumption from two to three standard drinks a day. And if we drink more than that, the risk for women is significantly higher than it is for men. Typical.

Turns out my years of 'keeping up with the boys' probably wasn't the best idea, but a big night here and there is fine, right? GP Dr Preeya Alexander says maybe not. 'Binge drinking is now defined as more than four standard drinks in a sitting. It's a lot less than many people would think,' she explains. 'And now they've said anything over four can increase the risk of accidental injuries such as being in a motor-vehicle accident or getting into a fight. We also know much more about any alcohol intake and its effect on health—if you're consistently binge drinking it can also increase the risk of certain cancers, heart disease and other health issues.'

Those other health issues she refers to include things such as fertility issues (as well as trouble getting an erection if you're a dude), liver disease and high blood pressure, but it's also depression and sleep issues. My friends and I used to joke about our weekend antics killing brain cells, which explained things like why I can never remember anyone's name or important details like what year I lived in certain cities or when the World Wars took place. So, I ask neuroscientist Dr Sarah McKay whether it's possible that I have genuinely given myself brain damage, and she says that while smashing rosé on the weekend might not kill brain cells, per se, that doesn't mean there's no impact. 'You are continually and artificially disrupting the communication networks at play in the brain,' she explains. 'You might not see physical brain damage, but it could impact your ability to learn and perform and be as healthy and well for the rest of the week. So, that might have an overall dampening effect.'

Damp is one way to describe me after a big weekend. Flat, doughy and downright depressed are others, as I would navigate 'may not survive Monday', 'too much Tuesday' and 'why did I do that Wednesday' before coming good, finally, on a Thursday—just in time to do it all again.

So, how do you know if you have a problem?

To answer this, I'm throwing back to my girl Brené (Brown; we're on a first-name basis in my head). She says that if you're asking yourself if your drinking is problematic, then, at the very least, it's probably not serving you. And, 'if you're scared shitless that your life won't make sense if you stop drinking', then you need to reach out for help, she shares on her blog.

This is a conversation I have with my friends often. It feels like we are frequently trying to cut down our alcohol intake and questioning whether our relationship with booze is healthy, which means it probably isn't. But life is prickly, and there's a store on most corners that sells a perfectly legal, relatively cheap and universally accepted solution—booze. So, when life rubs me up the wrong way (with not enough sleep, too much stress or my pesky expectations letting me down), it's easy to reach for a trusted friend, especially when it comes in a convenient bottle.

Indeed, there are plenty of people for whom 'partying on the weekends' doesn't turn out so well. A girl I was friends with in high school drank herself into such oblivion that she died from liver failure at age 33. I knew that things had escalated for her in recent years and that she'd burned bridges with a few of our friends, but that girl had a heart of gold. I'm yet to understand why things go one way for certain people and a different way for others. Maybe it's varying shades of mental health (or illness), or maybe it's just biology and luck.

Someone who wasn't prepared to find out was Maz Compton. You'll know her from your TV screen or radio, she's a media personality and author of *The Social Rebellion*, which she wrote about her decision to quit drinking. Now 'alcohol-free' (her preferred term) for six years, she tells me there was a time she was in a relationship with booze, and it was a shitty one.

'Alcohol crept into my life like a thief in the night and then took up residence in my house for a long time,' she explains. 'What I thought was a friend to comfort me only made me feel worse each time we connected. And yet, I felt like it helped me get through each week and to relax after a long day. It became a coping mechanism to deal with the life I had chosen. Every day for a long time I was offered a drink after work, during lunch, on a weekend. Before you know it you drink at every occasion: birthdays, funerals, weddings, bad day, good day, job loss, career promotion, new boyfriend, boyfriend dumped me, George died on *Grey's Anatomy*, they changed the size of Killer Pythons … and so on.'

So, Compton did what we should all do with shitty relationships: she ended it.

'It wasn't until I decided to do some serious spring cleaning that I realised the effect alcohol was having in a profound and negative way across all facets of my life,' she explains.

It was time, she says, to stand up and take responsibility.

'Only you are responsible for your choices. There is so much in our hands and we throw it away by not accepting the very choices we have each moment, in each day, to make wise and wonderful, empowered choices.'

I ask whether there are people in her life she feels would be better off if they stopped drinking too, and whether—given the positive impact giving up has had on her own life—she brings it up or leaves it for them to work out.

'I don't think anyone is ever truly honest about their relationship with alcohol until it becomes an issue,' she says. 'I wasn't—I would tell people I'd had a "few champagnes" when I knew I'd drunk the whole bottle. I'm not ashamed to admit that now, because I believe that my being honest will help others to not feel shame about their drinking behaviour but to understand it's unhealthy and that they have the ability and capacity to redefine it.

'The question I like to ask everyone is: "How is your relationship with alcohol?" Now, if you say, "Oh, I think I might be drinking a bit too much," or, "I would like to take a break but I don't know how to," then taking some time away from drinking would be a great solution. And if you say, "My relationship with alcohol is great," then I challenge you to take a month away from alcohol; if your relationship with alcohol is indeed great, this will be easy. But you may also realise during this process that your relationship with alcohol needed redefining, and so this is win–win.'

These days, instead of booze, Compton has a swathe of tools and techniques she uses to help her deal with whatever life throws at her.

'A lot of us sit in a space where we need something to help us "cope",' she says. 'Coping is not the key, dealing is the key! If you actually "deal" with your stuff you can overcome it, rise above it and move forward. To deal with my stress levels I used to drink a bottle of Savvy B, and now I meditate. To keep my mental health and self-image in check I exercise, I have a gratitude journal, I eat a nourishing and mineral-dense diet, I get eight hours of sleep as often as I can. I have healthy and fulfilling relationships and only a small number of them. I don't hang on to "things". I am careful with my impact on the planet. All of these choices help me feel content, which is a beautiful place to live life from.'

And if she had one piece of advice for her younger self?

'Go home and get some sleep, babe, you look tired!'

To Compton's point, bad behaviours are often in abundance because they help us withstand the poky, jabby stresses of everyday life, but they're often disguised as self-care, and that's where things get tricky. As you'll pick up in this book, I wholeheartedly believe in occasionally giving yourself whatever you want. Skip the gym. Eat the cake. Drink the wine, then drink it again. But I'm also no stranger to falling prey to that becoming the rule, rather than the exception.

So, what do we do with all this?

If this sounds familiar, I want you to consider your perfect storm—the times you're at your worst—and the conditions that contribute to you needing a crutch such as booze. Write it down—with pen and paper is best. If we know that alcohol, drugs, meaningless sex (if it makes you feel shitty after) and overeating are unhelpful coping mechanisms, we would be wise to dial them down, or at least keep a watchful eye over our use of them. Instead, we should ramp up helpful coping mechanisms before the chips are down, such as: exercise, eating well, sleep, talk therapy (with a professional or friend) and factoring in time for relaxation, mindfulness or a holiday. But we often don't know we need them until it's too late, and that's why making them regulars on our self-care roster is vital. Like getting the brakes on your car fixed before they fail. That's what clever people do, anyway. Clever people like you.

Bad-to-better takeaways

- If you feel like the dark side might be lurking, pay one of your friends to lock you up for the night.
- Don't drink too much on your wedding day, no matter how nervous you are.
- Save cranberry juice for rescuing you from UTIs, especially when there's white carpet around.
- If you're asking whether you have a problem, you might. Take a break and reassess.
- Get some helpful coping mechanisms on regular rotation before you desperately need them.

Lesson 8
Get Smart About Money

The best kind of freedom is financial

When I was growing up I had two financial experiences, both middle class but probably at different ends of that spectrum. Dad lived in a cheap rental, spent a lot of time on the dole and, though I never wanted for anything, it was a day-to-day existence, the type where you hunt under the seat of the car for coins to buy petrol. Mum, on the other hand, was fastidious about saving, started a moderately successful business and even managed to buy a cute little home in the fancy western suburbs of Perth.

When I got older and Mum met the man who was to be her long-term partner, I experienced real wealth for the first time. A successful businessman, he lived in a big house, had a boat, several cars and what felt like an omnipresent stack of $50 bills in his pocket, some of which would fall out wherever he went. I was too young to understand what any of it meant, but I lapped up the holidays and gifts, both of which are like crack to kids.

Before I knew it I was a private-school girl living in a big house in one of the wealthiest suburbs in Perth (and at the time of the mining boom, possibly Australia). The latest gadgets, VIP concert tickets and designer clothes became the norm, even though I was still blissfully unaware of the realities of paying for an impossibly privileged life.

Fast-forward a few years and the businesses, big house, $50 notes and fancy cars were gone. No longer did we go to the supermarket and not look at the prices, and I realise now what a ridiculous privilege it was to do that in the first place. Instead, Mum would call me from the supermarket and we would giggle about the fact that she only had enough money to buy shampoo *or* conditioner and which did we think hair needed more? I guess that's the thing about money—it's almost laughable how transient it can be, and if you don't come from much, how strategic you have to be to make more of it.

Now, I am no financial expert. Indeed, in my twenties I was nearly financially illiterate. So, what I share here is a result of my experience and my research only, it is not to be taken as financial advice—you have to get that from someone who actually knows what they're talking about. Take from it what makes sense and leave the rest.

You're already wealthier than you think you are

If you're reading this, there's a good chance you are already *incredibly* wealthy. Okay, maybe not in comparison to Kylie Jenner or even the richest kid at school, but in the scheme of the world, you've probably got a roof over your head, food in your belly and enough disposable cash (or a kind enough friend) to get you this book. So, if you've been feeling that the odds are stacked against you financially—they're actually firmly in your favour, even purely based on where you live and the fact you have the wherewithal to read this.

The cold, hard ~~cash~~ truth

After we lost all our money (and I use the term 'we' loosely ... it was really my stepdad's money and kind of Mum's and therefore mine by proxy), it took me years to adjust. And I don't just mean adjust to the new, frugal reality, but to really grasp the fact that if I were ever going to have any money, I was going to have to work my arse off to earn it. There was no well-meaning philanthropist (who wanted to adopt me) to open a trust in my name and hand me a 'welcome to the family' cheque on my 21st birthday. Instead, I was gifted a one-way ticket to adulthood with next to no financial skills.

For my entire twenties I lived paycheque to paycheque, with a penchant for spending and an allergy to saving. I didn't understand value, and blew every cent I earned (and more) on 'living': rent, bills and more rounds of drinks than I'd like to admit. I showered my friends and family with gifts, always splashing out on flowers and birthday presents, because giving felt good. I would borrow money from Mum for 'essentials' like a trip to Bali or a dress for a wedding, and while I would always pay it back (debatable—but she's not here to correct me, so you'll have to take my word for it), it didn't occur to me until much too late that if I didn't have the cash to buy/do 'the thing' I probably shouldn't buy/do 'the thing'.

Getting good at managing your money is a skill like any other, and probably one of the most important you will ever learn—because no one can sort out your finances but you.

Can money buy happiness? No, but it can buy comfort (and some really nice shit)

A study out of Princeton University found that, while money can't buy happiness, as you earn more you tend to feel better about, and more satisfied with, your life. Your emotional wellbeing, defined as the frequency and intensity of experiences such as joy, stress, sadness, anger and affection, also improves the more you earn, but once you can cover your basic living expenses (they use the benchmark of US$75,000 per annum in the study, which roughly correlates to AU$97,000 a year at the time of writing) the correlation drops off. If you're a low income earner, however, you'll be hit harder by the tough stuff in life such as divorce, illness and loneliness.

I hold a complex position when it comes to money. Would it be nice to be rolling in cash like the Kardashians? Sure, it'd be a fucking blast. Do I wish I had more of it? *Yes.* Do I ever feel like I have enough? *No.* Does it frustrate me that I didn't get my act together when it comes to money sooner? A thousand times yes. But it also annoys me that we spend a huge amount of money on really stupid things. I know people who think $3000 for a handbag or pair of shoes is a 'good investment'. Really? Are they likely to increase in value once you've shoved your stinking toots into them and walked them down a filthy street? I think not. I'd say it's likely the only dividends you will ever earn from said 'investment' is by way of compliments, probably from people who also own $3000 shoes, or at least wish they did.

No judgement here if Lamborghinis and Louboutins are your thing. But you can be filthy rich and yet totally bankrupt when it comes to happiness, and you can be on the bones of your arse and the happiest you'll ever be. Personally, I just want enough money to be able to do the things I want to do, take care of the people I love and not have to stress if something goes wrong and I need cash quickly. That's wealthy to me. That said, I surveyed a lot of people—mainly women—for this book and, almost without exception, they told me two things about money. 1: They wish they'd learned how to manage their money better and sooner. And 2: Not having enough of it is the thing holding them back from the life they want.

If you learn one thing from this chapter, let it be this: Your value is not tied to your financial worth, even though it might feel like a really tangible way to measure it sometimes. Even so, money is one of society's most quantifiable power currencies. I'm not talking about rolling around splashing cash on drugs, champagne and hookers in a scene straight out of *Hustlers* (or *Fear and Loathing in Las Vegas* if you need a reference that's pre 2000s), I'm talking about the power to buy a home you love. To buy your parents a home they love (or put them into quality aged care if and when they need it—that shit is expensive). To afford the option of private medical care. To support your loved ones in their endeavours, and surprise them with a holiday they deserve, or even to just be able to donate to your niece's cancer fundraiser without blowing the budget.

I come from a baseline of privilege; I had both exposure to possibility and access to educational opportunity. That said, I'm a journalist and I married a teacher, so the *Forbes* rich list is probably off the cards for me. But that doesn't mean I can't strive to be comfortable. And no matter what you earn, you deserve the same. I know that at the end of my life I will look back and think of the people I loved and shared it with, not the sales I made, the things I bought or the homes I lived in. But I also know that having money makes life easier. When you're less of a slave to the workforce, you have more time to spend with the people you love and on things you're passionate about, and this is only possible if you have money—which means you need to get strategic.

Extra strategic, if you're a woman

Back in the days when men brought home the bacon and women raised the children and 'ran the home', family finances sat in the male domain. These days we are less likely to be sold for a dowry of kangaroos, but we are far from equal: in many households we still carry the bulk of the burden of kid-wrangling and domestic duties, but we are still expected to earn our keep and come to a relationship with some financial value of our own, even if it's just by way of having a job. We are expected to meet men halfway, and yet it's far from an even playing field.

There seem to be three glaring issues of inequality when it comes to women and money.

1. **We work for less, starting from the very beginning.**

    We often choose lower-paid professions (such as teaching, child care and glamorous but poorly paid creative fields), and we still frequently get paid less to do the same job. At the time of writing, the gender pay gap in Australia is just shy of 14 per cent. Our counterparts in the United Kingdom do slightly better at just under 9 per cent, but if you're a woman in the United States you'll earn just 78 cents in the dollar compared to men. If this doesn't sound like a big deal, consider the impact over a period of time: if you're a university-educated in the United States, you will have $800,000 in lost compared to a man by the time you are 59. You read th rectly: $800,000! That's a nice home, outright, or 800 pairs of fancy shoes—your call.

2. **We take time out of the workforce to have a family.**

One of the most important jobs in the world leaves many of us at a major disadvantage. It slows career progression, earning capacity and superannuation contributions. Government-paid parental leave and companies with parental-leave policies help, but it doesn't solve the issue. After we take time out to care for young children, we are then less likely to operate in senior positions (and be paid comparable amounts) in the later stages of our career. Kind of ironic, given the people we are raising will one day work, pay taxes and contribute to the advancement of the economy in which we're busting our arses for a fair go.

The decision to raise children or get back into the workforce is one I know inside, outside and backward. Women feel split in two. On one hand we know how fast the time with our babies will go—before we know it they'll be grown up and won't want to hold our hand, hang out all day and dance to The Wiggles. On the other, we know that, sadly, the workforce isn't kind to women who take time out. Doing both is fraught with challenges too, leaving women feeling like rather than 'having it all', we are actually just doing a crap job of everything, which is unfair, given most of us have to work.

3. **We are not financially educated from an early age.**

If you went to high school any time before the last five years or so, there's a good chance you learned nothing about money while you were there. I mean, I studied economics and accounting and the only thing I learned was that I'm terrible at economics and accounting. This glaring omission from the curriculum is starting to be acknowledged but not in all schools, which means there are still plenty of kids growing up with literally no clue how to manage their money.

Financial education happens in the home too, so if your parents were rubbish with money, there's a good chance you will be too. Educating yourself now will only serve you (and your family) well, so here's what we're going to do about it.

First up, give yourself a quick win

Superannuation is the pot of money the government takes from our pay and invests on our behalf until we're 65 or so and ready to kick it with a piña colada. But according to the Australian Government's Workplace Gender Equality Agency, women retire with 47 per cent less super than men, and it's almost never enough to sustain us in retirement. It's the reason that if you are a woman and retired and on your own, there's a 40 per cent chance you will be living in poverty. *What the?* Think about it: You meet 'the one', and after a couple of years of dating the relationship is full steam ahead. You get married (or you don't) and you start a family. Over the next five years you have three kids, taking six months off for each one and going back part-time in between (or, you don't go back at all). The whole time, your partner continues to work and top up *their* super while you raise children. If that relationship doesn't last (and let's face it, many don't), there may come a day when you find yourself in a position where you can't afford a home and are too busy with the kids or too old to work. The Australian Human Rights Commission tells us that if this happens, there's a good chance you will end up one of the nearly 7000 homeless women aged 55 and over in Australia—a trend that has increased by more than 30 per cent in the past decade and continues to rise. That's one for the what-the-fuck files.

Now, to remind you, I'm not a financial planner. But here's how plenty of smart ones say to fix your super, in two simple steps.

- Make sure you only have one superannuation account. Your super fund can do a search for you to see if you have any lost super elsewhere, then they'll roll it all into the same place *for you*—it's one phone call and a five-minute job, promise.
- Work out how much you're going to need to retire (try the superannuation calculator at moneysmart.gov.au) and then contact your super fund and—if you can manage it—bump up your contributions even just by a tiny bit. Don't stick your head in the sand and hope for the best.

If there's diddly squat chance of you ever going and doing that, do some quick math. Work out how much super you're likely to earn before you retire (9.5 per cent of your annual income × the number of years before you book a hard-earned cruise). Then divide that by 20 (based on you retiring at 65 and living to 85). I'd hazard a guess you come up a little short of the amount you'll need to live a half-decent retired existence. If so, now is the time to do something about it.

Then decide what sort of life you want

There's no way around it, money is stressful. In fact, according to a 2015 survey by the Australian Psychological Society into stress and wellbeing, it's the greatest cause of stress in our lives. It's also one of the biggest sources of inequality, with some people earning incredible money doing things like 'influencing' and trading invisible currencies, and others earning peanuts doing our most important jobs (hello teachers, nurses, police, firefighters and aged-care workers).

I think it's important to be honest about what sort of life you want. Some people just want to earn a shit ton of money and don't really care what they have to do to get it. They want designer clothes, business-class flights and a big house in a nice suburb. Others want a simpler life: a comfortable home, a reliable car and an annual family holiday. Others again just want to live their lives in service (either to the community or servicing their own desire for bongs and X-box). Knowing where you sit is a vital first step in getting what you want, because it allows you to be clear about what you're aiming for.

The reality is, though, that if you want your financial situation to be different, you're going to need to make some tough decisions and back yourself on them. Hard. Don't worry if, like me, you had no financial education. Regardless of where you're starting from, the sooner you get your act together, the better off you'll be, and the fact you're reading this puts you two steps ahead of most. You don't need more money (yet), you just need a plan. The first thing we need to do is work out how much it costs you to live. Do up a (very rough) budget that covers your key living expenses:

- Rent or mortgage
- Food

- Bills: electricity, gas, water, insurance, phone, internet
- Travel: car, public transport
- Health and medical: private health insurance, doctors' bills, medication
- Extra essential stuff: haircuts, educational courses—but not Uber Eats.

Don't labour over it, there's a good, easy-to-use one over at moneysmart.gov.au if you like.

Now let's take a look at what you earn *after tax*. Check your payslip or your tax return from last year and then divide that by 52 to give you your weekly income. Consider any extra income too, from shares or shaking your tatas at Showgirls. Your living expenses should account for no more than 60 per cent of your income. If it's higher, you need to do some tweaking to cut costs, or you need to bump up your earning capacity by working more or selling stuff (not drugs, that's a bad idea, but, like, those golf clubs you bought on a whim and used once).

I believe that one of the most important books published in recent years is Scott Pape's *The Barefoot Investor*. A few people read it (it's Australia's second-highest-selling book ever, second only to *Fifty Shades of Grey*—horny fuckers), because it took a subject that had escaped most of us for our entire lives and made it comprehensible and accessible. You should 100 per cent buy and read his book (once you've finished this one) because it shares a simple and achievable plan that anyone can follow to create more wealth in their lives, allowing people to get out of the shitty debt most of us live in. Here's how.

Barefoot and broke no more

Once you've worked out how much it costs you to live, you need to automate your money so everything is accounted for without you having to be a slave to a formal 'budget'. You can spend what's in your kitty guilt-free, rather than trying to pay for your life with whatever is left after that big night out. Pape advises having three additional bank accounts to your standard 'daily' account, and recommends you have them all with ING because they have no fees and you can set them up easily from your phone, then name them as follows.

- **Splurge:** Spending money for non-essential but fun stuff (such as clothes and going out).
- **Smile:** Longer-term spending for holidays, gifts—things that will make you smile when you get/do them.
- **Fire:** Money to pay for financial fires you haven't budgeted for, such as blowing a tyre or an emergency root canal.

If you are spending 60 per cent of your income on living, 10 per cent should go into your 'splurge' and 'smile' accounts, and 20 per cent into 'fire'. In our house, we loosely work on 70 per cent living expenses, then 10 per cent each into splurge, smile and fire because we are idiots who live in the most expensive city in Australia, and arguably one of the most expensive cities in the world. It's not ideal, but it's reality.

Take responsibility for your financial flab

You know when you've put on a few kilos and you try buying a bigger shirt or wearing black to disguise it but you can't? Being financially 'flabby' is arguably more dangerous because it is easier to hide. You can blow all your money on rent, lease a Mercedes and max out your credit cards to keep up with the Joneses (or the Jenners) and no one will know. But *you* will, and it'll catch up with you. Which means you're going to need to pull your finger out, for a while at least. You need more *in* and less *out*.

Earn more: Ask for extra hours at work or take on some freelance projects, even just a few hours a week. Take a weekend job if you have to, or hit a monthly market where you can sell things you don't need. It's not forever, it's just for now. Even increasing your income by 10 per cent will make a big difference to your financial position.

Spend less: Asking yourself if you really need something before you purchase it is a quick and easy way to curb unnecessary spending. It's not fun, but it's worth it, and saying no more than you say yes gets kind of addictive.

Here are some ideas to help you rein in your spending (and remember, every dollar counts).

- Make extra dinner and pack lunches from leftovers.
- Invite your friends over rather than going out and tell everyone to bring something to share.
- Shop around for cheaper insurance.
- Set small but achievable savings goals. 'By 31 March, I'm going to have $1000 in savings. By 30 April, it'll be $1500,' and so on. Feel (really) good about ticking them off and celebrate hitting them with something you've been depriving yourself of, such as a cafe lunch or manicure. You've earned it, literally.

Mo money, mo problems

One of my biggest regrets in life is not getting ~~good~~ better at money sooner. I took a long time to buy a home (and to be honest, I'm probably in the last generation that'll be able to, at this rate), and when I did I didn't have enough for the deposit, so I had to borrow some and *still* had to pay thousands of dollars in lenders' mortgage insurance (that's insurance the bank makes you pay to protect *them* if you default on the loan). And that was just to get into a two-bedroom apartment. Around me, my friends were buying houses, trading up, taking extravagant holidays and I couldn't afford an apartment? My husband and I had six-figure salaries and no debt, we even managed to pay for his $30,000 Master's degree up-front. It felt like we were doing all the right things, and yet were so far behind.

But here's what you have to remember.

- You don't know anyone else's circumstances, because we're still not very good at talking about money. Maybe they got a head start by way of an inheritance from a loving grandparent or parent; maybe they've been saving their arses off for years; or maybe they're drowning in debt to keep up appearances. You just don't know.
- Sometimes it's all about timing, and people make good investment decisions or they get lucky. I have friends who now live in great homes because they bought their first shitty apartment eons ago, then the property boom hit and they were able to cash out with a whole lot more than they put in. If that's not you, that's not you.
- It's all about choices. I also have friends who have borrowed huge amounts of cash from their family (or the bank) because they want to live in a specific sort of home in a particular suburb. Pape refers to them as 'postcode povvos'. Don't forget, though: the bigger the house, the bigger the mortgage, the longer you're in debt, the more interest you pay and the longer you're tied down. No judgement, just choices.

There is no point comparing yourself to anyone else—that's their money story, not yours. Take the energy you're spending on them and focus it on yourself and your goals; you'll get there faster than you think you will. The aim of the game is to get debt-free as soon as you can. Knock over any credit-card debt, get into a home if you can so you have an asset and then pay it off ASAP.

How to get wealthy (if that's what you want)

All the people I know who have managed to 'do well for themselves' (without being born with a silver spoon in their mouth) have a few things in common. If that is your aim, consider whether these are for you.

DON'T BE SCARED OF HARD WORK

We would all love to do the bare minimum and still be wildly wealthy straight off the bat, but I haven't met anyone yet who has managed to achieve that. You kind of have to love working, because even if you 'love what you do', there are bits of every job that suck, even if you're getting paid well.

BE WILLING TO 'HAVE A CRACK'

I don't mean mortgaging your house or selling a kidney to bankroll your passion project (because I can't be liable for that), but there is often some risk involved with the projects that end up paying off. Having a crack can simply mean being brave enough to put yourself, and your idea, out there.

KNOW WHAT YOU'RE GOOD AT

You don't have to be the smartest person in the room or the best with people, but you need to be good at something. Work out what that is and then find ways to make yourself great at it. Those are the niches in which opportunities exist.

BE A MAGNET FOR OPPORTUNITY
Loyalty is awesome and often it is rewarded, but sometimes it isn't. Be open to opportunities to grow the business you're in or to do what you're good at somewhere else.

How to net yourself a more financially rewarding future

In my observation, there are a few ways to earn bigger bucks.

OWN YOUR OWN BUSINESS
You'll need to be prepared to work your guts out, but at the end of the day you will own it, which means you can sell it or derive whatever income you want from it while calling the shots.

WORK YOUR WAY INTO A BIG POSITION
If you are going to work for someone else, be prepared to put in long hours and some serious grunt to get as far as you can. The higher up the food chain, the more you're likely to earn.

INVEST
Investing is a way to own a small piece of other people's companies and reap the benefits when they do well. Don't be like those people on *A Current Affair* who invest their life savings in a bitcoin operation with a guy called Poncho, but accept that *any* investment comes with risk. The higher the potential reward, usually the higher the risk. Understand your risk profile; if you're averse to risk, put your money in something safe such as a high-interest account at a bank, where you'll be lucky to earn 3 per cent a year.

If you're willing to gamble a bit more (for people who are younger and can earn it back if they lose it), you could put it into the stock market where you might earn more, but you might also lose it altogether. Either way, be patient. As the world's most successful investor Warren Buffett says: 'Someone's sitting in the shade today because someone planted a tree a long time ago.' Be smart, invest small, re-invest the dividends and slowly increase your portfolio.

CREATE

People talk about 'residual income', and it's based on the fact that often our earning potential is limited to how many hours we have in the day. Creating something that isn't contingent on you physically doing it is clever, and allows you to continue earning after you've clocked off. For example, if you're a hairdresser, can you create a hair product that's missing from the market? Or if you're in child care, what about a toy, blanket or children's book you could import from elsewhere that you think parents would like? Think outside the box for random things the world might need. A woman called Roni Di Lullo, for example, earns $3 million a year making goggles for dogs, called doggles. Who'd have thought?

Now, these are all great ideas, but for true financial freedom, there's something more important than how much you earn or save or spend. And that's your relationship with money.

Milking the value of life

As much as I would like a bit more of it, I'm grateful for my relationship with money now. My family still has a long way to go before we're mortgage-free and as comfortable as I would like us to be, but we don't want for anything. And according to former NBA star of Chicago Bulls fame Luc Longley, that's a great place to be.

'Personally I feel like the people that are well reconciled with the value of a litre of milk and dig it when they pay off a chunk of their mortgage get much more joy out of money than people where it flows easily,' he tells me. 'I've seen so much ugly money that I actively seek out people who have a good, healthy relationship with money. When you get wealthy it's very easy to lose track of what things are worth to other people, because your perception of the value of things changes.'

Having lots of money still sounds awesome, but Longley says the dream can be better than the reality.

'The idea of earning money and paying off your own house feels like a rite of passage and part of the context of everyone's human experience that I didn't get, because my first paycheque at 21 was a million dollars,' Longley explains. 'It took a divorce, a global financial crisis and a stoush with the ATO for me to understand that money just didn't grow on trees.'

Longley says some of the most miserable people he has ever met are the wealthiest, because they can have difficult-to-understand emotional barriers and trust issues with friends and family.

'It has become a wedge in a lot of my friendships,' he says. 'As hard as I've tried, people get complicated around money.'

I ask him what it's like, however, to get paid really well to do what you love. He tells me that he is grateful to have earned well, but is quick to remind me that money isn't the answer when it comes to building a good life.

'I think the path to happiness is time to spend with your loved ones and on your curiosities and yourself, and that can be facilitated by money, but you have to already know the value of a litre of milk.'

What he means is that when we work hard to earn money (and aren't handed it on a silver platter), we truly know the value of simple, everyday things (like milk); it's a measure we have in common. When we're eventually able to bring more wealth into our lives, if we're smart we'll use it to facilitate the sorts of things that deliver real happiness—time with the people we love and exploring things we're interested in—rather than things that won't.

Substance over show

I'm not always my best self when it comes to money. I've made peace with the fact that we're probably never going to be financially 'rich', but I can sometimes get a little down-and-out when I fall into the comparison trap with friends who have family money, married into it or made it in a way I haven't yet been able to. I'm not exactly green with envy, but I can start to judge myself negatively about my own capacity to earn.

I'll stand in my room, huffing and puffing as I try to pull together an outfit that doesn't resemble old boots, a fifteen-year-old hand-me-down dress, a cheap T-shirt and that same old leather jacket I've been wearing for five years. My daughter, now well versed in dress-ups, watches my every move, modelling not only my relationship with my body but also my relationship with myself. She will request a 'dress' (top) and slip it over her tiny body, the fabric swimming to the floor. 'Cutie!' she will exclaim with a beaming smile, admiring herself in the mirror, and I can't help but feel grateful for a reality check I sorely need. To her, that top (also a hand-me-down) is a treasure. And yet I give myself a hard time because I can't afford the same clothes as the women with whom I am about to go to lunch (hello, first-world problem).

Deep down I know I am more than my clothes, and more than the house that holds the cupboard in which they are kept. And, yet, in that cupboard are more clothes than the majority of people around the world could ever dream of owning. There are $500 jackets (two), a $700 jumpsuit (honestly, WTAF was I thinking) and a $400 skirt, mixed in with $10 T-shirts and shitty old jumpers and mismatched socks. I don't have what many of my friends have, and in a lot of cases I don't aspire to, but my social-media feed is awash with women who look like they step out of a magazine or movie on a daily basis, and it's easy to feel (even though I know how constructed and filtered the image is) like I simply don't measure up.

I had to work through a lot of my own shit around money, worth and value before I was able to write this chapter. I am still learning that my value exists regardless of the car I drive or the clothes I wear, or where I sit on an airplane. But here's how I'm trying to think of it: It's like you're a Christmas tree—the value is in the tree. You can dress it up however you want with lights and tinsel and an angel that sits on top (saucy minx) but without the tree, there's nothing. And that, I wish I had learned sooner.

Bad-to-better takeaways

- Your value is not tied to your financial worth, even though sometimes it might feel like a really tangible way to measure it.
- If you're not great with money, find someone who is. No one is going to do it for you, but if you know someone good at it—family, friends, a professional—ask them to help.

- Be mindful when it comes to your money. Too often we just trust what we're paid and what we pay. I frequently 'tap and go' and then realise I paid $17 for a coffee without even noticing. Face palm.
- Don't compare! You don't know anyone else's circumstances.
- Make sure you're being paid what you're worth. More on that in Lesson 14.

Lesson 9
Being Good In Bed Is Easy
But loving sex is hard

The word 'slut' is the verbal equivalent of being slapped in the face. The shame-grenade does nothing to encourage a healthy relationship with sex, nor empower the people it's aimed at—even when it's used as a warning to 'protect' them. I've heard the term used to describe plenty of women, including myself, and ashamedly, I admit even using it in my younger years to negatively describe others (pot, meet kettle). In her book *Princesses & Pornstars*, Emily Maguire quotes an interviewee, Natalie, giving her the perfect definition of a 'slut': 'A slut is just a woman who has more sex or more sexual partners than whoever doing the labelling thinks she should.'

Bravo, Natalie, bravo.

Maguire goes on to question why promiscuity (which could also simply be considered experience and in any other realm, a positive) is still viewed, for women, in such a negative light. While men are still encouraged to sow their wild oats, women have a certain number of tickets they're allowed to punch before their 'value' (in some eyes) is affected. But of all the people (mainly women, but also some men) I surveyed for this book, only a small proportion (8.5 per cent of respondents) wished they'd had fewer sexual partners, and around a quarter wished they'd had more. The majority, however, said they were happy with their quantity of bedfellows, and I suspect that, rather than having genuinely 'nailed' the perfect number, this is a reflection of the fact that over time they have made peace with their sexual past.

As I've grown up, I've started to slowly piece together the role that sex has played, and continues to play, in my life. Many of us have a complex relationship with what happens between the sheets. Mine has been affected by the 'bad girl' persona I adopted to mask how frightened of the world I was. I was trying to be tough, but you didn't need to be Veronica Mars to see I was just scared. I was scared of myself, scared of not being loved, scared of getting hurt. I tried to model my behaviour on that of my male friends, because it seemed that the less they cared about people, the more people wanted them. There was carefree, back-slapping heroism that seemed to come from playing the field. Of course, deep down I was desperate for someone to fall for me—just like in the movies. But with no cameras around I just pissed people off and devastated myself when I was relegated to good-time girl, not the type you take home to your mother.

With some hindsight and a bit more perspective (oh, and hundreds of hours in therapy), I can see that my behaviour was fuelled by a troubling concoction of poor self-worth and an intense need to be sexually desired. Like most women I know in their thirties and beyond, I have let go of the what-*was*-their-name regrets from my youth, and even look back on most of them with a certain fondness. But it's amazing that something so pleasurable is able to cause us so much angst—regardless of whether you sleep with a hundred people, ten, one or no one at all.

Sexual self-worth

For most of my life, I built my self-worth almost entirely on being sexually desirable. I grew up watching Kim Kardashian and Paris Hilton build careers off the back of sex tapes, and Emily Ratajkowski gain international fame for being the extra-hot chick in a video clip. (Side note: I often wonder how the two other girls in that clip feel about that; they danced around like pretty sex slaves too and yet old @emrata got all the glory.) This is not new (hello Marilyn Monroe, Brigitte Bardot, Bettie Page) nor is it restricted to women (howdy Elvis Presley, Clark Gable, Mick Jagger), and with a quick scroll of your feed you'll probably agree it's not going anywhere. Sex will always sell—pop music, movie tickets, beer, underwear and pretty much any other product you can think of.

Someone who knows why is sexologist Dr Nikki Goldstein.

'We teach women that they get validated by being sexually desired, it's an ingrained idea in our culture,' she explains. 'All young girls or young people in general want to feel accepted, and they want to feel validated. Somebody wanting us sexually makes us feel good, it makes us feel powerful. We're validated for being a sexual woman, and that is a very powerful emotional high.'

Part of the challenge of growing up in a hyper-sexualised society, though, is that when you enact it in your own life, it tends to get you into trouble. We've come a long way, but sexually 'free' women are still judged negatively, and sex is still weirdly taboo—that naughty thing most of us do (and we even watch other people do) and yet we still struggle to talk openly and honestly about. For all of our twerking, equality-obsessed ways, a large proportion of our society is still very conventional—and it's part of the reason people can get so wound up over what is supposedly the most natural thing in the world.

'I think we're very fearful when it comes to sex,' Goldstein tells me. 'Religion has controlled us for so long—sex was something between a man and a woman, a husband and a wife. When we're unsure and fearful of something, the way that we find peace in that is to look for a norm. And we all want to feel normal, we all want to feel like we belong. But what is normal when it comes to sex? Is it two people? Is it three people? Is it once a week? Is it five times a week? We don't have anything to tell us what is normal and not normal with sex.'

The beliefs that matter most are our own, so rather than looking at our sexual attitudes and behaviours with judgement, it's important to reflect on where they came from in the first place.

Assessing your roots when it comes to sex

I always secretly wanted to live in a sex cult. Not a gross, awful sex cult where children are involved or women are there against their will, just one where (hot, cool) people could enjoy each other. I knew the reality would be very different, so a fantasy is where it stayed—but god only knows where that idea came from for me.

Goldstein says it is vital to assess our belief systems around sex if we want to have a healthy relationship with it.

'A lot of those deep-seated things around shame and regret and guilt come from ideals that we were given when we were growing up,' she explains. 'That might be religious, from our family or friends, from information that was in magazines like *Dolly* and *Cosmo*—so it's about looking at that belief system and challenging that.'

The way to do this, Goldstein says, is to write down your beliefs around sex. It's sexy homework, if you will.

'Some people say things like, "A woman shouldn't have sex on the first date,"' Goldstein explains. 'Then you have to look at—where did that idea come from? Is it from somewhere tangible? Or is it just something that's leftover from your upbringing? That way you can start to separate yourself from some of this backward belief system. Changing the belief system is how you can make peace with anything you have done, and also act on desires in the future.'

Let's assess yours. Write down everything you believe about sex and then challenge each belief by asking whether the source is credible. Get them onto paper so you can anal-yse (sorry, couldn't resist) them properly.

One of my misguided beliefs around sex was that being 'chosen' by someone was the ultimate vote of desire and therefore a tick for my self-worth. And I got extra points for being chosen by someone who already loved someone else, because if they were willing to risk their relationship, I must be really special. I can appreciate how fucked up that is now, but at the time it's what I subconsciously believed. I also believed that being good in bed was the best thing in life you could be, which is ironic because I definitely wasn't. I was self-conscious and only really there to please, which does not make for a great horizontal-tango partner.

If I'm honest, most of the time I kind of hated the actual sex part, but I craved emotional connection and found the build-up to sleeping with someone addictive—I loved the flirtation, the banter, the game. The 'choosing' in action.

The lowdown on lust

I adore lust. It's a dance: the locking of eyes, the subtle but tingly brush of a leg, the quickened heart rate in the seconds just before they lean in and kiss you. Back when I was younger, though, any time I fast-forwarded to the main event I was already second-guessing my decision. But I couldn't pull out now, could I? I mean, I had led them on, right? Now it was time to be a good sport and come through with the goods. *Screeeech!* (That was older me slamming on younger me's brakes.) Too many times I've done things I didn't want to do because I didn't know how to say no. It seemed easier to just get it over with than to utter a two-letter word. By night I channelled Samantha from *Sex and the City*, taking home anyone I wanted. But by day I was in the *Twister* of shame shitstorms.

'What gets a lot of women into these situations is that the chase is thrilling but the sex in itself is not mind-blowing,' explains Goldstein. 'The excitement comes from this desirable sensation of somebody sexually wanting you and you being a product of the society that we live in, which says that that is very powerful and rewarding for a woman.'

Powerful and rewarding, but also potentially damaging—especially if you do things you regret. Fast-forward to my thirties, though, and my perspective has changed. Do I *really* regret sleeping with 'guy from The Cottesloe Hotel'? No. Richard/Roger/Rainbow seemed very nice and we had a good time. Do I wish I could take back the arseholes who were (very) happy to be with me but then spoke badly about me afterward? I do. But honestly they're part of the reason I get to write this book, so I guess even they were worth it in the end.

Long gone are the days when your 'number' matters. I don't even know what mine is. The double standard when it comes to female sexuality, where it's fine for men to be promiscuous (encouraged and admired, even) but not women, is rubbish. What you do with your time and your body is your business, and your business only. Of course, I hold a complex position on this now, as a mother. The last thing I want is for my daughters to give themselves to people who don't deserve them. But there's another part of me that just wants them to enjoy sex (preferably when they're 45 or so, when I'm old and have no teeth and don't care anymore). I want them to feel the thrill of the chase, the rush of the intimacy and bask in the connection—all without guilt and judgement. I want them to be safe, looked after and in control. If only it had been that way for me.

Sex Ed, for adults

I was pretty eager to get rid of my virginity, kind of the way I suspect people feel about chlamydia. My boyfriend at the time was a bit of a hoodlum, which in suburban Perth basically just meant he was obsessed with Tupac, spent most of the day smoking bongs and dabbled in petty crime. In other words, a total catch. At that stage my sexual education consisted of rolling a condom (which broke) onto a banana in hysterics at school, the sealed section of *Dolly* magazine and hormone-fuelled chats with brave souls who had gone before me.

On that fateful day I drank a few glasses of my drink of choice at the time—Baileys on ice (god bless a young metabolism)—and steeled myself for what I knew was going to be a painful but necessary step toward becoming a woman. In shocking news, it was nothing like I'd seen in the movies—I was on a mattress on the floor with Tupac thumping 'Keep Ya Head Up' in my ears (which, with all due respect to Mr Shakur, is hard to do when you feel like someone is performing penis surgery on your hymen). It was predictably clumsy and awkward, and I was glad when it was over. I skipped into school the next day thrilled to have parted ways with my V plates.

I stayed with that boyfriend for a few more months and we had sex a few more times, but I was never really into it. I think he nicknamed me 'dead horse' (how lovely) because I would just lie there, frozen, not sure what to do. I wasn't sexually awakened, I was just going through the motions, a theme that would continue until I was much older. There was one guy I was obsessed with who, after me telling him I wouldn't sleep with anyone unless they were my boyfriend, asked me to be his girlfriend, slept with me and then dumped me the next day. Instead of recognising that he was a class A dick, I questioned myself. Was I not very good in bed? Did he not like me? Why wasn't I good enough to be his girlfriend? I was hurt, embarrassed and rejected, and I slept with that arsehole on and off for the next fifteen years.

Like so many things in life, as adults we tend to stop learning, exploring and teaching ourselves when it comes to sex. It's like driving—you don't really get better or worse at it, you just kind of keep doing it, maybe less frequently than you used to. But the benefit of getting older and wiser is that you can learn to really enjoy sex, to see it as an awesome hobby you get to practise with your forever person, your now person, or a whole football team of people (maybe avoid an actual football team, though, because that never seems to play out well). I think the best people to practise with are ones you love and trust. All the women I surveyed for this book, without exception, told me that the most sexually rich times they've had in life have been with long-term partners rather than racy one-night stands. So, there's that.

Libido status: lazy at best

Like many women, I can turn desire on and off like a tap. The less I have the less I need, and the more I have the more I want. Anyone in a long-term relationship can attest to the tenseness that can bubble to the surface when a couple hasn't had sex for a while; you can both feel it and know what needs to be done to fix it. And once it's time to make babies, sex takes on a different meaning. All of a sudden you experience sex for what it was originally intended—to procreate—and it's amazing. But once babies come along, things change. Date nights get traded for late (late) nights, which means you barely have enough energy to lift your fork to your mouth let alone have sex, lingerie makes way for maternity bras and windows of opportunity to get laid on the couch or frisky at the movies seem to evaporate.

Even without kids, though, long-term partnerships can stray into vanilla territory. And before you know it, you're daydreaming of those lust-fuelled years where you made a quick dash to the alley with the guy who looked like 50 Cent but most likely wasn't. So, how do you keep it interesting and invite more excitement into a bedroom that has become 50 shades of basic? You open your mouth. For a chitty chat. With your clothes on.

Ask questions such as:
- What turns you on?
- What do you like in the bedroom? What do you hate?
- What have you always wanted to try but never had the chance or been too scared to bring up?
- If you watch porn, what do you go for?
- What's the most exciting sexual experience you've ever had? Careful here ... you'll need your ego in check in case the answer doesn't involve you. If real feelings are involved, maybe ask about their favourite sexual experience you've ever had together.
- Where's a place you've always wanted to have sex? Maybe it's the kitchen or the car or an airplane bathroom (gross, I don't get the appeal, but you do you, boo).

Then, here's the only trick you need to know about being great in bed

Outside the bedroom setting, I've asked a lot of people what turns them on. Their answers have almost always been the same: someone who 'loves it'. They don't care whether you can do circus tricks with your vagina or if you have cellulite on your butt, they just want to be with someone who unashamedly loves sex and is there to enjoy it. But I know firsthand that is easier said than done. All sorts of things hold us back from being able to truly enjoy sex—previous experiences, expectations as to what sex 'should' be, hang-ups about our bodies, a lack of understanding of what works for us, not to mention all of the cultural, religious and societal influences.

So, how do you turn yourself on to enjoying sex?

WORK OUT WHAT YOU LIKE
Spend some time getting to know your body, and not just your genitals. Do this on your own first, then you can educate a partner.

ASK FRIENDS WHAT THEY LIKE
You share everything else, why not get specific about this? Choose your location wisely so you can really get into the nitty-gritty, lubricate your talking machines and get chatting.

TRY TO GET OUT OF YOUR HEAD
We hear a lot about mindfulness, and it can (and should) absolutely extend to sex. Thoughts will still come and go, but try to focus on your body and what you can feel. Stay in the moment.

REMEMBER THAT SEX ISN'T JUST ABOUT PENETRATION
The sex we see in the movies tends to focus on climax, but sex isn't just about penetration nor about having an orgasm. So, if you struggle to 'get there', maybe forget about 'getting there' and just enjoy the ride. In the wise words of John Farnham (who I'm sure would be thrilled to be quoted here): take the pressure down.

PULL OUT SOME INSPO
I'm not down with porn as the main form of sex education for young people ... but for adults, it has advantages. It's a wondrous catalogue of genitals, showing that all shapes, sizes and colours are out there, which can help you feel more confident about what

you have. It's also an idea generator, giving you new moves to try. And lastly, it can get you in the mood, even if you don't feel like it. Dopamine is famous for its role in our brain's reward system. When we eat food we like, have sex, win on the slots or—you guessed it—watch porn, dopamine levels in the brain go gangbusters.

(Side note: If you're not in a long-term relationship, you are in the enviable position of being able to work out what you want, and what you don't, both inside the bedroom and out of it. I can't tell you how many women have told me they wish they'd had more sexual experiences before they were attached. Enjoy it, because once you're knee-deep in a mortgage and kids you'll be thinking about that-time-with-what's-his-or-her-name faster than you can knock back your weekend Merlot.)

A cautionary tale about being sexually generous

When I was in my early twenties the company I was working for secured the rights to shoot a documentary on a national pole-dancing competition. I was to produce and host it, and I was desperate not to fuck it up. I was anxious as hell, though, not just because of the gravitas of the opportunity, but also because I had convinced myself I had HIV. Never wanting to kill the mood, instead of protecting myself in the moment, I would stupidly 'roll the dice', which is kind of the behavioural equivalent of finding a pill on the street and throwing it down the hatch, crossing your fingers and hoping for the best.

Next, I would pray I hadn't been exposed to any disease. I'm talking on my knees, hands in prayer pose, cry-begging the universe to protect me—a totally logical approach for a science-loving, non-religious person. I would take myself off frequently for testing, shitting myself that *this* was the time I would be told my life was over. I was certain I was going to be punished for my sins, so my brain would operate on all sorts of fallacies. I could see lesions on my skin, I'd get dizzy, had chronic headaches and wake up in a sweat (which on a quick Google search all but confirmed my self-diagnosis). These days HIV isn't a life-threatening illness, the drugs can basically make the virus undetectable in your blood and people with it can live long and healthy lives. But back then it still felt like a death sentence.

I knew I needed to get to the doctor, but I couldn't face the music before the shoot. I had to hold it together so I didn't let anyone down, and then I would deal with the inevitable. Mum was thankfully in town when shooting day rolled around, and I managed to pull her in to assist on the shoot because I needed the support. I was a nervous wreck. I couldn't focus on anything other than how my life was about to change once I heard 'those words'. As soon as we wrapped, Mum and I bundled into the car and went home, where I collapsed on the bed and surrendered to sleep, relieved the day was over.

The reprieve didn't last long. The next morning I woke up paralysed with fear and couldn't leave the house. I lay on the couch sobbing with Mum hovering nearby, understandably wondering what the fuck was going on, so I reluctantly told her I was 100 per cent certain her pride and joy had been a bit of a hussy and contracted a life-threatening illness. I would later learn that Mum had had (genuine) HIV scares of her own over the years; once she even had a positive test result that turned out to be false. She had also buried one of her closest girlfriends as a result of AIDS. The two had travelled together to Mykonos for a European summer of debauchery and both lusted over the same dude, even bickering over him. Her friend 'won', got lucky with Mr Mykonos and scored HIV in the process, which later progressed to AIDS and took her life. Turns out Mum was the lucky one after all.

As I lay prone on my couch of self-induced terror, Mum called a doctor to the house and, while rational me knew that it was medically impossible, I was hopeful he would circumvent my need for a blood test and tell me on sight that I didn't have HIV. Instead, he took one look at me and said I was having a severe panic attack, prescribed some Valium and said I needed to go to my GP as soon as I was up to it to face my fear head on. No shit, Dr Sherlock. The truth is, I believed a diagnosis like that was what I deserved for leaving myself vulnerable and exposed. But mostly I think I felt ashamed for being sexual. This was dumb on so many levels. First, it illustrates just how emotionally immature I was, still subconsciously believing that there's a dude in the sky with a clipboard dishing out diseases to naughty boys and girls for punishment. Second, there's not a single part of me that thinks anyone who acquires HIV should feel ashamed of their diagnosis, and yet I applied the twisted thinking to myself.

A few days later, I sat in the doctor's surgery, waiting for my results.

'Casey Beros?' said the grim reaper.

I jumped up before she'd finished my surname, but then dragged my feet through the wet concrete that had replaced the floor and finally—after what felt like a two-hour walk—sat down on the chair in the doctor's consulting room.

'What can I do for you today?'

Not much, aside from handing down my death sentence, said my brain.

'I'm um ... just here for the results of my ah ... recent tests,' my mouth stammered as I spiralled into a full out-of-body experience.

I watched her face intently as she opened my file on the computer and clicked through various tabs, tapping on the keyboard for what I'm certain was hours but in reality was probably seconds.

'Chlamydia: negative. Syphilis: negative. Gonorrhoea: negative. Hep B: negative. HIV ...'

I tuned out at this stage, the bright lights of the pearly gates calling my name. When I came to, the doctor was staring at me, concerned.

'I'm sorry, what did you say?' I asked the reaper.

'Negative. Your HIV test is negative.'

'Negative like not good news? Like I have HIV?' I asked, confused.

'No, negative as in clear—you do *not* have HIV,' replied the lovely doctor, who must have subbed in for the reaper while I was out of consciousness. I thanked her and floated out of the room, relief washing over me like a cool shower on a hot day. I looked up, put my hands in prayer and mouthed, 'Thank you.'

The best sex is safe sex

Do you know what the solution is to this entire debacle? Condoms. Run-of-the-mill, sex-ed-banana, available-from-literally-every-supermarket/pharmacy/convenience-store-in-every-suburb condoms. If I had my time again, I would make them a non-negotiable, every time, until I was in a long-term, exclusive relationship with someone I trusted and we had both been tested. Makes sense, right? So, why is it so hard to use them, given we've had that message drilled into us time and time again?

'You do get kind of get caught up and you feel guilty, you don't want to ruin the moment by ... "Oh, can you put this on?"' explains GP Dr Preeya Alexander. 'I encourage my patients to make it their blanket rule. You need to say to people, "Look, I need to protect myself." And as a GP it's not actually chlamydia that I'm worried about—although chlamydia is everywhere, so you should be worried about it—but HIV and syphilis are still issues in heterosexual populations too.'

Alexander says condoms are amazing if they're used correctly, but they're not fail-safe, and not just because they can break.

'They don't actually mitigate the risk of something like genital warts or herpes,' she explains. She adds that women should carry their own condoms, and we shouldn't discriminate: 'You know, the really hot guy with all the accolades gets exactly the same treatment as the not-so-hot dude without them.'

In other words, be nice to your vagina

Years ago I saw a documentary about labiaplasty and became fascinated by 'designer vaginas'. I hadn't yet watched enough porn to realise that the spectrum of what a 'normal' vagina looks like is vast and varied. All I knew was that I wanted a Barbie panel; neat and tidy with no extra bits. I took my time and got multiple opinions, but eventually sought out the surgeon from the documentary and set up an appointment. Even after he showed me pictures of a million vaginas and assessed my own, I was still convinced I wanted to go ahead and scheduled the surgery. I'd done my due diligence, but I was in my early twenties and nowhere near mature enough to weigh up the emotional and physical consequences of my decision.

If you don't know what a labiaplasty is, it's a surgical procedure where you change the size and/or shape of your inner labia. Essentially, you slice away any 'extra' and toss it, like you would the pastry offcuts if you were baking a pie. I decided to lump together two surgeries on two completely different body parts because I'm a sadist and figured I'd kill two birds with one scalpel—a bald patch on my head (which I'd had forever; Mum said it was where god had kissed me on the noggin, the doctors said it was alopecia—and no offence to Mum or god but my money is on the docs) and the poor tiny bit of extra labia down below. I don't remember much from before the surgery, but boy do I remember after. I was in a world of pain and couldn't wait to get out of the hospital and home where I could moan and eat ice cream until I felt better. I staggered into a taxi and rode the whole way home with my sore head in Mum's lap, and a thick pad between my legs, tender from someone *cutting off a piece of my vagina.*

My recovery was slow and far less fun than I expected. Not even endless snacks and back-to-back *Dawson's Creek* reruns could compensate for the intense pain as my wounds healed, inhibiting my movement and capacity to shower or do pretty much anything for myself. I spent five days lying on a mattress on the floor in the lounge room (where the TV was; this was before the ease of watching Netflix on your laptop in bed) wishing I could take the whole thing back. But bit by bit, my labia slowly looked less like I had allowed someone to attack it with a scalpel. As I healed physically, it dawned on me that what I essentially signed myself up (and paid handsomely) for was genital mutilation, and I am now deeply ashamed. It makes me shudder to think of my children doing the same thing, or ever believing they are not 100 per cent perfect as they are.

What the hell was my problem with my vagina in the first place? It had always served me well, never caught an STI (though not for want of trying) and rarely led me astray. It has been waxed, lasered and stifled by lycra to within an inch of its life, and as the gatekeeper to my ovaries it has facilitated bringing two beautiful babies into the world. While I convinced myself I was doing it for me, in reality I was doing it because I thought it would be more attractive—mainly, to men. But the net result wasn't actually more confidence in the bedroom. All I really got was some lost sensitivity … and I'm still waiting for my vagina-of-the-year award.

Moral of the story? Your sexual self-worth isn't tied to how perfect your body is, and it's also not diminished by how many (or how few) people you share it with. Embrace the parts of you that enjoy feeling sexual; that pleasure is one of the greatest we get.

Bad-to-better takeaways

- Your worth has nothing to do with how sexually desirable you are.
- Get good at sex on your own first, then choose partners who deserve you to practise with.
- Get clear on where your beliefs come from around sex. Are they serving you? If not, it might be time to upgrade them.
- Sex is so much more than the actual act—and you're allowed to talk about it.
- Think of condoms as your seatbelt: essential for your safety and a non-negotiable for every ride.

Lesson 10
Let Go of the Idea of 'The One'

Embrace all of your 'ones' instead

I don't believe in 'the one' but rather, that (if we're lucky) we get a few of them, and they each come into our lives to teach us something different. If you ask anyone who has spent some time dating and playing the field about the loves in their lifetime, there are often common themes. There's the first love (where you think you'll die from the pain when you break up), the outlier (where you have no idea what you were thinking but they were totally necessary), the man-meth bad boy (or girl) who is addictive and bad for you, and your 'this is it' person. Let me introduce you to mine. Well, three of them. I'm saving the best for last in Lesson 16.

The first love

I got my first tattoo when I was fifteen, the perfect age to make a permanent decision. I don't know why I was so desperate to get 'inked' (what all the true fuckwits call it, including myself at the time), but I think it made me feel grown-up and tough, like the world couldn't mess with me if I was willing to inject black ink under my skin. I chose the Japanese symbol for 'desire' (cringe); who knows why, I've never been to Japan and literally all I'd desired by that stage in life was a pony (which I got) and boobs (which were coming).

After a few beers for Dutch courage, my friend and I went to a mid-level-dodgy tattoo parlour, not dodgy enough that we'd end up with hepatitis but just lax enough to not ask us for ID. I went first, and almost passed out from the pain, which only reinforced in my underdeveloped brain just how brave I was. I felt panicked (probably my gut telling me to *run*) and I will never forget the surprising loudness of the tattoo gun or the feeling of the needle tearing through my skin—hot, prickly and painful. My friend opted for a similar symbol (or maybe it was the same, I can't remember) on her tummy, and we parted ways with our $100 and skipped out of there like the heroes we were.

Two decades later and I still have a (patchy, faded) reminder of my terrible decision poking proudly out from my swimmers at the beach, a stamp of the trampiest variety to let everyone know that at some point in my life I was that girl. Since then, another two tattoos have joined it on my body, just to really drive the message home. One is a tiny heart on the inside of my middle finger, a reminder to love myself even when I feel like flipping the bird at the rest of the world. The other I got with the love of my young life. Matching, of course.

I stuck with my Japanese theme (at least I'm consistent) and added the symbol for 'love' below 'desire', like chapters of a Japanese book I can't read. A quick Google search confirms they loosely represent the words I'd wanted, but honestly they could have meant 'dick' and 'slug' and I would have had no idea. I'm pretty sure the only thing my tattoo artist was fluent in was murdering buckets of KFC. Years later I would learn that the two symbols together effectively means 'loves sex'—which, while not untrue, is also not ideal to have permanently tattooed on your back.

First love came into my life when I was nineteen and freshly back from a year in Europe; wiser, worldlier and—thanks to the so-called 'Heathrow injection'—10 kilos heavier. I had known him for years, but when I came back we fell hard and fast, and if I remember correctly we decided we loved each other and were shacking up within weeks of hanging out. We set up house in an apartment (an investment of Mum's, which I was fortunate to be loaned), both relishing the novelty of having someone to belong to. We even got a dog, one I would eventually claim in our 'divorce' settlement and who would be my best friend for sixteen years.

Before things turned bad, they were intoxicatingly, breathtakingly, incomparably amazing. I was certain he was my soul mate and that we would be together for the rest of our lives. Early in our relationship, though (before we were officially 'in' one), I went out one night and—much later in the evening—called an ex. Before I knew it I was in a cab to his house, and I woke up the next morning in his bed with a sore head and a guilty conscience. I tried to will it away but I couldn't and eventually came clean, hoping we would be able to move past it.

For the next decade (yes, ten years—I'm a slow learner when it comes to men) we tried. I never regained his trust and though all we really wanted was each other we frequently hurt one another in futile and immature attempts to 'get each other back' as we navigated breaking up, making up and everything in between on what felt like almost a weekly basis. We weren't yet mature enough to compartmentalise what had happened and truly move forward. There was too much water under the bridge and we both knew it, but we held on for dear life anyway.

We'd have one eye on each other and the other on someone else as we desperately tried to get over the relationship. It never worked, so from time to time we would give things another go, but it would always fail for one reason or another; we were jealous, angry and hurting—not exactly the ideal emotional environment in which to build a solid relationship. After about three years, during one of our 'off' periods, I decided to move to the other side of the country. I knew if I didn't put a continent between us we would just keep getting back together, and that wouldn't work for anyone.

He felt left behind and resented me more, yet still we couldn't let go. He even moved over at one point, we got a house together and I thought we had finally turned the corner to a new life together in which everything would be perfect. But our wounds followed us wherever we went. They weren't in locations or other people, they were inside us—and the damage was irreparable.

My only stipulation for him moving over and us getting back together was that he wasn't allowed to just not come home after a night out, which seemed like a fairly reasonable request. I didn't trust him (red flag), I'd given up drinking for a while to prove he could trust me (redder flag) and my expectation was that he would come home when he said he was coming home (the fact this was not a given should have been the reddest flag of all). He played ball for a couple of months, but then he dropped it, hard, and when I woke for about the fifth time, at 5 a.m., to an empty bed, I called.

Me: 'What are you doing?'

Him: 'Just hanging out.'

Me: 'Right, so ... are you coming home?'

Him: 'Yeah I'm coming now, just waiting for a cab.'

Three hours later, no prizes for guessing who wasn't home.

I packed a bag, called my best friend and asked if I could stay with her for a bit. He and I spoke later that day and when he informed me that his priority was to head back to the pub rather than catch up to apologise, I told him my priority was to break up rather than stay together. He laughed and told me to get over it, fully expecting that—yet again—I would forgive him. But I meant it when I said this was his last chance, and I didn't give a fuck if he'd packed up his life and moved to Timbuktu for me—the writing was on the wall.

The next morning he went surfing down the coast (still clearly not in a hurry to patch things up), so I hired a truck, drove to our house, packed up my things and left. For weeks afterward he used every trick in the book to try to get me to come home, from guilting me financially about how he would afford the house on his own (not my problem), to him moving all the way to Sydney for me (again, not my problem given he'd broken the only rule I'd set) and pulling out the tally of who had caused more hurt in our relationship. But none of it mattered, the relationship was over and I knew it.

It took me years to get over him. I still feel my heart drop into my gut whenever I see him or hear his voice. But slowly, over many years, we managed to build some semblance of a friendship. I thoroughly enjoy seeing him occasionally at a mutual friend's wedding or a barbecue if we're in the same city, at which you'll have a hard time finding two people who like each other more.

Timing is, quite frankly, a bit of a bitch. Sometimes you'll meet 'your person' before you're ready, and, eventually, someone else might end up reaping the benefits of your hard work. But they weren't your person forever, they were just your person for then, and for whatever reason their new person is what they need for their next chapter, just as you will find in yours.

The outlier

You know that saying: 'If you stop looking for love, it'll find you when you least expect it'? That happened to me in 2013.

My best friend and I had started a business running health retreats and were keen to secure a base in Bali, Indonesia, where it was warm, appealing for travellers and cheap to operate. Before I moved my life there, I took a job managing a restaurant to save some money in my native Perth. And it was at this very restaurant that the outlier entered my life. A well-known Australian actor, on screen he is impossibly charismatic and talented, and in person he is naughty, funny and one of the most intelligent people I've ever met. I had no idea I would end up hanging out with him that night, let alone fall into a wild and loved-up adventure with him for the next few months.

I was struck by how much (and how quickly) I wanted to be around him. That first night we drank, laughed and ended up back at his hotel; I knew he was leaving the next morning and didn't think I'd ever see him again. But over the next few months we kept in touch and got together whenever we could. I felt safe with him, and we would spend hours discussing everything and nothing.

I even flew out to a little mining town called Kalgoorlie to meet him, spending a couple of precious days together where—at the famous Kalgoorlie Hotel and after several (many) beers—we exchanged makeshift wedding rings in a makeshift wedding ceremony. We had both been pretty vocal about how marriage wasn't for us, so we thought it was hilarious, but also felt an intense connection that we wanted to mark as a moment in time.

The next day we agreed that, while our 'marriage' was neither legitimate nor conventional, we wanted to be our own version of husband and wife, just to each other. We wouldn't confine the other to any sort of monogamous promise, but we would be together in spirit and in person whenever we could. To commemorate the trip we bought rings. I even sent Mum a photo of our hands decked out in our rings saying 'Guess what?!'—which is an appalling thing to do to your mother but also *very* funny. (Side note to my girls: Please don't ever do that to me.)

In all seriousness, though, it felt good to belong to someone. I liked being a 'wife' even if I wasn't a real one. Our lives kept moving and we organised for him to come up to Bali so we could have a week together. He hadn't had time off in forever and needed a break. I worked out for weeks and made sure I was waxed, manicured and pedicured to within an inch of my life, with my hair done and a perfect Bali tan. I couldn't wait to see him and to have more time together than we had ever had. As I drove out to pick him up from the airport, I was nervous with anticipation. As soon as he came through customs, though, I could tell something wasn't right.

The outlier wasn't typically the neatest of fellas, he almost always looked like he'd smoked a joint and possibly slept in a car. Looking back, actually, a lot of my boyfriends looked like that …

there's clearly something in 'bedraggled' that appeals to me. When he saw me his face lit up, but his eyes seemed dark and empty. He looked rougher than usual, but I put it down to a long flight (I mean, who *doesn't* look like shit and smell like farts when they get off a red-eye). When we got in the car I asked if everything was okay and he said he was just overwhelmed to be there. I tried to buy it but spent the cab ride with my head on his shoulder and my heart in my stomach. Something was wrong.

It's an understatement when I say he came to Bali with nothing. He got off the plane with the clothes on his back and a newspaper in a plastic bag. He reasoned we would buy him some board shorts, a T-shirt and thongs, and while I applaud his non-materialism, it felt like he didn't give a shit for a girl who had spent weeks physically and emotionally preparing for the week of a lifetime. He had even lost his ring, something I felt had connected us over oceans and countries. We splurged on a beautiful hotel and tried to get into holiday-mode by drinking cocktails and cuddling in the infinity pool, but he seemed kind of detached.

We muddled on, but things weren't right. By day we would ride our motorbikes to the beach and he would put on his headphones and play music so loud he couldn't hear my directions, meaning I'd lose him and have to turn around and chase him down. By night we would go to dinner at a beautiful restaurant and he'd blow his nose loudly and deliberately on the cloth napkin. It felt like he was testing me, but I couldn't work out why.

Over the next few days, the outlier fell apart. He was a one-man circus; happy one second, angry the next, beside himself with sadness in another. I tried consoling, inspiring, holding and scolding, but nothing worked. Within a few days I had friend-zoned him, stipulating that we needed to get him well if we were to continue a relationship. My gut was screaming at me to run but my head was reasoning I had to stay. Looking back, I didn't really know how to help him. I could see glimpses of the kind, hilarious and intelligent man I'd fallen for, but in other moments he was a complete stranger. One minute he would calmly agree he needed help, and the next he'd be telling me I was overreacting to the whole thing. My head was spinning.

Things went from bad to worse, but I figured I would get us through the next few days, get him on a plane home where we could get him some help and then see where things landed. I needed some space, so I headed to the gym to blow off some steam. Running on a treadmill, I listened to Kesha sing about how she brushes her teeth with a bottle of bourbon (which confuses me somewhat but I'm here for it). A song like that is a red flag to a bull and combined with exercise endorphins it's a recipe for disaster. I convinced him to come to a party that night, which is so not his scene but I needed a break from the energy between us. I figured a few drinks, some dancing and other people around couldn't hurt and might lighten the mood.

When I'm anxious, I tend to drink much faster than I should—it's like the liquid quells the rising feeling of panic in my throat. Ideally, I would drink tea. Or kombucha. Something that doesn't have the ability to impede my brain's basic functions, but unfortunately none of that was on the menu that night. We teamed up with a bunch of guys, friends of friends of mine, and went back to their villa for an after-party. I was flirting up a storm; I think I wanted him to see that I was desirable to other people, hoping it would shock him out of his 'behaviour'. I can see how ridiculous that is now and wish more than anything I could go back and whisper in that girl's ear: 'It's not his behaviour, it's his brain. Kill him with kindness and then reassess.'

It got late and I ended up lying on a day bed with one of the guys. Our clothes were on and we weren't making out or anything, but I think he had his arm on me and … put it this way—it looked bad and wasn't in any way appropriate behaviour. (Side note: If you think this is the part where I do nothing wrong and it's all a big misunderstanding, don't worry, I'll well and truly fuck things up in a minute.) The outlier came looking for me and begged me to talk to him, but I was done talking. The past week had left me so emotionally drained that, in my immaturity, all that was left to do was detonate, so I turned into a monster, telling him with the subtlety of a sledgehammer that I had zero fucks left to give. He disappeared, and I tried to block the whole thing out the only way I knew how.

I tried calling him the next morning but his phone was off. He'd headed to the airport and hopped an earlier flight home. We spoke when he landed back in Australia and miraculously managed to smooth things over. The relationship was finished but the friendship was still there. To anyone reading this thinking I'm a c*nt, I don't blame you. I hate the way I handled things. But I'm human and I make mistakes. All I know is that I owe him an apology, a hug and a beer. And I can't wait for that day to come.

Maybe you've experienced your own outlier. If so, don't forget—everyone comes into our life for a reason. You will always learn something, and you might just find yourself expanding your horizons while you're at it. Don't discount people because they're not who you think you should be with, and don't see a relationship as a failure if it doesn't work out. Mourn the loss, take the lessons, dust yourself off and get back on the unicycle.

Man-meth (or wo-man meth)

Sometimes, bad boys (and girls) are like meth: addictive and bad for you. You know them—they're devilishly good-looking, full of witty banter, 'one of the boys'. They convince you that *you* are the *only* one, and in fact they adore you so much they can't even get it together to be with you. They also manage to concurrently convince a number of other smart, intuitive people of this very same thing. It's kind of like the polygamous version of Romeo and Juliet, but none of the Juliets know, for a while at least.

Remember the guy I told you about who slept with me and then broke up with me the next day? The one I then slept with for the next *decade* and then some? He has something over me (and a number of women I know) that I can't even articulate. It's like magical man-meth dust, or something. Had I actually gone on to share a life with him it would probably have been miserable, because I know exactly what he's like, and yet when he messages—as he does every year or so just to make sure I'm still on the hook—my heart skips a beat, even though I am blissfully and happily married.

I ask Dr Nikki Goldstein what the fuck is wrong with me and why so many of us fall into their trap. She says that, again, it comes down to validation.

'We are taught to believe that if you can change them and they fall for you then you are so worthy,' she explains. 'Normally that person has issues with commitment, they like having lots of one-night stands and multiple partners. So if you're able to win that person over and they change their ways for you, then what does that say about you?' In my mind—that I was a legendary sex goddess who deserved some sort of parade or at least a spot on *Who* magazine's sexiest people list.

I longed to feel I was worth changing for. But allow me to let you in on a little secret about my bad boys: Some of them got married and had kids and they reined it in a bit, but they didn't *really* change. Thankfully I have largely outgrown feeling special for gaining their attention (aside from my main man-meth, he still gets me every time), but my point is: you don't want to end up with that guy (or girl). You want to end up with the one who actually wants to be in a relationship with you, not because you were able to eventually wrangle them into it—but because you're amazing and they know it.

Just like real meth, man-meth can make you act like a lunatic. When you have their attention you feel like you have superhuman strength, and when you lose the high, you come down hard. Man-meth can take a formerly confident, glowing, happy person and turn them into a paranoid, sleepless, scabby mess. And they're tricky AF because they know exactly how to push your buttons and play the game. My rule of thumb is this: If it sounds like a duck and it looks like a duck—it's probably a fucking duck. Straight to man-meth rehab for you, sister.

Your 'this is it' person

One of the things I learned from my 'marriage' to the outlier was that I was longing to belong to someone. I spent a few more months in Bali but decided it wasn't the right fit for me or my business. I had a deep desire to be part of the media landscape in Australia and a rubber arm that saw me partying way too much on the hedonistic island. Acknowledging I couldn't have my Bintang and drink it too, I moved back to Sydney. I was still partying a lot, but deep down I was lonely. In my attempt not to 'look' for a partner, instead I just looked in all the wrong places, hooking up with guys I would never settle down with. The truth was, I wasn't acting like the sort of person they would want to settle down with either.

And then I'd finally had enough—of the late nights, the feeling like shit, the worry about people talking badly about me. I decided to get my life back on track. I worked as much as I could, went to yoga, dialled the partying down a few notches and prayed for the world's kindest man. And, the universe delivered. He deserves his own chapter, so more on him later.

Finding 'the one' is a numbers game

Dating these days is like an all-you-can-eat smorgasbord of people in your pocket. You don't have to get dressed and go out, you can 'swipe right' and pick up. Based on ease of access, finding 'the one', if that's what you're looking for, has never been more of a numbers game. Just like securing a great job or new apartment, you apply for a bunch and hope you get a call back. If I had my time again, I would date everyone. Especially now you can (kind of) get to know someone through your phone. If nothing else, you'll meet interesting people who might become friends.

If that's you—take the pressure off, have fun and relish your singledom. On the way, though, you're going to have to go through a few duds. You'll have great dates, terrible dates and dates that make you lose faith in humankind. You'll be rejected and you'll reject people (kindly, I hope). But like Lotto, you've got to be in it to win it.

Bad-to-better takeaways

- When you break up with your first love it will feel like someone has ripped your heart out of your chest and put it through a garlic press. You'll survive, I promise. And if you've already been through this, you know what I'm talking about, you survivor, you.
- Don't cheat. Ever. It's not worth it. Break up and then do whatever you want, but not before.
- If you're fighting a lot, you're probably not right for each other. Bickering is okay, a healthy debate is fine, but proper fighting—yuck. Cut your losses and move on. And if you don't trust them, walk away. Life is too short to be with someone you don't trust.
- Bad boys (and girls) hook you in because we love nothing more than the validation of getting the attention of someone who is hard to get. Be smarter than I was and spare yourself.
- If it looks like a duck and it sounds like a duck—trust me, it's a duck.
- Drop your expectations and be open to all sorts of people. Every relationship we have teaches us something we need to know about ourselves.

Lesson 11
Friends Are Like Wine

They make everything feel better

Meeting one person who ticks all our boxes is akin to finding a singular food that satisfies all our nutritional needs (and desires). How lucky it is, then, that we have different friends to cheer us on, lift us up and hold our hand when life pelts us with lemons.

The sense of belonging that comes with besties is a feeling unlike any other—they're the family you choose. But as beautiful as they are, just like any other relationship, friendships aren't always straightforward, and it makes breaking up incredibly painful. 'Never!' you might be thinking. But, especially as you get older, it happens for a whole range of reasons. Geography, families and different life stages can get in the way of what was formerly a vital union for you, and it can leave you confused and heartbroken.

When I was growing up I didn't think I would ever drift apart from my closest friend. We spent every minute in each other's pockets—riding horses all weekend, eating chips with filthy hands and singing along to Mariah Carey. As we got older, though, things changed. All of a sudden she was into make-up, clothes and boys, and I just wasn't there yet. Over the coming years we clung to our friendship but had less and less in common. The final straw was her inviting me to a 'cool' Sydney party, where she left me to go and hang in the VIP section with her then-boyfriend. That's when I knew it was done. But I still miss her, even many years later. We connect here and there, but it never sticks. And when I see a picture of her on social media, my heart still sinks a little, just like seeing an ex with their new lover.

Sex and the City sold us an impossible dream that we would be BFFs forever. I should have known not to trust those bitches after they said I would be able to afford designer shoes on a journalist's wage, but I bought into the eternal-friendship narrative anyway, hard. Sure, relationships are complex, messy and much more glamorous on TV, but over years of building lifelong friendships, that's what I expected them to be—for life. In reality, though, as we get older, our circle tends to become more like a few sparse dots in the vague shape of a circle, maybe, if you joined them together with a pen.

So, if you're looking around wondering where the hell all your mates went, don't worry—it's just your life spring-cleaning to make room for all the good stuff to come. I know this is easier said than lived. I used to be devastated when a friend and I would drift apart; it felt like I had failed. But a step back in a friendship is simply that and shouldn't be seen as a failure at all. It's just two people's lives moving in different directions, sometimes temporarily. And sometimes, you acted like a dickhead. That's right, you. There is no question that in my bad-girl days I treated friends badly, and I lost some of them because of it. I have to take that on the chin and find solace in the fact that these days I strive to do better. It's hard not to take personally, but I wish I'd learned sooner that friends move around like chess pieces. Some move closer, some move further away and some move off the board altogether. And all of that is okay.

Diversify, baby

You don't wear the same pair of undies every day, so you can diversify when it comes to your friendships too. Sure, you might have a core group of pals, but be open to new connections. There could be cool colleagues at work or uni, or people you meet via an exercise class or hobby. Be open-minded; some of my dearest friends are decades older than me and have been the best mentors (and friends) I could have ever asked for. They consistently show me that getting older isn't something to be feared, but in fact, if I work at it, life only gets better and better.

I have many different types of friends. Naughty friends I bonded with over late (late) nights, healthy friends I connected with because of our shared love of wellbeing, mum friends as a result of similarly aged tiny people and friends I've been thrown into situations with through work, school and hobbies.

Here are a few types of friends you might have in your pocket.

THE SMART ONE

While like attracts like, I also believe you can level-up when it comes to your mates. Surrounding yourself with people who are smarter and better at life than you will always serve you well.

THE INSTANT BESTIE

You told each other your life story over margaritas—on the day you met. You can't believe how comfortable things feel, and how quickly. Before you know it, you start to 'miss' them—cue endless emoji-laden chats like you're passing notes in high school. It's the friendship version of falling in love and it feels good. Swoon.

THE GOOD-TIMER

You spent Saturday nights licking the walls and Sunday mornings lying in bed laughing until you cried about your adventures the night before. They know your deepest, darkest secrets—most of which took place after 2 a.m. If you're dancing on tables they're there, if there's champagne, a fancy party or a weekend away they're all over it, but bring on the harder bits in life (the ones you really need your friends for) and poof—they're gone.

THE CLIMBER

You grew up together but then your lives moved in different directions. You still adore each other but truth be told, while once upon a time money or status never mattered, all of a sudden it does. You start second-guessing what you're wearing when you catch up and aren't invited when there's a fancy dinner, reasoning that you couldn't have afforded it anyway. But there's no getting around the fact that they've upgraded to newer, shinier friends—and it hurts those pesky feelings of yours.

THE INCONSISTENT CONSISTENT

You know those friends you don't see or speak to for months (years even) but when you do things are *exactly* the same? There's something invaluable about these people, and a catch-up every so often is just enough to fill your cup and remind you why you love them. It's maximum bang for your friendship buck.

THE LISTENER

They're not your coolest/funnest friend, but they're always, *always* there for you. They're the one you call when things aren't going your way, and they are always ready with a willing ear and a pep talk. They're a good friend, a good listener and a good person, and it would be a good idea to hold on to them and take care of them too.

Go with your gut

I've heard it said that the best judge of a friendship is how you feel when you leave someone. If you feel good after you've spent time with them, that's a winner. If you feel bad, you might have some assessing to do. If someone bullies, judges and belittles in your presence, making jokes at other people's expense, you can bet your bottom dollar they'll do the same thing to you, leaving you feeling exposed and vulnerable rather than like they have your back no matter what. Sometimes people act like that because they're unhappy and sometimes they're just arseholes. You'll need to determine which it is and then make the call as to whether you stick around or politely extricate yourself. Here's what I know: your gut won't lie to you on this one. If you feel crap when you leave them, it's probably best to park that friendship for a while.

Friends = happiness

There's a big, long-term study out of Harvard that has been going for more than 80 years and aims to identify the predictors of a long and happy life. In 1938 during the Great Depression, researchers started to follow a group of 268 men and are still tracking the ones who are alive now, as well as a bunch of their kids (who are in their fifties and sixties). In the 1970s they added another 456 men to the mix (and in later stages of the study they've started looking at women too), giving us a long-term picture of lives outside our own—the choices they've made, the things they've done, and how that has affected how long they live and how happy their lives have been. The researchers closely studied their health, relationships and how well they do in what sort of careers. What they found is this:

The quality of our relationships is the biggest determinant of our happiness.

They can be relationships with lovers, friends, family or people within our community. Over money or fame, having strong and satisfying relationships has a protective effect on our health and happiness, helping delay the 'falling apart' of our bodies and brains as we get older. While getting old might seem a million years away, knowing that the depth of your relationships is perhaps the most vital tool in a happy and healthy life is a valuable lesson to learn early, because it will help you determine which ones to fight to hold on to (and which ones to give the flick).

Social media and dating apps give us instant access to more people than ever before, and yet we are lonelier than ever. According to Swinburne University's 2018 Australian Loneliness Report, one in four adults considers themselves lonely, more than half of us say we lack companionship and a quarter of us are highly socially anxious. You don't have to be alone to be lonely (you could be surrounded by people and still feel that way), and you aren't necessarily lonely if you enjoy spending time alone. Rather, loneliness is a sign that, perhaps, your current relationships aren't meeting your expectations or needs.

Belonging is a biological imperative, it's what keeps us alive. Back in the day, splitting from the pack would leave us vulnerable and exposed, guaranteeing an untimely death, so it's little wonder we place a huge emphasis on our relationships.

So, what constitutes a deep and valuable one? Here's what it looks like to me.

YOU HAVE EACH OTHER'S BACK, UNCONDITIONALLY

There's not much any of my friends could come to me with that would make me turn on them. You need someone in your life in whom you can confide when you've really, truly fucked something up knowing they'll be there for you regardless. And vice versa.

YOU RESPECT EACH OTHER

You won't always see eye to eye, and that's okay. But you don't trash each other because you're always operating from a baseline of ultimate respect.

YOU BOTH PUT IN *AND* GET OUT

Friendship is kind of like a bank. You make deposits, take withdrawals, earn interest over time and even take out a loan here and there. What you're trading is your time and energy, and it has to work both ways. If their account is overdrawn and it doesn't look like they'll make a deposit any time soon, you need to switch banks.

YOU CAN TALK TO THEM ABOUT PRETTY MUCH ANYTHING

I've never understood people who hold their cards close to their chest. Part of the joy of being human is connecting with others on a deep level, and that means being able to be vulnerable; they have to love you at your worst if they get to love you at your best.

YOU CAN CANCEL ON EACH OTHER JUST BECAUSE

You need friends who say, 'No problem—look after yourself!' when you have to cancel last minute. Not ones who make you feel guilty for doing what you need to do.

To work out if someone is a good friend, ask yourself these questions.
- How do I feel when I leave them?
- Can I be 100 per cent myself around them?
- Do they bring out the best in me?
- Are they there for the good bits *and* the bad bits?

If you get a negative vibe on any of those, I'd reassess. You can keep them as a friend, but don't go above and beyond for them, because I suspect they won't be around forever. Also consider what they would say if they asked themselves these questions about you—are you being as good a friend to them as *they* deserve?

Check mate(s)

You probably have friends in your life you just know you'll be friends with forever, right? Well, according to one research study, you lose half your network every seven years. In my study population of one, I can attest to the fact that you'll look back on friends you were sure were your forever people, and for one reason or another, things don't pan out that way. Just because someone has been attached to you at the hip for a period of time doesn't mean they'll stay there. It's like chess—they can move out a bit then they might come back in *or* they might keep on moving out until they're just a bunch of awesome memories. That's okay!

Breaking up

When a romantic relationship ends, you usually have that awkward conversation where you sit down and blame everything on each other, or on yourself if you really want out of there, then you amicably part ways or one leaves the other in a puddle of confusion and ice cream. But with friendships, more often than not things change slowly over time, and rather than sit down and thrash it out you just sort of stop trying. There's often no closure, but you'll still need to grieve it like you do the demise of any other relationship—with self-care and time.

Lower your expectations

For the longest time I was tripped up by my expectations of people, particularly my friends. If their effort didn't match my effort, I'd feel let down. If they didn't handle something how I would have handled it, I'd feel angry and hurt. I was needy—outside of my job, my friends were my world; we had grown up together and in my eyes (and heart) we were family. As we got older, though, and I saw them less, I felt kind of ripped off. I'd signed up for life, and yet it felt like some of them were happy to just drift apart, like, *Thanks for all those years, I'm doing my own thing now.* Things were changing but I wanted them to stay the same, even though I knew deep down they couldn't.

Still now I have to remind myself that it's usually my expectations hurting me. People are just busy living their lives. But wait, shouldn't we be able to have expectations of the people closest to us? Sure. You can expect them to be kind, to give a shit, to show up. But you can't expect them to behave as you would, nor as you would like them to. And remember that people have their own stuff going on—not everything is about you.

Friendships are like icing on cake: you can survive without them, but who would want to? Choose yours carefully, remember that it's a privilege to be your friend, and it's an equal privilege to be theirs. Treat them with kindness and respect, and don't be afraid to move on when it's time, even if it's just for now.

Bad-to-better takeaways

- Friends are like chess pieces—they move around: closer, further away, off the board completely. That's normal, natural and okay.
- No one said there's a limit on how many friends you are allowed to have. Diversify!
- Go with your gut. How you feel when you leave someone is a really good gauge for whether they deserve their spot in your life.
- Hold on to the ones who have your back no matter what—they're like human gold.
- Try not to let your expectations get in the way. Enjoy people for what they *are* rather than focusing on what they *aren't*.

Lesson 12
Know That Things Will Go Wrong
Embracing the darkness of the bad times

Warning: This chapter deals with grief, sexual abuse, addiction and loss—of relationships, jobs and pregnancies. If you need to, please feel free to skip ahead.

When I worked on health retreats, I learned quickly that everyone is walking around with emotional scar tissue. It's often invisible, but it's a safe bet that many of the people you pass in the street, avoid eye contact with in the lift or rub shoulders with on your morning coffee run are mourning, recovering, healing and trying to overcome obstacles others would find insurmountable.

I'm going to go out on a limb here and assume you've been through something shitty too. You, me and every single person I know. And that's because every minute of every day, all over the world, people experience terrible, traumatic things. As you read this, people are saying goodbye to someone they love. They're being beaten, tortured, abused. They're having the worst moments of their lives, and no one gets to skip the inevitable hurt that comes with being alive.

There are no tricks, no hacks, no short cuts. Rather, this chapter is about acknowledging some of the shitty things that can happen to us and offering you solidarity in the knowledge that there are other people out there who go through them and that, if nothing else, the dark times will help you learn a whole lot about yourself. It's not about pumping you up so that the hard things aren't hard, they will always be hard. It's about coexisting with and even embracing the place where we learn just how resilient we are and are reminded of what's important to us.

Someone adept at shepherding people through hard times is Zenith Virago. If you've never heard of Zenith, here's her in a nutshell: Originally from the UK, she married her high-school sweetheart and had two children before walking away from everything to start a new life in New Zealand as a 'dyke' (her word), then eventually settling in Byron Bay where she had a baby for her best gay male friend 'not to co-parent—as a gift' and then became one of the area's most loved celebrants before evolving into a deathwalker, guiding people and their loved ones through the process of, well, dying. So, like, a pretty standard, run-of-the-mill life. I sit down with Zenith over coffee and she tells me about a poem by Rumi called 'The dissolver of sugar' and says we can apply its sentiment to all suffering in our lives.

'It's like dissolving one of those sugar cubes in a cup of black tea, you drop it in and it dissolves so you can't see the sugar cube, but it's in there and it makes the tea sweeter,' she says. 'And I think that often in difficult situations, if you can learn to dissolve them within yourself, you're sweeter for that experience, you're humbler and more grateful, even if that gratitude takes a couple of years to manifest. Things that look like disasters are actually often gifts.'

If you feel like you've been dealt a shit sandwich, there's every chance you have. And no matter what you do, you can't deny the following.

- You can spend your whole life learning and end up with a brain tumour that wipes you out in six weeks.
- You can spend a million hours training your body for the Olympics, only to injure yourself a week out.
- You can give your life to charity or public service and be assaulted (or worse) on your way home from work.
- And you can be a total arsehole and be absolutely fine.

The topics I discuss here are by no means exhaustive, they are simply some of the shittier things that many of us will go through at some point. I could write a book on each of these and barely scratch the surface, so at the back of this one I have included some resources that are a good starting point if you need support. Please know that, just like everything else in life, this book (and its author) are imperfect. If something here doesn't gel for you and your beliefs, again, please feel free to jump ahead.

So, where to begin this cheery chapter? Let's start with the biggest emotional dumpster fire of them all.

Grief: when you lose someone you love

If you've ever lost someone, you'll know how uncomfortable grief is. We don't like to be around it or talk about it, and certainly not to feel it. We're understandably afraid of grief because it represents loss, and none of us wants to lose something important to us. However, if there's anything in life that's guaranteed, it's that we're all going to experience grief, likely many times, so it's worth wrapping our heads around.

In 2014, Nora McInerny had what can only be described as a clusterfuck of a time, losing three of her most important people in a matter of weeks: her unborn child due to miscarriage, and both her father and her husband to cancer. As she explains in her TED talk titled 'We Don't "Move On" From Grief. We Move Forward With It', grief is one of those things you don't 'get' until you do, and it's only then that you understand 'you've been touched by something chronic, something incurable. It's not fatal, but sometimes grief feels like it could be'.

I know Nora's story. We lived it in 2019 when my mother-in-law received the same diagnosis as Nora's husband: glioblastoma, which is a fancy word for a particularly aggressive form of brain cancer. While Nora had three years to say goodbye, we had six weeks. Her decline was so quick I still can't quite believe it happened. We'd seen her just a couple of weeks prior on one of her weekly trips to Sydney. She would stay with us on Sunday nights, when I'd torture her with an episode of *The Voice* or *Married At First Sight*, before she took care of our daughter on Mondays while I went to work before driving the three hours back to Canberra. Week in, week out. Most people I know think their mum is pretty awesome, but my mother-in-law was an actual angel. She baked and sewed and helped with the kids, but more than all of that, she was a pleasure to be around: smart, funny and kind—and sick, only we didn't know it.

After a long drive she and her husband pulled up at home, and as they made their way up the stairs, he spun around to a crashing sound, expecting to see his frustrated wife and whatever it was she had dropped. But crumpled on the stairs wasn't a bag of shopping, it was my mother-in-law, head on the pavement and out cold. On inspection of a decent gash to her head, they piled back into the car and headed to the emergency department. Doctors gave her an MRI to ensure she didn't have any bleeding on the brain, and what they found would change the course of our lives, and particularly hers, forever.

A biopsy confirmed our worst fears. Two tumours growing rapidly in the left hemisphere of her brain, the reason we (on reflection) had seen subtle changes in her in the months preceding the fall. Changes we had put down to her being tired or having a migraine, something she had suffered from her whole life so wasn't out of the ordinary. In plain terms, brain cancer is a bitch of a disease. Survival rates are awful and it kills more kids than any other disease in Australia. Even though someone dies from it every seven hours here, it's rare compared to other cancers, and as such it is badly funded and poorly understood. For my mother-in-law, as it is in so many cases, nothing could be done. Even with second, third and fourth opinions from leading neurosurgeons, the cancer was growing so quickly that there was no way to catch up with it. The kindest course of action was to take her home, rug her up, love her with all we had and say goodbye.

Because I have worked with and for some of the most powerful people in health care in Australia, I had lulled myself into a false sense of security that if the shit ever really hit the fan health-wise, for me or someone I cared about, I would be able to fix it. Or at least I'd be able to get us into the very best hands and those hands would be able to fix it. I had convinced myself there was some magical hospital club that people who know people could access that could fix pretty much anything. But there isn't, and they can't.

My husband set up residence in his parents' home to care for his beloved mum, and we maximised quickly dwindling time with our favourite woman. I massaged her hands and feet, gave her facials and told her stories, even when she stopped responding to them. We wrote a card from her for my husband's 40th birthday—which she would miss. We threw my daughter a lounge-room party for her second birthday—the last her 'Ma' would attend. And we found out the sex of the baby in my belly she would never meet—a girl we would name in her honour. We cried and laughed and watched *Who Wants To Be A Millionaire*, and I said all the things I needed to say, even though she could no longer tell me the things I needed desperately to hear. That she wasn't scared. That we would be okay. And that somehow, she would be watching over us.

Just weeks later we sat in the family home without her, watched by photos of happier times hanging on the walls. In the corner sat her empty chair. The woman who had given her whole life to her family was gone. Time had gone too fast, and yet was all of a sudden standing still.

There are no words when someone is going through what my mother-in-law went through, but I gave it a go anyway in a letter that my husband read to her because I knew I wouldn't be able to. I suppose it was my way of starting the grieving process and saying goodbye. I told her how much I loved her and how I appreciated everything she had done for us, and that I would never let our girls forget her. That I would take care of her son and her husband and make sure we stuck together. I apologised for making her watch terrible TV, sitting like judges of a reality show in a row on the couch, eating on our laps. Had I known those days were so limited I would have set the table more often and gathered us around to soak up every minute we had together. But I didn't, because I always thought there would be a next time, lots of next times.

One of the things I've learned is that, even though it feels like it sometimes, life isn't happening to you, it's happening around you. Your job is to learn how to operate within it; the good bits, the bad bits and the really bad bits. Because life is a lot of things, but it's sure as hell not fair. And regardless of whether you believe there's a bearded dude sitting up in the clouds playing director, or you are manifesting what's happening to you via your crystal quartz, or it's all a big conspiracy being handed down through the 5G network, sometimes really shitty things happen to really good people, and we don't know why.

The best we can do is to get good at rolling with the punches and try (even when it seems impossible) to be grateful for the lessons they deliver.

MOVING FORWARD WITH GRIEF

'Grief doesn't happen in a vacuum, it happens alongside of and mixed in with all these other emotions,' says McInerny. 'You can and will be sad and happy and grieving and able to love in the same year or week, the same breath.'

Watching my husband navigate life without his mum all but confirms this for me. Rather than moving progressively and chronologically through the stages of grief as I had naively expected, he quietly shifts through them daily. Hourly. Sometimes by the minute. He loves me and his girls more than anything, but without his beloved mum, life almost doesn't seem worth it. If you strip away his adult clothes, his important job and the fact he's in charge of two small children, he's still just a little boy who wants his mum. Without her, he wants to get into bed, pull the covers up and not get out. But he can't. Because life goes on regardless of whether or not we want it to.

I stuffed my grief deep down so I could hold it together to look after him, our toddler and the growing baby in my belly. But the grief found its way to and through me, often in unexpected ways. Chronic stress headaches became my own suspected brain cancer, and I panicked I'd be gone in six weeks too, until an MRI confirmed I was cancer-free. Then my worry shifted. Was that pain in my belly gas or ovarian cancer? And that sore knee was probably bone cancer, right? I mean, it couldn't possibly just be wear and tear, could it? Not sure what else to do, every day I got up, took care of my family and went to work. By all accounts, I was 'holding it together', but really I wanted to hide. I was devastated not just that that could happen to someone so special, but that it could happen at all.

Outwardly I reasoned that his mum lived a full and wonderful 68 years on the planet. She was still so young but during her life she had found love, travelled the world, had two children she adored and watched them both become successful, fulfilled, adored adults with families of their own. I can reconcile that she had a great life, even though she should have had at least twenty years more. What I can't reconcile is when it happens to people at the beginning of their lives. In my tiny circle alone, brain cancer has also taken my friend's 23-year-old brother, my doctor's 38-year-old wife and my family friend's seven-year-old niece. And brain cancer is just one disease.

I don't say any of this to scare you, I do it to acknowledge the fact that while no one deserves to have their life snatched from them, that doesn't mean it won't happen, and knowing that is mildly terrifying but it's also a call to arms to live our lives like every day is our last, because it genuinely could be.

HOLLY'S STORY

Holly Butcher was born in Grafton, in regional New South Wales. Her mum, Wendy, is a teacher's aide for kids with special needs, and her dad, Ron, a school teacher. She was a happy little girl, full of life. She excelled at sport (hockey and squash, in particular) and at school before going on to university to become a dietitian. She loved the outdoors and holidaying at the family beach house. She had a great group of mates, was fit and healthy and had met the love of her young life, Luke. By all accounts, life was good.

Then things started to go wrong. She would go for a run and get a sore knee. She would get stomach pain but put it down to something she ate. When the pain got too much she saw a doctor, who didn't send her off for a scan because she was young and seemingly healthy. And yet the pains persisted, so Holly did too. She finally managed to get an abdominal scan and while she was awaiting the results ended up in hospital, where after more scans, biopsies and a nail-biting wait, she was eventually diagnosed with Ewing's sarcoma—a rare cancer that occurs in the bones or the soft tissue around them. Holly was 26.

Wendy recalls receiving the devastating news. 'I thought to myself, "No cancer's good, but is it a good one?" But the answer was, "No, it's, like, the worst one,"' she tells me.

Holly started chemotherapy two days later, diligently following her prescribed regime. While these days the treatment isn't usually the incessant throwing-up you might have seen in the movies, chemotherapy is still kind of like the human equivalent of weed killer. It kills the cancer/weed, but it kills healthy cells too, and it's no walk in the park. Six months later, though, things were looking up for Holly. A scan revealed no growth of her cancer and she was seemingly headed for remission. But just three weeks later, Holly approached her mum with a message from her gut. 'It's back, Mum,' she said. 'I know it's there—I can feel it.'

Holly was right, the cancer was back. Three surgeons performed a twelve-hour surgery in a last-ditch attempt to rid her of the disease that was invading her body, and while the surgery was 'successful', six weeks later Holly had shadows on her liver, lungs and kidneys. From there, she deteriorated rapidly. As sick as she was, Holly managed to sneak in one last family holiday to the Whitsundays, requesting the best catamaran (because WTF wouldn't you), where she spent a week with Luke and her family, lapping up the weather and holding her favourite people close.

'She was just a nice person to be around, that's the hardest thing for me,' says Wendy. 'Her whole being was always good. She didn't take crap. Everyone liked her. She was honest to the core; if she thought you were being full of shit, she'd tell you. What you saw was what you got, she never put on airs and graces, she was just Holly—a girl with a beautiful smile.'

On 4 January 2018—just fifteen months after her diagnosis and at the tender age of 27—Holly passed away peacefully with her family and Luke by her side. Later that day, Luke and Holly's brother Dean posted a letter Holly had written to her close friends and family on her Facebook page. It was her way of saying goodbye, and it went mega, mega viral. It's full of truth and well worth looking up, I've put a reference in the back of this book.

I never got the chance to meet her, and I never will. But I feel a deep connection to Holly and her story, because it reminds me what an incredible privilege it is to be here, even if we've had to go through some shitty stuff along the way. It's a reminder to take stock of the gift that is your life, and to feel gratitude for the fact that there are millions of people around the world that would give anything to get back to their washing-hanging, family-hugging, TV-watching lives. The same one you're living right now, that possibly never feels quite enough.

Sexual abuse: when you lose something that should never have been taken from you

If you've ever said or done something dumb and woken up with the world's worst shame hangover, you'll know how I felt on Mother's Day in 2009. I held my breath as the phone rang out, clinging to the hope that the floral Ugg boots and lovely card I'd sent Mum prior would cancel out the call I'd made that morning. They didn't.

It goes without saying that calling your mum to wish her a Happy Mother's Day when you forgot to go to bed is a terrible idea. Within the first three seconds of our call, Cluedo knew and promptly told me off, conveniently inviting me to unleash the fury I had been harbouring against her for years. Our call ended with me calling her a c*nt (Happy Mother's Day) and her justifiably hanging up. But before you withdraw your vote for my Daughter of the Year award, let me explain.

I am one of the one in five Australian women who has been sexually abused, and one of the majority of those whose abuse was at the hands of someone they were supposed to trust. Now, it wasn't in any way Mum's fault, but for a long time I was really angry about it—with him, with the world, and, perhaps unfairly, with her. My experience of abuse has had a profound impact on every area of my life from the bedroom to the boardroom; my relationships, my self-worth and my capacity to go after the life I deserve. When someone hurts you, especially when you're too young to understand it, it takes something from you that you never get back. The abuse runs through you like your DNA, no matter how much time passes.

It's the reason I have never let my girls sleep at a home with a man in it without me. I am on high alert any time we stay anywhere there is another man in the house with us, even if the girls are within five feet of my body, and even if the man is someone I, on paper, should trust. At family events I head count the men constantly like a secret service agent guarding the president, and subtly shadow any man venturing anywhere near my children. It doesn't matter who they are and whether they are twelve or 80. I cannot relax, and I won't, probably, for the rest of my life.

Sexual abuse (which can also be referred to as sexual assault) is defined by our government as any sexual activity you have not consented to. It refers to a broad range of sexual behaviours that can make you feel uncomfortable, frightened or threatened, including: rape (forced unwanted sex or sexual acts), indecent assault, child sex abuse/assault (using power over a child to involve them in sexual activity) or incest (sexual offences by relatives).

There has been a lot of talk about consent in recent years post the #MeToo movement, but the term still conjures suggestions of a verbal exchange: 'May I?' + 'Yes, you may' = consent. But consent is far more complex than that.

Consent means being old enough (over the legal age of consent) and freely agreeing to the sexual activity. Someone who is drunk, drugged, unconscious or asleep cannot freely consent. A person cannot freely consent if they have been forced, tricked or threatened. Consent can be taken back at any time and non-verbal signs such as turning away, pushing someone's hand away, or not responding to touch are all signs someone wants to stop; they don't have to verbally or audibly say the word 'no'.

So, the definition is clear, but the abuse itself and how it transpires often isn't. I know I gave no indication that I was open to what happened. And yet, I spent years racking my brain trying to think of *anything* I did that could have brought it upon me. At seventeen I was almost an adult, and I was certainly trying to behave like one (or at least, how I thought adults behaved). But in the eyes of the law—and in my underdeveloped brain—I was a minor. And it had more of an impact on me than I will ever be able to put into words.

Dr Gemma McKibbin is a social researcher from The University of Melbourne who studies child sexual-abuse prevention. She says that, while they exist, when we think of sexual abuse we need to scrap the notion of the creepy priest or paedophile hanging around the school gate—instead, it's the guy behind the counter at your local shop, that quiet dude at work, and the 'lovely' father at school. Maybe even someone in your own family.

'Around 90 per cent of sexual abuse actually occurs in a family context,' she says.

She adds that the impact is far-reaching, both in the short and long term when it comes to mental health, physical health and the ability to form lasting relationships, and that the damage doesn't correlate with any particular 'level' of abuse. As in—victims don't have to be raped to be messed up by the experience.

'It can form the entire landscape of their life for the rest of their life, the lens through which they see and interpret every single experience they have,' she tells me. 'Girls may internalise, taking responsibility for the abuse and maybe finding themselves in other abusive situations, whereas boys may externalise, which is why some boys go on to perpetrate abuse. Girls need to be able to express themselves sexually, to play and flirt and have fun and know that adult men will respect that. It's the same old feminist argument that it's never the fault of the victim; not what she's wearing or saying or whether she's had two drinks or ten.'

SO, WHY IS IT SO RAMPANT, AND WHAT CAN WE DO ABOUT IT?

One of the things I have noticed about porn these days is that it not only fantasises youth and being underage, but it also seems to hero familial sexual experiences; 'My stepsister loves to X,' and 'My stepmom gives the best Y.' I ask McKibbin about this, given it seems to me like a disturbing case of cause and effect when you consider how mainstream porn has become.

'I find it really challenging and appalling, to be honest,' she admits. 'My position is: whatever you want to do as consenting adults, you know, if you want to get tied up or whatever, that's your business. As long as you're not abusing children or animals or each other, that's okay. But for children who are now exposed to porn so early and in such mammoth quantities and such explicit material, it's very worrying, and we are doing a massive disservice to our children by enabling access to that material.'

Given how systemic the issue of sexual abuse is, I ask McKibbin if we can fix it, and how she would fix it if she were in charge.

'It's really not rocket science, it's very doable,' she says. 'Sexual abuse remains so hidden and secret, and that means nobody can talk about it in a sensible, informed way—it brings such emotion and discomfort. We need a measured public-health response. We need interventions that are perpetrator-focused, and by the time they reach the criminal justice system it's too late.'

McKibbin's point is that supporting victims once abuse occurs is like putting the ambulance at the bottom of the cliff. To prevent the abuse from happening in the first place, we need to get better at talking about it—and being okay with the terms we use to do so. In recent years, there has been a shift away from calling victims, victims. The preferred term has become 'survivor' in an attempt to empower the person involved, but while I'm all for empowerment, the challenge is that it implies victims are weak. 'Playing the victim' has become part of our vernacular, usually to disempower someone. And McKibbin says this is an issue.

'Some girls really don't want to identify as victims,' she tells me. 'We're all meant to be "survivors", but you can't be a survivor if you haven't acknowledged the victimisation. So, girls put on this kind of brashness, this bad-girl persona, but in some ways we can't ever recover or hold the perpetrators to account unless we acknowledge our own victimisation. Sexuality should never, ever be exploited for anyone's purpose, and my main message to victims is it's never your fault. Never, not one thing that happened, nothing you did; the perpetrator is absolutely 100 per cent responsible at all times.'

I know firsthand what it's like to live feeling like something has been taken from you. For the longest time I didn't know what to do with the damage, so I tried to hide it, but it was written all over me—in my relationship with myself and others, and most certainly in my behaviour.

So, what helped me get through it? A few things:

- **Talking.** I've done hundreds of hours of therapy with both professionals and friends. Because I grew up in a small town, when the news of my abuse broke, there were other versions of the tale going around that positioned me as the instigator. It hurt me beyond belief, but I knew I would never be able to set everyone straight so instead I got good at telling my story to the people who had the guts to ask me. That sort of transparency has served me well and these days I can tell the story like I'm talking about someone else.
- **Time.** They say time heals all wounds, and while I'll have the emotional scars forever, time has certainly helped me make sense of what happened and make peace with it. It has taken the sting away.
- **Perspective.** I would imagine the same thing happening to my seventeen-year-old niece or (later in life) my daughters. What would I say to them? How would I look after them and coach them through it? Would I tell them they were 'ruined' and their life was 'over'? Hell no! So, I eventually learned to stop saying those things to myself.
- **Camaraderie.** Finding people who understand what you've been through and truly 'get it' is a godsend. Seek out those people.

These days, rather than fight what happened, I've made a home for it. I imagine it in a little black box tied up with a ribbon, and I allow it to live inside me. I get it out sometimes to take a look when I need to or when someone asks me about it, then I put the lid on and put it back. The experience didn't ruin me, but instead it just revised, reshaped and refocused me. And taking back your power after it is taken from you feels good.

Addiction: when you lose your way

Back in Lesson 7, I told you about a friend of mine who drank her way to liver failure by the time she was 33, and I shared with you that I've always been respectfully fascinated by the way—without oversimplifying it—it can be all fun and games for some, while others end up with their lives torn apart by addiction. What I do know is that good times are a slippery slope, and instant gratification—especially for people who are hurting, which I would argue many (or most) of us are—is a common and easily accessible salve. It's the reason substance-use disorder (or addiction) is the third most common mental illness in Australia; with around one in twenty of us using too much alcohol, tobacco or other drugs, both the illegal type (such as cannabis, speed, ice, cocaine and heroin) but also prescription medicines too (hello painkillers and sedatives).

I don't know why addiction never happened to me, I certainly gave it a crack (pardon the pun, I've never done crack). My genetics were against me and my behaviour did me no favours, nor did the company I occasionally kept. So, when you're young and having fun, how do you make sure you fall into the camp that doesn't end up with an addiction disorder? First, it's important to understand what addiction is, and you don't have to be sticking needles in your arm to be an addict. Addiction is a physical or psychological need to use a substance, and it can be as simple as not being able to rein it in after a few wines with your friends or say no when a plate gets passed around at a party. It makes sense: feeling good feels good, and we all want more of that.

So, how do you spot the signs of addiction, in yourself and in people you care about? You might recognise the following.

- You need the drug (or more of it) to feel comfortable, or you feel dependent on it.
- You withdraw from family and friends, or avoid people who don't do that drug.
- You experience problems with relationships, study or work as a result of use.
- You use drugs to cope emotionally with the stresses of everyday life.
- You participate in dangerous activities due to drug use, such as driving under the influence.
- You lie about how much you are using, to others and/or yourself.
- You regularly empty your bank account to have a big night.
- You sell belongings or steal to pay for drugs.
- You feel crappy when you're not on the drug, also known as withdrawal.
- You feel anxious, angry or depressed or lose weight as a result of use.

What do you do if any of this sounds familiar? By now, I hope you've found yourself a good GP. If you haven't, please put that at the top of your to-do list. Ask your friends who they might recommend. If money is an issue, find someone who bulk bills or speak to the practice to see if there's any way they can bulk bill you or decrease the gap. Once you've found them, book an appointment and tell them what's going on. If you can, take them some 'data' and be specific: How much are you using of what drug and how often? Be *brutally* honest, with them and with yourself. Start there, and I've also included some resources for organisations that can help at the back of this book—including free counselling services.

DON'T TAKE IT FROM ME, TAKE IT FROM SOMEONE WHO KNOWS

By her own admission, J had a sheltered upbringing. Curious and inquisitive, she enjoyed international travel with her parents where she got a taste for different cultures and the big, wide world. She lived in a nice, stable home in the suburbs where she attended a private girls' school and had plenty of friends. With her parents focused on their careers, she rebelled for attention; a well-trodden path for well-to-do kids. By twelve she was smoking cigarettes, at thirteen it was pot, and she quickly progressed to heavier drugs.

At seventeen she met the man who would be her first love, a 26-year-old with a penchant for violence, control and speed (and not the Keanu Reeves/Sandra Bullock movie-on-a-bus variety).

'So, all of a sudden there's this seventeen-year-old girl out there in this world, still really sheltered and starting to use drugs,' she explains. 'I had all this energy and wisdom and intelligence, but nowhere to use it and I was heading down this really dark road. That relationship became abusive, he was jealous and controlling. I'd be in tears after ten minutes of waking up every day. He was just such an arsehole.'

An arsehole with a lot of power over a young, impressionable woman. Desperate for independence from her family, J wanted to do everything on her own, and there was no shortage of people ready and willing to take advantage of a child wanting to operate in an adult's world.

'I had everything in my name, the lease, the power bill, all that,' she explains. 'So, of course things like my credit rating went down the drain because, you know, the bills would get stuffed up and a lot of the houses that we had were in my name, so I got blacklisted from renting and from a young age everything started to stuff up for me.

'I've realised now that when you take drugs from a young age you don't grow up emotionally, it just stops time,' she explains. 'The drugs were a numbing tool for me, a way to escape my uncomfortable feelings of guilt, anxiety, depression, not belonging and being unworthy of love. They make you go against your values and beliefs, which creates a lot of inner turmoil but also creates constant arguments with your family because they can't understand. From an early age I lost myself and started trying to be someone I wasn't.'

There to help were her ever-reliable drugs of choice: marijuana, speed and, eventually, heroin.

'I could have been awake for two weeks straight, but otherwise I'd get up in the morning and have a shot of speed or heroin first thing and then you know, go on with my day.'

I ask where she got her money from, given she didn't have a job.

'Money came from all over the place, like Mum and Dad. I used to lie and get a lot of money out of them, and then just, you know, Centrelink, and I did a bit of dealing here and there.'

It strikes me at this point that doing drugs, whether it's lines in the bathroom of an exclusive club or shooting up in a dingy rental, isn't just about the high of the drug, it's about the high of belonging.

'Once you sort of get in that network, everyone helps everyone out,' J explains. 'You all put your pay together so you've got a bigger amount, so you get rich on payday and by the next day, you've got nothing for the next two weeks. It was really depressing. You have your high and once you come down you come down really hard because you've got nothing around you. You're like, all I want is a fucking burger, you know what I mean? And you can't even do it because there's nothing there. And that's how I lived for a long time.'

Not even good news could drag her out of the spiral.

'When I found out I was pregnant I'd already previously had a couple of abortions and I just couldn't do it again. So I was like, "Okay, I am going to try and make this happen." It was really hard not to use during the pregnancy. I did fail a couple of times here and there but I sort of managed to stop and I even breastfed for six months, so that was really cool.'

Over the next two years J had two more babies, making her a mother of three under the age of three, something that would overwhelm even the steadiest of women, let alone one heavily addicted to drugs. I find it hard to reconcile that image with the smart, articulate and sweet woman I'm talking to. As we start to get into some of the heavier details of her life, she suggests we break and continue the following day so her son can't hear the stories that would follow. Like the time she ended up in prison for armed robbery.

'Taking drugs impaired my judgement, it made me violent and angry at my family, myself and with society. I found myself breaking the law and running my body into the ground relentlessly over and over again, which affected my physical and mental health as well as my relationships with my one and only brother, my mother and father.'

Even so, by all accounts jail time helped get her on the straight and narrow. She got clean, made friends and did every educational course she could, grateful for a second chance. It's about a year after she gets out that I interview her, and it seems like she is trying to turn things around. Sure, she doesn't have a job and is smoking in her room, but her bed is made neatly behind her, and she speaks to her son, who might be around five now, in a caring tone, managing his needs like a good parent does throughout our chat.

I leave our conversation filled with hope for J, and excited to capture and share the rest of her story, especially when she tells me she would like to publish a book of her own one day. And then, she disappears. Slowly and silently. She misses our next interview, apologising and rescheduling for another day, but then she misses it for the second time. After the third failed attempt, I lose hope and start to worry. I send a message asking if everything is okay, to no response.

I hope she is, and that one day we get to finish our interview. Because on her good days, I think she has infinite wisdom to share.

Break-ups: when you lose your +1

You know how in romantic comedies when the main character breaks up with someone and she's devastated but she's like ... cute devastated? Then she whines about it to her best, unassumingly hot friend and realises they're actually made for each other and everything finally makes sense? If only real life were like that. Until someone invents an app specifically for breaking up with people (Flicker? Breaker? I'm open to suggestions) we're going to have to face facts: at some point we'll probably have to navigate the emotional minefield that is a break-up, and there's no way around it—break-ups suck, regardless of whether you're doing the breaking or the taking.

WHEN YOU'RE DOING THE BREAKING

I once broke up with someone because I didn't like the way he stood. Yes, stood. Like, stood up vertically in space. On his feet. You get it. There was also the guy who perpetually smelled like garlic, the guy who used to get drunk and pull his penis out at every party we went to and the guy who ate a goldfish out of a tank to be funny. Winners.

The truth is, I was never very good at breaking up with people. More often than not I'd just fade away until they got the picture, never brave enough to have 'the conversation'. If I had my time again you already know I would date everyone and then have 'the conversation' with all of them, because who cares! It's a conversation! Older me feels like that, but I cast my mind back to the days I wasn't mature or confident enough to have those conversations and feel the 'ick' creep over me. The 'ick' was when I knew a relationship was over. All of a sudden I hated the way they looked at me, spoke to me, touched me, kissed me (ew) and I just *knew* I had to get out of there.

I'll go into more detail on how to handle conflict in Lesson 14, but let me say this about romantic break-ups: staying with someone for any reason when you know you don't want to be together is cruel. Set them free, give them the chance to find someone who loves their turtlenecks and toenails. But for Pete's sake (or Pat's or Pam's)—be kind. Be straight up. Don't lie, but maybe curtail your desire to tell them you hate the way they stand. They don't need to know that and probably can't help it.

It is totally acceptable to tell someone they're simply not the right fit for you, that you've enjoyed your time together but it has unfortunately come to an end. In an ideal world we'd all high-five and move on, but while the words are simple, we find them hard to say because we worry about hurting feelings. But remember, feelings are transient. So yes, getting broken up with sucks, but it doesn't suck forever. Of course I'm probably oversimplifying things if you've been together a long time or there are complex issues, all I'm saying is that we can over-egg these things and draw them out, making them more emotional than they need to be. It's simple: you're simply not the right fit for each other. No harm, no foul.

Thank them for sharing time with you because time is one of our greatest assets and if they've given you some of theirs, that deserves some gratitude (even if they're a bit of a dick). Every relationship we have teaches us something we need to know about ourselves, so focus on what you *gained* rather than what you lost. Thank you, next.

WHEN YOU'RE DOING THE TAKING

Even when you come to a 'mutual' decision about breaking up, I think many of us still feel a pang of 'Why didn't they want me?' even if we didn't want them. And when it isn't mutual, it can be even harder to take; 'But I thought it was going so well, I don't know what happened!' Rather than thinking there's anything wrong with you, think about this. You know when you go into a clothing store and try something on that looked awesome on your friend or the model or mannequin but then you try it and you have to rub your eyes a few times to see if the monstrosity in the muu-muu staring back at you is, in fact, you? Relationships are exactly the same. What works for you may not suit her or him or them. And what vibes for them might be a genuine non-negotiable for you (like wooden necklaces, for example).

When someone breaks up with you, they're actually doing you a major favour because they are *setting you free*. Free to focus on yourself, your friendships and your passions. Free to find someone who values and adores you exactly as you are, and free to not have to share your precious time with someone who doesn't see you as anything other than the best thing since sliced bread.

There is simply no point staying in a shitty relationship. Regardless of whether you're doing the breaking or the taking, focus on the *reality* of the relationship, not the *potential*. Don't hang in there until they outgrow their bad behaviours, because there's every chance they won't, especially not while someone as incredible as you is there to hold things together for them. Toxic relationships erode your happiness and zap your energy, and no one needs that shit—life is hard enough as it is.

Here are some unhealthy ways to get over a break-up:

- Fill a bath with Chardonnay and get in (though I don't hate it …).
- Ugly cry into a tub of Connoisseur every night for a month.
- Blitz yourself with drugs and alcohol to get away from the feels.
- Quickly replace your ex with someone else.
- Expect to get over it in a week.

Here are some smart, healthy ways to get over a break-up.

- Fill a bath with warm water and bath salts, then get in with a glass of Chardonnay (or even better—tea).
- Ugly cry into a tub of Connoisseur while watching something all empowerment-y with a girlfriend for a big night in.

- Blitz yourself with exercise and meditation to sit with and move through the feels.
- Quickly replace your ex with no one but yourself and a community of people who build you up.
- Give yourself time.

Remember, your value doesn't depend on someone else's ability to value you.

Abortions: when you terminate a pregnancy

I just want to give you a heads-up here. Nobody really told me what it was like to have an abortion before I had one, and I don't want you to go through the same thing. And there's a decent chance you (or a friend) will; a third of Australian women experience an unintended pregnancy in their lifetime, and around a third of those will end in abortion.

There are a couple of ways to end a pregnancy these days. One is called a medical abortion, where you take a couple of pills a day or two apart that end the pregnancy and (in most cases) encourage your body to expel the cells on its own. The other is a surgical abortion, where doctors manually remove the cells from your uterus. Which is best for you is a decision for you and your medical professionals. Taking pills sounds easy, but it's not necessarily a walk in the park. Also know that what is available to you will depend on a couple of things: the laws in your state, how far along you are and your medical history. So, explore your options as early as you can.

A surgical abortion is a simple procedure, but it's still a procedure. Once you make it past the pro-life campaigners out the front, you'll sit in a waiting room with other sinners and then eventually be taken to a room where you'll talk through your decision with a nurse. Once you're through that bit, they will ask you to take your bottoms off and pop on a gown, before they lead you to a cold, bare room with what is just a medical bed but looks like it could double as an appropriate location for war crimes.

Your feet will be put in stirrups, giving the doctors and nurses a decent view of your lady parts and access to the cells they need to remove. Before you know it you'll be groggy but awake again and—if you're lucky—you'll be offered a cup of water and some bickies, which you'll gratefully accept before slowly getting dressed, grabbing your things and heading home. You'll be tired and possibly a bit sad, and you'll need someone to drive you and maybe stay with you a while. Order in, watch a movie (preferably one in which people don't have babies) and give yourself a big cuddle.

Talk to your friends, the ones you trust most. Speak to a good GP and see a psychologist if you can for support. Some clinics have counselling services attached to them too, so use them. And remember that no matter what anyone says, choosing what's right for you is always the right decision. But a word from the wise: do yourself a solid and avoid this conundrum in the first place if you can by taking charge of your contraception, just like we learned back in Lesson 9.

Getting fired: when you lose your job

Losing your job makes for one of the tougher days in life. Whether it's because the company is being restructured, your role is no longer required or you're simply not the right fit for each other, there's a sense of rejection that comes with parting ways with an employer that can be hard to shake. Actually, they've given you a great opportunity to refocus on what it is you want and go after it. Need some examples of people who've done just that? Glad you asked ... Oprah, JK Rowling, Steve Jobs, Madonna, Hillary Clinton, Walt Disney and Anna Wintour to name a few. Even some of the most successful people in the world have come up against an employer not needing their services anymore, and many say it's one of the things that set them on the path to their eventual success.

But while that all sounds quite romantic and inspiring, let's think through this practically. You lose your job, your income and your daily purpose. What would you do? You might sob into a bottle of red (or a tub of ice cream, or both), cry to your partner/parent/friend/hairdresser about how it isn't fair and WTF and then you'd do what you do best and get on with it. What would that look like? You might do up your CV, ask for a new reference, pimp your LinkedIn and start the hunt. No income? You'd dive into your savings. No savings? You'd dive into your parents' guest room. No parents/guest room? You'd lean on a friend and take out a loan. You'd be okay. And you might just find yourself landing something better or dedicating some time to that project you've been thinking about forever. Once you understand what you'd do, worst-case scenario might not seem so scary. We'll dive into that in more detail in the next chapter where we talk about professional success and finding that *thing* you were born to do.

So, what do we do with the shittier parts of your story?

In any country, city or even cafe you will find all sorts of stories about race, gender, abuse, heartbreak, grief and disappointment. And those stories inform who we are, how we behave and how we view the world. But it can't all be sunshine and rainbows, because then how would we appreciate the good times when they roll around? Crappy things are guaranteed to happen, to all of us. How we rise (eventually) after some of our toughest times is, I think, one of the greatest challenges we face and one of the toughest lessons we can learn. But the dark times are the ones in which we get to test just how resilient we are, and affirm that we are indeed made of tough stuff.

Bad-to-better takeaways

- Bad things happen to good people, mediocre people and terrible people every day. It's just the risk of living—and no one is exempt.
- Going through awful things can make you more understanding, more patient and more grateful. Like dissolving a sugar cube in a cup of tea, the tough times make you sweeter for them.
- There is a 100 per cent chance that at some point you are going to lose someone you love, and grief is a personal and complex experience. Allow yourself the space to live it.
- Don't ignore signs and symptoms when it comes to your health and don't take no for an answer if you feel something's not quite right—you know your body better than anyone.
- When it comes to abuse of any kind, it is never, ever your fault. Ever.

Lesson 13
What You Need to Know About (Professional) Success

Someone has to win, so it may as well be you

When I was in high school we had one of those parent–teacher days. Mum and Dad managed to not kill each other for an hour while we sat with my teachers and talked about the sort of career they thought would suit me. Based on the 'do what you're good at' approach, they suggested journalism because English was my best subject, and broadcast journalism specifically, presumably because I didn't look like a smashed crab. Until that day I'd had no idea what I wanted to do, so this gave me some much-needed direction, but it also reinforced my need to be 'special'—because in my juvenile mind, only special people could get a job on the telly.

By the time I was in Year Twelve my partying was well and truly out of control, but I miraculously managed to complete my final exams with a good enough grade to get into my chosen university course of journalism. How is beyond me, given the way I was behaving, but I think I have always been good at knowing the bare minimum I need to do to achieve a goal. My school principal told Mum that she sincerely hoped I would fail so I'd get the message that I couldn't simply cruise through life. Don't worry, Mrs Brown, while I wouldn't fail then, I'd come to fail plenty.

The road to success is not linear

Fast-forward to a few years ago and I landed my dream job—hosting a health show on a commercial TV network. I auditioned multiple times, screen testing with different talent line-ups and shooting a pilot for the network to seal the deal. I wouldn't allow myself to believe it was happening until we had a signed contract, and even then I would temper the excitement in myself and the people around me until we were literally on the air, because I knew it could be taken away at any moment; television is fiercely competitive and production is volatile—a show can be happening one minute and not the next for a whole range of reasons, most of which are entirely out of the talent's control.

When I knew we were going into production I took my agent out for a big, fancy dinner. We drank champagne and revelled in the moment, I felt like I was finally 'on my way'. What I had dreamed about since that fateful day in the school hall was actually happening and it put a spring in my step like the universe had validated that I *was* special/good enough, because now I had the achievement to prove it. The experience was better than I could have ever expected. I'd found my tribe with my co-hosts, hair and make-up artists and producers who believed in me. I loved the work, and while the show wasn't going to win any Logie awards, we were finding our groove. The production company was happy, the show was drawing enough of an audience and the network was satisfied. We were told to prep for a 40-week run the following year, and I was over the moon. Not only did I get to do my dream gig, but I was actually good at it.

Halfway through the season, I landed back in Sydney after shooting in Melbourne, exhausted but deliriously fulfilled. I planned to get a cab home from the airport, but as I made my way to the taxi rank I got a text from my husband saying he was coming to get me and would be there in five minutes. I didn't think much of it; he's thoughtful and always trying to make my life easier. As I typed out my reply, my phone rang. It was my agent.

'The network has cancelled the show,' she said in a calm and measured tone, kind of like the one I imagine a hostage negotiator would use.

I giggled, thinking she was fucking with me. We'd just had the news we were going to a bigger run, so that simply couldn't be the case. My brain quickly caught up with my lips, though, when she didn't giggle back.

'I have the head of the production company on the other line, I'm going to patch him in.'

My heart sank as I absorbed that this was no joke. As the lines connected, my husband rounded the corner, parked and jumped out, giving me a sad but knowing smile—my considerate agent had given him a heads-up. As soon as I heard the two voices on conference call, I lost mine. For the twenty-minute ride home I tried to listen carefully to the reasons while going in and out of awareness, taking deep breaths and doing my best not to cry. The rising lump in my throat prevented me from saying anything, so I just sat there mute.

The head of the production company praised my efforts and said it had nothing to do with me or my talent, and that they weren't sure how or why things had changed so drastically but that it had 'come from the top' and they were putting *Judge Judy* back in our time slot, the juggernaut seemingly rating better than a brand-funded program about health and wellbeing. The axing was effective immediately, so today had been our last day on set. As we pulled up at home and the call wrapped up, I managed to croak out the words: 'I'm so sorry, and I'm so grateful for the opportunity. Thank you from the bottom of my heart.'

I hung up and burst into tears. My husband wrapped his arms around me and held me close as I sobbed into his shoulder. Then he held my hand and walked me and my bag up the stairs to our apartment in silence, where he turned on the bath, poured me a glass of my favourite wine (of which he'd bought two bottles in case I wanted to drown in it), undressed me and put me in the bath, then undressed himself and got in behind me. I said nothing, crying quietly while he lovingly rubbed my back as I sank into the warm water and my new reality. My dream job was gone, and I was devastated.

I wish this was the part where I told you I woke up the next day with a renewed vigour. That I bounced back, dusted myself off like the warrior I am and got on with it. But none of that is true. I was heartbroken, and it took me years to get over. With a little hindsight, of course all I have for the experience is gratitude. While I was still finding my feet then, now I am a more practised and confident presenter; I *know* I can do that job. So, the next time an opportunity like that comes my way you won't be able to stop me, and you can never take away the fact that I made one of my dreams come true.

We imagine that the road to success should be a fairly straight line if we make the right moves. We know there will be bumps, but still we expect that if we keep working hard, we'll eventually reach our destination. Rather, what we end up with (if we're lucky) is a sort of 'heartbeat' pattern, moving up and down but, hopefully, loosely trending upward. Over time we will see that we're getting somewhere, but it's easy to miss the incremental successes when they are disguised in the grunt of the day-to-day. It's like a game of Snakes and Ladders: you roll the dice and sometimes climb up, other times you slither down, but most frequently you're edging slowly toward the finish line.

Defining success

The term 'success' tends to conjure images of material wealth, fame or accolades, things we're conditioned to believe lead to a better life. 'She's very successful,' would have us believe that she has it all together. She must, to have achieved her goals, right? Maybe, maybe not. More likely, what she has is a plan. A plan and some gumption.

But before we can get to a plan, we need to know what success means to you. Is it being a CEO, owning your own business and flying at the front of the plane? Or is it owning your own home and being a great stay-at-home parent? Or maybe it's a 9 to 5 you don't hate and weekends with your family? Remember, when you get to the end of your life you're not going to be focused on how many deals you sealed, so while professional success is awesome, let's keep it in the perspective of the *life* you're building, not just the #lifegoals you want to hit.

Take the example of writing this book. I could define success by the following.

- Achieving the goal of writing it.
- Writing it and getting it published.
- Writing it, getting it published and selling 1000 copies.
- Writing it, getting it published and selling 10,000 copies—putting me on the bestsellers' list in Australia.
- All of the above plus making *The New York Times* bestsellers' list.

Which of those qualifies as success for me might be completely different to what it is for someone else, and it might mean different things to me at different times in my life. Right now, it's just a privilege to be published, but if this book is a success, I might use a different yardstick to measure my next one.

What do *you* define as success? Not your parents, your friends, your community or your social-media feed, but *you*? Write it down and stick it somewhere you can see it. Remember, this is not about your goals, it's about your definition of success.

If I had done that, it might not have taken me so long to cultivate the inclination to really strive. Even though my body and brain were slowly moving me toward my 'goals' (though I don't think I ever called them that), it would be years before I would foster the work ethic to get up early, work late and every weekend (and holiday) pretty much ever. Deep down I think most of us are inherently lazy—bad girls are no exception. Which is a bit of a spanner in the works if you subscribe to the notion that success is 10 per cent talent and 90 per cent hard work.

How to get around it

We assume that when we find our 'thing' or when we're in the right job or working on the right project, dedication to it will flow thick and fast—that we won't struggle to commit to it in the way we might have in the past. But this is simply not true.

In her TED talk titled 'How to Stop Screwing Yourself Over', US relationship expert and media wizard Mel Robbins says: 'In any area of your life that you want to change, there's one fact that you need to know: You are never going to feel like it. Ever. It's very simple to get what you want, but it's not easy. You have to force yourself, and I mean force.'

This couldn't be more true. Most of us would much rather sit on the couch punching through episodes of our favourite series than working up that business plan we've been talking about for years. Acknowledging that it's going to take some real grunt, and that grunt might feel icky, will help when it comes time to ignite it. Successful people all have one thing in common, no matter what field they're in: they work really, really hard. They don't hit the snooze button, they get up and work out. They don't put off making that difficult call, they pick up the phone. They miss dinners with friends and holidays with family, and prioritise the work over the fun stuff, not every time, but a lot of it.

This truth is uncomfortable, but it's one you'll want to make friends with if being 'successful' at anything is on your life list. There will be moments (lots of them) when you'll want to kick and scream and give up—but you can't climb the mountain without doing the work. It will be slow and painful and hard, but if it's what you want, it will be worth it. It's worth noting, though, that striving isn't for everyone—cruising is just as viable an option; after all, it's what most people do.

Someone who chose not to is Michael Jordan, widely known as the best basketballer of all time. If you think he's a curious case study in a book for bad girls, stay with me. Jordan played fifteen seasons in the NBA and won six championships with his team, the Chicago Bulls. In 1993, at the height of his career, he retired and set his sights on a new challenge: minor league baseball. The guy is a stupidly gifted athlete, so jumping from one sport to another might not seem like a stretch, but he essentially became a rookie again. The world was watching, and he was the butt of many a joke as people compared his incomparable basketball prowess to his mediocre results in baseball while learning the ropes. But he just did what he does best—applied his legendary work ethic, and he ended up playing 127 games. I know nothing about baseball, but apparently that's no mean feat.

In Netflix documentary *The Last Dance* Jordan's coach describes his work ethic—the best he had ever seen. 'He would hit early in the day, he'd hit off the breaking ball machine, he would come in after regular batting practice, hit some more before the game, and then would hit again after the game. You could see it just building and he kept getting better and better and better.'

By all accounts, Jordan was no picnic. But you don't need to be an athletic freak to borrow from his attitude to work and apply his dedication to success. Luc Longley was Jordan's teammate, and is one of Australia's most famous basketball players to date. He knows what it takes to get really good at something.

'It takes a certain type of person to immerse yourself in something, and ... the fundamental ingredient for that is a deep curiosity in something and in yourself,' he tells me. 'I didn't set out to be the world's best basketballer but I got more and more curious and that drove my daily habits and my practice. To expect that lots of people might find that in their lives is unrealistic, but I think if you have you've been given an incredible gift.'

Longley says you have to find a way to love the work, because merely chasing the rewards—even at the top—is futile.

'That day-to-day practice of being "great" might not come with rewards for years or they might not come at all, so you have to be able to enjoy the process of the practice and not worry about the destination or about being great right away.'

I ask what it's like to be at the top of your game, something many of us aspire to but few will experience. His answer surprises me, and yet, it doesn't.

'I wasn't at the top of my game,' he shares. 'Nineteen years since I've played and I still think more about the things I should've done better and could've done better to be a better player than I do the things I did great. My body finished before my mind was ready to, so I felt like there was unfinished business. Now more than ever, though, I feel proud of it, and the primary, almost sole reason is because my children can look at it and go, "Wow, Dad, you really had a crack."'

I know from my own successes that goals are elastic. As soon as you arrive at them, they stretch or change into new goals, in further, trickier territory. That can be a good thing and allows us to push ourselves further, but if we can't stop to pat ourselves on the back when we get there before limbering up again, it's like being on a treadmill to a destination that doesn't exist. Instead, we need to learn to embrace where we're at right now, rather than living for the peaks and dreading the troughs. Even the 'bad' bits are good, and the 'nothing' bits in between are even better—because you don't know what's just around the corner. When you're too focused on the outcome, you miss the ride along the way, and that's where the good stuff is, but, as Longley says, you have to divorce the outcome from the intent.

Think about the Olympics. For all the people who end up with a medal, there are hundreds or even thousands of others who come up short, sometimes by one hundredth of a second. They train for years to race, often for a minute or less. They know they can't all be on the podium, but they give it a red-hot go, not just to have the chance of winning but also because they love the hustle.

Focus on building a successful life

We grow up seeing 'successful' people (such as Jordan) get attention because they are living interesting lives, and we want to be interesting too. Even if we don't dream of private yachts and Maseratis, we still want to live in a nice house, drive a nice car and buy nice things. There is comfort in not having to struggle, and in an ideal world we would all earn a decent crust doing something we love. But the world is far from ideal, and it means that for most of us, we won't get to do our dream job, or live our dream life, every day.

Our society is built on having people who are willing to do a vast range of jobs to service the needs of the people in it—and there are people achieving success in all of them. But we aren't all going to be wildly 'successful', which is why working out what's important to you (and how best to build it into your life) is vital. It's about defining what a successful life is to you, and then going after that. And that might mean making some tough decisions around what you can and cannot be. But just because you decide you can't be something professionally, doesn't mean you can't weave it into your life somehow.

The case for having a crack

During one of our 'off' times, my first love went to Aspen for a ski season. He worked in an internet cafe and spent an inordinate amount of time on the phone to me rather than doing whatever it was he was supposed to be doing, which allowed me to convince myself that he was missing me. Ah, hindsight—I love you but you always show up too fucking late.

Even though he had left me in the dust to chase snow, blow and babes (let's call a spade a shovel), we decided to meet in Europe to torture each other a little while longer. I saved up, bought a plane ticket, packed my bag and landed in London, but without working visas or European passports (WTF were we thinking) work was—spoiler alert—hard to find. We shacked up in a friend's pool house in Surrey, miles away from potential work or even any shops. While we were waiting for someone to predict our whereabouts and offer us jobs, we did what any self-respecting twenty-somethings would do and ate everything in sight while watching movies. The gluttony was inconveniently timed with a meeting I had with a modelling agency, the owner of which was a friend of Mum's who had been keen to meet with me. But after months of eating and drinking, my hopes of bringing in some cash that way were over faster than I could put away a block of chocolate.

My first love decided to head back to Australia, but rather than go with him, I went on to the US. I had just spent all that money to get overseas, and even though I was running out of cash, it had been a dream of mine to spend some time in America, and I was deluded enough to think I could make it work there, for a while at least.

I landed in New York City and found a place to stay; a 'room' in a small theatre that was between productions right near Times Square. Some crafty dude was renting the space out to people like me who were desperate for a slice of New York life. He used the thick theatre curtains to section out five or six tiny areas, each of which had a single blow-up mattress, a stool and a lamp. I was lucky enough to secure one of the front rooms that had a small sliver of natural light, and I covered the filthy black wall with photos of my family, friends and dog to make it feel like home.

I showered in the tiny bathroom and cooked two-minute noodles in the tiny kitchen. I walked everywhere, rarely needing the subway given everything I needed was within a few dozen blocks. This is going to blow your mind and is one of my biggest regrets, but I didn't do anything you would expect me to have done while I was there. No Empire State Building, no Metropolitan Museum of Art (or museum of any kind), I don't even remember going to Central Park. All I did was walk the short distance to the gym where I took classes and rode on the bikes so I could watch MTV, then walk to my waitressing job at an Irish restaurant down past Wall Street, and go to a handful of dance classes at the famed Broadway Dance Center.

There was one time I went out with a photographer friend, but the night culminated in him giving me some sort of pill (which put me on my arse) and then him disappearing, followed by me calling Mum in Australia to help me find my way home by counting the street signs of the grid-style Manhattan streets.

'Forty-second, Forty-third …' I would say as I miraculously maintained some semblance of forward motion.

'No, no, Casey—that's up. You want to go down, go the *other* way,' said Mum down the line from Australia, no doubt cursing the day I was born.

I eventually found my way home and now thank my lucky stars that was the case, because the outcome could have been so different.

Anyway, back to me being a hermit *in New York City*. It was 2006, so there were no streaming services, no social media, just a few songs on my brick-sized iPod and a book or magazine for company at night. I convinced myself I was simply committed to my goals, but the truth is I was still under my first love's thumb, and while he was in Australia pretending I didn't exist, I was too scared of losing him to get out into the world and live. I needed to work, though, so I could afford to stay, and I did whatever I could: waitressing, helping on music-video sets and showing other people around my theatre rental for a discount on my rent when the landlord couldn't be there. Scouring Craigslist for work one day, I saw an ad for dancers. I called the number, told them I had experience (I didn't) and sent them a photo, and they said I could have the gig.

A week later I rocked up to my first professional dancing job at Saks Fifth Avenue with literally no idea what I was doing. It was a private party for some sort of autumn launch, and I was thrown into a room with a bunch of (real) dancers and handed a costume of fluffy white shorts and matching boots with a maroon bikini top and bunny ears. I made friends with a girl called Meredith (fuck knows if that was actually her name, I may have subbed that into my memory because she kind of not really looked like Meredith from *Grey's Anatomy*). She took me under her wing and told me we would dance in fifteen-minute shifts in different sections of the party. We were dancing on raised platforms, as the DJ spun fun tunes and drag queens teetered on heels around us, and I felt like I'd pulled on that costume and entered another universe. I was far from the best dancer there, but I'm pretty sure I had the best time. And I had 100 per cent winged it to get there.

I did a few more dance gigs while I was in the US, doing the best I could with the few dance skills I had. I knew I wasn't good enough to be a professional dancer but I didn't care, it was fun, I earned some money and I was 'good enough'. While I would never make a career from dance, I loved music, movement and (anxiety aside) people, and would later turn that passion into a great little side hustle as a Barre instructor, cranking my favourite songs and making every class as fun as I could. I'm glad I was able to recognise that professional dance wasn't going to be my career, but I'm also grateful that I knew I could weave it into my life somehow.

Success doesn't always happen to the 'right' people, or even the best people for the job

I once heard an Aussie comedian and popular television host say he realised early on in his career that 'the person who wins in life is the person who stands up and takes the prize', and there's something about this that really resonates with me. In fear of 'tall poppy syndrome' (something Australians are notorious for) we never want to come across as being too big for our boots, so we stay small. We keep quiet. We don't say things like, 'I deserve this,' or 'I'm really good at that,' even if we think/feel/believe it.

Do you ever think about the fact that for every Michael Jordan/Pablo Picasso/Lady Gaga, there are a dozen more just like them (maybe even better) around the world who—for one reason or another, be it circumstance, timing, luck, self-belief, finance—didn't make it? Of course there are! Some of the world's most talented people are flipping burgers and washing cars, they're single mothers working for minimum wage, and old, disgruntled grandfathers living on the pension because for them, 'success' just hasn't happened. There are also people running countries, at the helm of multinational businesses and on world stages not because they're smarter or better than the next person, but because they worked hard, got lucky—and believed they deserved it.

In other words, they figured out what they wanted, worked out how to get it and then (the most important bit) enjoyed the ride. And now it's time for you to learn how to do the same.

First, figure out what you want

It might be following in our parents' footsteps, chasing friends into industries that sound cool or simply a case of how things pan out, but we often fall into things. And more often than not, I believe it's because we don't really know what we want.

So, what do *you* want?

We can't all become millionaires off our side hustle or even work doing something we're passionate about. But there are a few questions you can ask yourself to help gain some clarity around what you want, because you deserve an amazing life, whatever that looks like.

WHAT'S YOUR WORK STYLE?

Do you enjoy the stability and low risk of working for someone else, and a guaranteed paycheque regardless of how a business performs? Sometimes just having a job you don't hate that pays the bills is a noble enough goal, allowing you to spend time on your passions or hobbies on the side. Or would you prefer all the risk (and all the potential reward) of building a business of your own? You'll need to be ready to work harder than ever and fail (a lot) but it will be yours. If it does well you do well, and if it doesn't you don't. There's no right answer here, but it's an important distinction to make up-front.

WHAT ARE YOU PASSIONATE ABOUT?

I know—I just rolled my eyes too. But this is vital in working out where to place your effort, because if you're going to spend a third of your life at work, you may as well earn a living doing something you're genuinely interested in. Do you love kids? Maybe child care or teaching is for you. Are you amazing with your hands? Perhaps massage or physiotherapy is calling your name. Do you hate people but love spreadsheets and data? Maybe you're a researcher. Are you awesome at partying? PR or events could be your jam. You can do a job that's 'meh' to give you time for the 'yas' outside of it, but even better is to do something you like and get paid for it.

So, How do you find your 'thing'?

A lot of people say to think about what you would do tomorrow if you had the day off. The challenge is that, being honest, a lot of people would like to lie on the couch or head to the beach, which kind of limits your options. Which is why I think it's better to think about it like this: *What are you doing when time stands still?* When you don't care about anything other than what you're doing? When I'm interviewing someone, presenting or writing, dancing or riding horses, time stands still for me. I'm not thinking about anything other than exactly where I am. An hour could pass and it would feel like ten minutes.

We tend not to pay attention to these cues, especially when they are related to fun or leisure activities, because we don't think we can make a living from them, but I disagree. I have an ex who desperately wanted to be a pro surfer. I was all, 'You can be whatever you want, baby!' And he was all, 'It's too late, I'll never make it.' I'd break out the tiny violins and give him a kick up the arse, but while I admit the odds were stacked against him (he was 'too old' in his mid-twenties and probably not quite good enough) I encouraged him to see the opportunity in the passion.

Okay, maybe he couldn't be a pro surfer. But here's what he *could* be:

- A manager of elite surfers.
- A surf teacher, running surf retreats.
- A brand rep or on the marketing team of a surf brand.
- A surf writer or videographer.

You get the picture. Focus on the *passion* and open your mind to the opportunities. He chose to do none of the above and instead picked a job that allowed him a lot of free time to do what he loves most—surf. And that's just as viable an option.

Remember, there's not just one way to achieve what you want. Some careers have specific pathways you need to follow. To become a doctor you have to study medicine, or if you want to be an electrician you have to learn the trade. But there are lots of careers where different roads lead to the same place. A girl from my high school wanted to get into TV, so she did work experience on school holidays at one of the local TV networks. By the time she finished her journalism degree she'd been at the network for years, slipping easily into a reporting role before landing a plum job reading the news. Smart girl. My holidays were spent being a nuisance, so instead I took a few extra years to complete my degree and then when I finished I moved to Sydney and targeted the person I thought I could learn the most from. The timing was right, and when that company decided to do a TV show, I was in prime position to reap the benefits, gaining vital skills both in front of and behind the camera. We both achieved the goal, we just got there in different ways.

GET EVERY BIT OF EDUCATION YOU CAN

Our education system, quite frankly, gives me the shits. The world has changed and yet our knowledge model remains the same. The timing forces us to make decisions about what career we want before we've had the chance to actually try anything, corralling us into subjects before we understand why we should study them, which gives us a silly score that does or doesn't allow us into university. If you follow that path, by the time you're in your early twenties you've got a degree you may or may not be interested in pursuing in terms of a career (and might not even be relevant in a rapidly changing world), or, if you got stuck into a trade, you might be years into a job you're not sure you want to spend the rest of your life doing.

Just decades ago, people would have one career in their lifetime. Women would get married and have children early, and making it to your sixties was considered elderly. These days, you're more likely to have seventeen different jobs over five different careers and most of us will work through our sixties and live well into our eighties, so we have more time to work before we retire and kick the bucket. And it seems a shame to spend so much time doing something you chose when you had braces and acne. I think we should get into the workforce sooner by tipping the scale of study toward more work experience, try a bunch of different things and then study them to give us the knowledge and tools to do a job we're genuinely interested in.

DON'T TALK YOURSELF DOWN

Even long after we've left school, many of us have a hangover of never feeling like we quite fit in, but our thoughts are not reality, so if you've ever said to yourself that you're not good enough, you'll never make it, you're too fat/ugly/stupid/weak—that needs to stop today. Catch yourself every time, acknowledge the thought and promptly tell it to fuck off. Don't resist or dwell or try to fight those thoughts—they will come—but stop paying them attention. They simply aren't true. You have probably spent years (or decades) bullying yourself, and while you're not going to be able to click your fingers and stop, try to be more aware of your thoughts and see what happens.

HAVE A GO

I surveyed and interviewed a lot of women for this book, and when I asked them about regret, the resounding answer was not leveraging their talents enough, AKA: not truly having a go. I think this takes a lifetime to learn, but being aware of it is a step in the right direction and a valuable lesson to take on as early in life as possible.

Back in my day (she says, shaking her cane), you only got a ribbon at a school carnival if you came in a place. I think it went from first to fifth to give more kids a chance at taking home a little coloured strip of polyester, and I'm almost certain they spread the love by putting on extra races with fewer kids. But these days, you get a ribbon just for having a go. There's a lot I like about this, instilling in kids a sense of achievement for putting themselves on the line. But the trouble is that when we grow up, there's no one waiting with a ribbon to congratulate us for going to work. The only reward for having a go, is having a go. And I spent many years not having a go out of fear of failure.

Here's how I see it now. Every time you take something on, you learn something new about yourself or you gain a new skill, and those skills almost always transfer to something else in the future. Will you fall flat on your face? Possibly. But the much greater likelihood is that you'll come through unscathed and be kind of stoked with yourself for having a crack. So, what if you viewed everything as an opportunity to learn something, regardless of the outcome?

I can't tell you how many things I've stuffed up because I put too much pressure on myself to be 'successful'. Especially for big shoots where I'd be presenting, or even screen tests or auditions, I would over-prepare, not sleep, and pause everything else in my life until I got through that *thing*. Not only could I not enjoy it, I would also make myself sick with nerves. These days I try to take a different approach. I replace, *You have no idea what you're doing* with, *Even if you fall on your face, what an amazing opportunity to build your skills.* I sub, *They will never, ever choose you* for, *How great that you can get in front of them, and who knows what might come of it in the future.* And rather than tell myself, *You are in no way good enough for this* I say, *You have just as much chance as anybody else.*

You have to get to a point where you have faith in yourself and your skills, and the self-compassion to be kind to yourself regardless of the outcome.

Now, we need to work out how to get it

I get nervous when I do any sort of public speaking. Even in a really informal setting (like when you have to go around a circle of people and introduce yourself) my heart races as my turn gets closer, and I stammer my way through familiar details such as my name, where I come from and why I'm there. I can't tell you how many moments have been ruined in my life due to can't-think-straight-and-about-to-spew-on-myself nerves. These days, I ask myself whether I'm nervous or actually excited. I tell myself that those butterflies in my stomach and jitters in my hands are because I am excited to get to do what I love. This isn't always 100 per cent true (as in, sometimes I am just genuinely nervous), but a little trickery can go a long way.

Being nervous about something shows you care, and that is never a bad thing, personally or professionally. Nerves are good for performance, and if you can harness the power of that nervous energy it can actually do wonders, making you sharper, more reactive and more energised.

'If you look at an elite athlete, a professional sportsperson, when he or she walks out onto whatever field or court they are playing on, they don't want to be totally relaxed because then we don't necessarily perform at our best,' explains Dr Tim Sharp, whom we met earlier. 'We need a certain level of arousal to increase our reaction time, our thinking time, our performance. A lot of singers and actors get quite anxious before they perform, but they can utilise that and channel it into positive energy, and that's the same for any of us in our daily lives.'

START SMALL

Too often we set ourselves too big a challenge. Giving the entire kitchen a spring clean is such a big job that it feels insurmountable. Instead, begin with the cutlery drawer. The first step of any goal is the hardest, but if you can take that and just get started, you're on the way. Don't worry about all the steps to come, you'll get to them later, just take the first one.

GET HUNGRY

If you want to 'make it' (whatever that means), you're also going to need to get, as my mum would say, a bit hungry. For the record, I'm always hungry—but she's not talking about snacks.

Hunger for success looks like making an effort, picking up the phone, offering your time for experience and knocking on doors. It's so simple and yet so hard to do—we're good at championing other people but rubbish at doing it for ourselves. The starting point is simply saying the words: 'I'm looking to get some experience in …' Make a list of ten people or organisations that might be able to help and hit them up, one by one. Success is a numbers game, and I'd hazard a guess that you'll get a response from at least one of them.

When you reach out and ask them for a mentoring session, you'll disguise it as a coffee. Here's a script:

Hi _____,

My name is _____ and I'm an aspiring _____. I'm reaching out because I really admire the career you've built, and I'd be so grateful for the opportunity to pick your brain about your incredible career over coffee (on me!) or over the phone at any time that suits you.

Is there a time next week you could spare half an hour? I'll fit in with whenever you're able to make work.

Thanks in advance, looking forward to connecting with you.

Most people love nothing more than talking about themselves and are usually happy to give up time to do so. It's like free, ego-boosting therapy, making them feel successful and important. Some people (who feel too successful and important) will not respond—fuck you very much to them and reach out to someone else. The people who are kind enough to give you their time will likely become your cheerleaders and are worth their weight in gold. Because everyone appreciates someone having a go, and you only need one opportunity for your life to change.

Here are some questions to ask on your coffee date:

- What are the best and worst things about what you do?
- How did you get to where you are? What do you think made you successful?
- What lessons have you learned along the way?
- What mistakes have you made?
- What would you do differently?
- What's your advice for getting into the industry?
- What do you think the future holds for the industry? Where do you see it in five or ten years?
- Where would I be smart to spend my time upskilling? Are there any courses or study you would recommend I do?
- Is there anyone you can connect me with that you think would be worth me talking to?

If it's going well, ask if you can shadow them for a day. Tell them you'll work for free and that you'd love the chance to watch them in action. Most people won't say no to free labour, and who knows who you'll meet along the way. Best-case scenario: you learn something and make good contacts (or impress the shit out of them so they keep you in mind for a job). Worst-case scenario: you find that what you had in your head is actually not for you, which is a very worthwhile way to spend a day because it allows you to invest your energy elsewhere without wondering if that thing was for you.

BTW, I don't believe we are ever too old or experienced to do this. Once I worked out health journalism was my thing, I pursued it relentlessly. I still do. And if I switched careers or moved into an area of journalism I wasn't familiar with, I would do the exact same thing.

GET (REALLY) GOOD AT WHAT YOU DO

Trauma cleaner Sandra Pankhurst said: 'No matter what I do, whether I'm a prostitute or cleaning dunnies, I do it 150 per cent—I do the best I can at it. It's just a matter of applying yourself to do the best you can do.'

Right on, Sandra.

She also told Sarah Krasnostein, the author of her book *The Trauma Cleaner*, 'I've had more cock than hot dinners,' which makes me really, genuinely like her a lot, because brutal candour is a beautiful, endearing thing.

Being good at something takes consistent practice and a curiosity about your craft. What you're after is specialised knowledge, and that comes from truly immersing yourself in and understanding something, so you are the person people go to when they need answers on that thing. It also comes from doing something over and over and over again. Experience allows you to troubleshoot anything and become a natural (even if it's taken you years) and when you stuff up or things go wrong, that experience only makes you better at your thing.

HAVE A CONTINGENCY PLAN

I was seven when I started my first business breeding budgerigars and selling them to pet shops. I read everything I could to set them up for procreation success. I knew I would need at least one girl and one boy, because biology. For the none of you interested, you can tell male budgies because they have a blue patch of skin above their beak (called a 'cere') and in girls it's pink. I would also need some breeding boxes and something to line them with so they were comfy. No one likes getting it on in a wooden box.

Back in those days, success for me was defined as enough money to buy myself a decent lolly bag from the deli ($2 would get you a bag as big as your head) and possibly a little somethin' somethin' from the toy store. That or more budgie equipment, my memory fails me so I can't be sure, but kudos to me if I was reinvesting my profit. I bred all sorts of colours, with the going rate $7 for green, $8 for blue or white, and $9 if they were yellow or multicoloured. If I got lucky I could net up to $54 for a batch, and I'd have two or three couples going at once—I was like a tiny budgie pimp.

While my enterprising skills were impressive, my contingency plan left a lot to be desired. A big storm came one night and blew my aviary over, letting my treasured budgies out to fend for themselves. These weren't wild birds proficient in storm wrangling or fighting off predators; they were pampered suburban birds, on a diet of carefully selected seeds from a box and with a grand total free space of around 4m². I never saw them again.

The benefit of being seven, I suppose, was that it was far less distressing to lose my entire business overnight than it would be to lose a career or business I had spent years building now. Which is why I think it's vital to have a contingency plan. If Covid-19 taught us anything, it's that your life can be one way one day and up-ended the next. Businesses that were turning over millions of dollars a year were forced to shut their doors, and many didn't survive. Unemployment skyrocketed and hundreds of thousands of people in Australia alone were out of a job. But you don't need to be hit by a global pandemic to require a contingency plan. Strategies change, businesses fold, and the people who run them have to make tough decisions sometimes. So, if the rug were ripped out from under you tomorrow, what would you do? Knowing the answer to that will make it easier if that time ever comes around, and for most of us, for one reason or another, it will.

And lastly, buckle up

One of my favourite motivational speakers is an Australian guy called Keith Abraham, who says, among other things, that in order to succeed, you have to fall in love with difficult. You have to welcome it, embrace it and even invite it. If you do the hard things now, Abraham says, your life will be easy, and if you do the easy things now, your life will be hard. Think about it this way: If being successful were easy, everyone would do it—right?

Walt Disney was turned down more than 300 times when he was trying to get finance for Disneyland—now one of the most visited tourist sites in North America and, according to *Forbes* magazine, one of America's most profitable companies. Almost everyone said no, but someone said yes. And Disney knew he would find that one, as long as he kept going and didn't let the rejection deter him. Like Walt, the most successful people I know are *drivers*. They flog their wares like a salesperson in a marketplace whose livelihood depends on it. They are undeterred by the word 'no', seeing it as simply one step closer to their 'yes', allowing them to be fearless when it comes to failure.

THE BEAUTY IS IN THE STRUGGLE

Oprah addressed the graduating class of Harvard in 2013, sharing with them some wisdom about failure off the back of her TV network, OWN, turning out to be a bit of a flop. Here's what she said: 'If you're constantly pushing yourself higher, the law of averages predicts that you will at some point fall. And when you do, I want you to remember this: there is no such thing as failure. Failure is just life trying to move us in another direction … learn from every mistake, because every experience, encounter and particularly your mistakes are there to teach you and force you into being more who you are.'

When we look at successful people, all we see is the culmination of where they are now. We don't see the years of blood, sweat and tears, the trial and error, the confidence-crushing knocks and the failure.

'If you are at home, and you're sitting on your couch and you're watching this right now, all I have to say is that this is hard work,' Lady Gaga told the audience while collecting her Oscar. 'I've worked hard for a long time, and it's not about winning. But what it's about is not giving up. If you have a dream, fight for it … it's not about how many times you get rejected or you fall down or you're beaten up. It's about how many times you stand up and are brave and you keep on going.'

Putting yourself out there takes guts and opens you up to all sorts of criticism, but the most important opinion is the one you have of yourself. For all my years believing I deserved a 'special' job, I have also always known that there is honour in hard work, no matter what you do. My mum has worked hard her whole life, still now juggling three or four jobs at an age when she was hoping to be winding down. She never complains, she just digs in and gets it done, and I am so inspired by that. You don't need a 'special' job to be special.

MOTIVATION IS A FINITE RESOURCE

If you've ever taken on any sort of project, be it a work or study thing, or a change in your lifestyle such as eating well or starting an exercise regime, you'll be familiar with the inevitable waning that occurs once motivation starts to wear off. But as we learned in Lesson 6, motivation is a finite resource. It's like the battery on your phone—it will last for a while but at some stage you have to plug it in, leave it alone and charge it up.

Athletes don't train flat-out, year-round. They have periods of intensity, periods of rehabilitation and periods of complete rest. For much of my career I have felt like there was only one speed: 456 per cent. I have worked in some capacity on most days for the better part of the past decade because I can't switch my brain off. But some down time doing nothing is vital; sometimes we need to do-tox our to-do lists and just chill the fuck out.

Executive coach Vanessa Bennett taught me that people are always going on about needing more time, but time is fixed—there are only 24 hours in a day, and seven days in a week—and that will never change. Energy, on the other hand, we can create more of with things like good sleep, exercise, coffee, nutrition and having a passion or purpose. And when you have more energy, you can do more with your time.

YOU WILL PROBABLY ALWAYS FEEL LIKE AN IMPOSTOR

We tend to downplay our abilities. It's a way of staying safe, of not coming across as narcissistic. But impostor syndrome is almost universal, and I have come across very few people who don't suffer from it. I come up against impostor syndrome all the time—like I've pulled on my mum's clothes, shirt sleeves dragging on the floor, high heels swimming on my feet. I walk out of meetings and have no idea what anyone was talking about. I don't even know what I was talking about. I still can't believe I'm in charge of two children, that anyone would entrust their lives to me and that the gatekeepers at the hospital thought it was a good idea I take them home.

No matter how successful someone is, there is almost always doubt in the back of their mind, wondering if they're good enough (and marvelling at how the fuck they got there)—you just can't hear it. And most people I know feel like that, every day, no matter how accomplished they are. Make friends with that, because in all your flawed, self-conscious glory, you have as much to contribute to the world as anyone else.

Remember my friend Dr Nikki Stamp, the cardiothoracic surgeon we met back in Lesson 3? She is one of the most professionally successful people I know, so I asked her whether there's anything she would change if she could start over.

'I would do a lot differently,' she tells me. 'I'd stop focusing on this idea of stratospheric success—that you have to be the best and most accomplished. I wish I had taken into account when I was choosing my career all of the other things in my life, that I had thought through my whole life at the beginning—that I'd looked forward.'

I'm reading between the lines here, but I think what Nikki is talking about—aside from wishing she had that crystal ball we would all like—is that she wishes she had learned sooner that professional success isn't the most important thing in life.

'We only want to celebrate our successes because we're so terrified of our shortcomings and how they define us,' she adds. 'I wish I'd learned to cultivate this sense of being good enough a lot sooner to give me comfort in those icky moments where we compare ourselves. I still do that.'

Success is relative, whether you're just starting out, somewhere in the middle of the pack or on top. The more you achieve, the more you expect and the more that's expected of you—so being super successful may not be all it's cracked up to be, and you can't take the trophies with you when you go.

Bad-to-better takeaways

- Success is not linear, and champagne moments are few and far between. Sometimes the most powerful lessons come from the lows, so learn to love the grind.
- There are many different types of success. Get crystal clear on what success means to you so you know what you're aiming for.

- You will always feel like an impostor. Always.
- How do you eat an elephant? You cut it up. Just focus on the first step—that one is the toughest. The rest will follow.
- The reward for having a go is having a go. Every single thing you do is an experience that lends itself to something else.

Lesson 14
Get Good At Conflict

How to have tough conversations

No one likes conflict. We have a deep desire to be liked and not 'rock the boat'. I'm no different, though in my younger years my big mouth often got me into trouble anyway. It took me a long time to learn that avoidance of conflict is the reason so many of us settle for less than we are worth, stay in bad relationships and put ourselves last. It makes sense; our brain is hardwired to keep us from harm, and an altercation with our lover or standing up to our boss is fraught with danger. But getting good at having those inevitable tough conversations is one of the greatest skills you will ever learn. Few of us are naturally good at conflict, though, so to upskill you'll need some practice—for those times you have to thrash it out with your boss, your beau or your bestie. Here's how.

Be prepared

Going into tough conversations unprepared is like going into battle without a gun. (Side note: I'm vehemently against gun violence and use the analogy purely to illustrate the point.) Think through your argument and make notes to take in with you so you can't get off track, because we tend to lose our train of thought when we're nervous. Keep notes brief; just dot points or simple statements.

Before you have 'the chat', consider these questions.
- What's at the heart of the issue here?
- Where are you willing to compromise?
- Where aren't you? What are your non-negotiables?
- What do you need moving forward to resolve this?

As much as you can, document everything from the conversation. Dates, times, discussions and what is agreed. This will give you some data to draw upon down the road if you need it.

Go in with a potential solution

No one likes someone who brings the issues but not the tissues. Ask yourself: In an ideal world, what would this look like for me? How would I solve this if I were the one in charge or the only party here?

Finding a solution doesn't mean sticking around if you're getting a bad deal. The 'solution' might be parting ways, but be clear on what you want to achieve as a result of the conversation. If it's available, have a couple of options you would be comfortable with up your sleeve, so you have more chance of finding a resolution that works for you both.

Seek first to understand, then to be understood

It's easy to go in so pumped up with our own perspective that we can forget to really listen to the other side of the story. So, go in with the initial intent of hearing them out. You don't need to rehearse in the moment (you have your notes to support you); instead, focus on what *they* are saying. Really hear them and repeat it back so they know you have heard and understood them. Thank them for sharing their perspective, because you know firsthand these conversations are hard to have. Empathy usually helps diffuse a tense environment. Ask questions if anything they're saying isn't clear, and try to put yourself in their shoes. Can you see where they're coming from? Now it's time to calmly and clearly lay out your perspective so it's easy for them to understand in return.

Breathe and buy yourself time

When we're nervous or anxious, we tend to over-speak. You know, where verbal diarrhoea pours out of you like champagne escaping a bottle. Take a slow, deep breath before you say anything. Speak slowly and clearly, maintaining eye contact. Don't rush. Say only what you need to say and nothing more. If you find yourself racing, take a moment, take another deep breath and start again.

Use assertive language

Being assertive allows you to communicate your position with respect for someone else's. It doesn't come naturally to everyone (myself included), but like any other skill it can be learned. And it's worthwhile, because it can help build your self-esteem and earn the respect of others. It's about not fucking around—if something doesn't work for you, it doesn't work for you. Saying no when you need to shows you respect yourself, and that shit is impressive.

You know when your boss asks you to take on more work when your plate is already overflowing, and your gut is screaming 'Please dear god *no*!' but the words that come out of your mouth are, 'Of course, no problem!' Being too passive isn't taking one for the team, it just leaves you stressed, angry and resentful.

On the other hand, being too aggressive makes you look like a self-righteous bully, which won't get you the result you want either. You need to be like the three bears with the porridge—just right(ly assertive). Here's how *not* to do it.

'Hey, I was wondering if maybe we could have a conversation about X because I kind of sometimes feel like possibly you're a little bit Y and it would mean the world to me if you could just ever so slightly adjust your behaviour so that I can survive but also if it's too much trouble don't worry it's not really that big a deal in fact do you have anything else you want to lump on me okay brilliant can't wait good chat bye.'

Here's what to focus on instead.
- Use 'I' statements. Rather than, 'You're wrong,' say, 'I disagree.'
- Keep it simple and be specific: 'I'd like you to help with X.'
- Get good at saying no. You don't need to explain your reasoning, but if you do, keep it brief.
- Practise. Write it down or talk it out with a friend first.
- Try to put your emotions aside, especially if it's a professional conversation. Don't let clear messaging get lost in emotion. Stick to the facts.

What to do when they're not listening

Rinse and repeat. Fifty times if you have to. Say things like: 'To repeat myself, I'm not comfortable with X,' or, 'I'm not willing to Y, and my position hasn't changed.' Also remind them you have politely listened to their perspective and are asking to be truly heard in return. Sometimes adults can be like overgrown toddlers—they need someone to be in charge but they really don't like it when someone (you) steps up. Bad luck to them.

Stand in your superhero power

You know how Superman wears his superhero suit under his clothes? Imagine your power suit underneath your clothes, so you can use strong, open body language and feel powerful when you need to. This is about standing up for yourself in a calm and measured way, and that's a kick-arse thing to do. Feel the power in that (even if deep down you're shitting yourself).

Pull in an objective third party

Sometimes you can't get there on your own. You're so bogged down in the detail and your position that no matter what you do, you can't seem to find common ground. Bring in someone else to help facilitate the conversation, whether it's a paid professional (a mediator or counsellor) or just someone objective who understands and can help bridge the gap. Be really clear with them about what you're trying to achieve so they can help you get there.

I have always relied firmly on other trusted opinions prior to going into any difficult conversation. I'd seek multiple views on anything from an argument with a friend to whether I was being undervalued at work, and while I fully appreciate the need to learn to trust your gut and stand on your own two feet, I always gained a huge amount from opening myself up to alternate viewpoints. They almost always ask a question I haven't thought of, or bring something new to my attention, and I ask them to play devil's advocate and put themselves in the other party's shoes so I can be aware of anything I might not be considering. It's like taking your blinkers off.

Of course, don't share sensitive information that isn't yours to share in the process—people have a good radar when it comes to loose lips; it makes them feel like their secrets wouldn't be safe with you, and that's just not the sort of girl you are.

Take responsibility

It's rare we don't play some part in the conflict that finds us. Asking yourself what role you played and taking responsibility for that is a crucial piece of the process. What could you do better next time? An apology—where warranted—goes a long way. It's cool to take responsibility for bad behaviour.

Pick your battles and your timing

Never put up with bad behaviour for an extended period of time, but timing is vital in getting the result you want. If it's personal, find a calm time when you can be together and no one has to rush off. Create space to have the conversation where you won't be interrupted by other people, phones or the TV. If it's professional, request a set time to have a meeting. If you know your boss or colleague is often late, flustered and grumpy in the morning, set it for the afternoon (maybe after they've eaten lunch so they're not hangry). And if you know they have to leave at 4.30 p.m. to pick up their kids or head out to another meeting, don't set it for 3.30 p.m. Choose a time when you know you'll be able to have their full attention and run over if you need to.

Understand your value and don't be scared

Nothing makes you want to do three nervous poos in a row like a difficult conversation. To ease the jitters, think about how good you will feel on the other side once it's over and done with. If you're stressing over worst-case scenarios, give yourself some time to consider them. He'll break up with you? Okay—if your requests here are reasonable and he does, then he's a dick and you don't need him. You'll meet someone else, I promise. Your boss will give you the boot? That's hard to do these days depending on your type of employment, and if you're a valuable employee (which you probably are) they will be looking for a solution too. Rehiring and training someone new takes time and money—two things businesses hate to lose.

Be one step ahead

If you know this person well, do your best to anticipate their responses and be ready with yours. A well-thought-out argument considers both perspectives, so that when they challenge you, you have already thought through what your position might be. Try to solve the problems before they are presented to you.

Let's say you're asking for a pay rise. You think your boss's response will be that the business can't afford it, or that there's a current pay freeze. So, on top of doing your research around comparative roles, rates of inflation, your own data about when your last pay rise was and how your role has expanded since then, think through how you can help your boss or business achieve their goals. Think commercially from the business's perspective, meaning you need to find the money (or bring in more of it) so that giving you a raise doesn't put the business out. But let's say you're in admin, without direct access to more customers or increased revenue. All is not lost—you just need to get creative.

You: 'I'd like to talk about increasing my pay.'

Your boss: 'Right, well, we can't afford it at the moment, and you know there's a pay freeze ...'

You: 'I'm aware. I've been doing some research, and comparatively in the market my role is offering around 10 per cent more than what I'm on now, and given that my role has expanded significantly since I started and my last pay rise was in 1842, I'd like to explore how we can get me closer to my market value, because I'm committed to the business and I'd like to stay here, but I also need to consider what's going to give me the best return financially. I've come up with a list of admin costs I think I can bring down—paper that's 10 per cent cheaper, office cleaners who are $5 an hour less and a water dispenser that will save us on the number of water bottles we're buying for meetings, with the added benefit of making us look and feel like environmental heroes. I've done the calculations and that adds up to around $10,000 a year in savings, and I'd like you to increase my pay by $5000 a year—so the business will still be $5000 a year better off, even after giving me a raise.'

At this stage, you're speaking their language as well as showing initiative and commitment to the business. Even if a pay rise isn't possible right now, you've put in the request. Ask when they'll be in a better position to have that conversation, then put that date in your diary as well as a reminder two weeks prior that it's coming up. Make notes of exactly what was discussed, and when your two-week reminder pops up, request another meeting, revisit your data and ask yourself all the same questions again:

- How has your role changed?
- Have you picked up the slack anywhere?
- Have you brought additional value to the business by way of new ideas, increased revenue or saving on costs?
- What have been your 'wins' since you last caught up?

- What are your objectives within the role for the next six to twelve months? And how will they deliver value to the business?

Show them you have a plan that works in their favour. If it's win–win, it's hard to refuse.

Also, don't forget that more money isn't the only lever here. Perhaps if a pay rise isn't possible right now, they might look at more flexible working arrangements such as working from home one day a week so you can save on travel costs, dropping your days or hours slightly so you can monetise some of your time elsewhere, or having them cover your lunch costs a couple of times a week. Think outside the box.

When it's personal

If the conversation is personal—with a partner or friend—tread extra carefully. Emotions can make us say things we don't mean, and they're hard to take back. Starting those conversations with something like, 'Obviously we're here because we care about each other, so let's have an open and honest dialogue so we can find a way to move forward,' sets a positive tone for what can be tricky terrain. Be kind and solutions-focused, because no one likes having emotionally draining conversations over and over again.

Remember, too, that the people who know us best are also best at rubbing us up the wrong way, so if the conversation starts to escalate and you feel someone is getting frustrated or losing their cool, there's no harm in bringing the intention back in, or suggesting you park the conversation to pick it up again in a day or two. Sometimes it takes us a long time to work through things that are difficult or painful, or that tickle in places we don't want to be tickled.

Bad-to-better takeaways

- Get clear on your non-negotiables and ideal outcomes so you know what you're aiming for.
- Wait your turn to speak and really listen to the other side—repeat it back so they know you've heard them.
- Breathe. Speak slowly. Don't rush. Be clear and concise.
- Don't be scared—you are valuable, worthy and prepared. If it's a reasonable request that's met with an unreasonable response, then you might consider your options.
- Make it win-win by genuinely considering their position and how you might improve things for both parties.

Lesson 15
Forget Fame

Being 'average' is more than okay

I always thought I would grow up to be famous. God knows for what—I can't act my way out of a paper bag, I was an average model at best, I can't sing (though if I turn the music up really loud sometimes I think I can) and I'm certainly not 'influential' on social media. In an era when many of us are told that we can grow up to be whatever we want to be, it's unsurprising that what that translates to is seeking out a life that appears to come with all the perks—attention, freedom and lots of cash.

I assume our obsession with fame is largely linked to our sense of self-worth, of wanting to be a 'somebody' versus a 'nobody'. Of course, wanting to be liked, admired and respected isn't new; from an evolutionary perspective, it has always been the case. We have an innate desire to be adored, and one way to achieve that validation is via fame. In essence, we all just want to feel special. It's the reason that every day, people around the world try their hand at getting on a reality TV series, no matter what they have to build/share/cook/do/date/disclose in order to get their fifteen minutes. For a lucky few it's a legitimate path to bigger and better things, but the media is never short of sob stories from people who wind up feeling chewed up and spat out.

Think about every reality show you've ever watched: of the twenty or so contestants, who do you remember? The nice, normal person who came seventh? Nope. It's much more likely you remember the villain, or the one who created the most drama and therefore got the most airtime. Growing up on a staple diet of people behaving badly on TV teaches us that bad behaviour is not only acceptable, it also gets you attention and potentially even fame.

We love watching celebrities rise (*That could be me one day*), and fall (*Thank god—they're just like me*). Because of the massive perks of being famous, it's easy to set aside the fact that celebrities are still real people with feelings that get hurt. We reason that hardcore trolling and bullying online 'comes with the territory'. As such, it's no surprise that we see stars fall victim to substance abuse, legal battles, disease and even death. Because at some point you stop being a person and you start being a commodity.

A career in the public eye is by all accounts a bitch of a pursuit, and yet, if what you feel you were born to do happens to be something in it, then I understand that intrinsic pull. But it's not easy, and that's worth being prepared for—as is truly considering your motivation for wanting fame in the first place. Because if you think it's going to make you more 'special' than anyone else, you might be sorely disappointed. Scandinavian countries call it the Law of Jante—the idea that no one is more valuable than anyone else. It's about fitting in, rather than standing out. It's not like Australia's tall poppy syndrome where we cut people down when they get a bit too big for their boots, but about knowing that no matter who we are or what we do, none of us is more important than the other. And they kind of know what they're doing on the happiness front, consistently rating among the happiest countries in the world even though most of the time it's dark and freezing.

A girlfriend of mine has always wanted to be an actress. She's been in LA for the past decade and has landed a couple of minor roles, one with a former Hollywood darling we were all hoping would be her big break, but she hasn't 'made it'. Almost every time we speak, regardless of whether she's up for it or not, I coach her like I'm Tony Robbins and then get off the phone feeling like a hero. I truly believe in her and all I want for her is the success she craves. She's talented as hell as both an actress and a writer, and I have no doubt that if she keeps going, works hard and gets lucky, she'll end up in the Tina Fey/Kristen Wiig/Maya Rudolph camp. But it hasn't happened for her yet.

I ask her about that drive to be famous.

'I still hold on to the idea that there might be a chance, and I think it has kind of ruined my life in a sense,' she says. 'Because I am always living the idea of who I should be as opposed to who I am. It's given me a sense of entitlement, that I'm special (for no real reason) therefore I deserve to be handed something or appreciated for something just for being me. It's an irrational and delusional headspace to be in, which doesn't support reality and sets you up for failure. You aren't able to see the good things in your life to be grateful for or the small wins because it doesn't match your expectations. You are constantly self-loathing because anything that falls outside of that idea in your head is a failure. It's all or nothing, which is a very hard way to live and means you are in constant suffering.'

This might seem like an intense depiction, but I think you'd be hard-pressed to find someone in her position who didn't feel the same way. And there are a lot of them.

Researchers from the Queen Mary University in London have looked into what quantifies and predicts success in show business. They say that if you want to be an actor, you're looking at a 90 per cent unemployment rate and a 2 per cent chance of working enough to make a living. Not great odds. Think about it in the context of Hollywood: for every actor you can name, I'd guess there are thousands more just like them. All talented. All ready. All hungry. So, what's the difference between the ones who make it and the ones who don't? Luck and timing. Luck to get in front of the right director at the right time, to be the best on audition day and 'fit the brief' and that all of the stars align for the project to go ahead. Then timing of who else is in the market at the time, of when a project gets launched determining how well it does and of what is popular and happens to fit that bill. That's not to take away from preparation, talent and hard work, of course, but those alone are not enough.

So, if the public eye is where you want to be, here are some tips from someone who has never 'made it' but has sat on the sidelines, watching, for quite some time. There are a few things that seem to make the pursuit of life in the public eye (a little) easier.

Focus on the craft, not the by-product

For me, there are two types of people in the entertainment industry: those who need to do a certain job, of which one of the side effects happens to be fame; and those who want to be famous because it looks like a cool life—and they will do anything to achieve it. It's a safe assumption that the people in the former camp are more likely to keep going and be happier while they're at it, because they are driven to do their thing and if fame comes with it, it comes. Being really honest about what is driving you will help you keep your eye on the prize, and may make it more likely to happen.

Have something else

Very few of us can derive a living purely from fame-inducing activities. Even though my dream was a TV show, I'm lucky that I have been able to fill my career with other related work: writing this book, producing content for clients and working with other talent. If you are desperate for a job in the public eye, it's a good idea to consider what other jobs you could do in your industry that would allow you to make a living *and* increase your specialised knowledge so you're an even better actor/singer/dancer/YouTuber. You could: write, produce, teach, edit, be a runner or assistant on set or go into casting ... and so on. Immerse yourself in the industry you want to be a part of while you wait for opportunities to do what you do best. Best-case scenario: all that extra work makes you even better at what you do and when your time comes you're well positioned to take advantage because you've had more time to practise your craft. Worst-case scenario: you've built a career in an industry you love, which you can still enjoy, even if the 'fame' thing doesn't work out.

Give it a timeframe

If you take stock of the tip above, you can simultaneously pursue your craft while building a career and you can take less notice of this one. But if you're going to throw everything you have at something (and there are plenty of people—my LA friend included—who would argue that's the only way to get what you want) then I suggest putting a timeframe on it. 'Making it' can take years and years (think: Morgan Freeman, JK Rowling, Susan Boyle), so the only way to ensure you don't lose your entire life to something that isn't going to pay off (unless, I suppose, your parents are willing to bankroll your endeavours) is to define what success looks like for you (as we did in Lesson 13) and then set a timeframe in which to achieve it. Regularly assess how you're tracking and be flexible. Remember—things rarely work out the way we think they will.

Beware the pitfalls of 'social' media

Ah, social media. The term itself makes me giggle. Have you ever seen a family or group of friends 'spending time together' but every single one of them is glued to their phone? You'd think Zoomers or Millennials would be the worst at it, but I would argue that Baby Boomers—AKA my parents—take the cake. There is not a time or place mine think it's inappropriate to pop off for a quick scroll of the feed or their turn on Words With Friends, even mid conversation. Of course, the dopamine hit that social media apps are designed to deliver—that feeling of being wanted, needed and 'liked'—is like crack to us too, and there's every chance you're an addict.

Nothing facilitates the comparison game like social media. It's a popularity contest in your pocket, available to you at any time of any day. These days someone is as likely to hunt you down on Instagram as they are to Google you. It's a business card, a way of showing the world what you do and how to contact you.

It's free marketing if you're a 'brand' or you have a business, and so I totally get why people pour time and energy into it, but the people I know with lots of followers openly admit that the thing is a relentless beast. I imagine it's quite strange having people 'follow' you (that used to be called stalking) and viewing your life through the lens of what will make good 'content'. Ugh, how exhausting.

Let us also not forget that most of what we see on social media is complete BS. I love seeing models and wellness 'influencers' posting about their clean, green, post-Pilates lifestyles on Mondays after I've seen them emerge from the toilets with a suspiciously itchy nose on Saturday night. I applaud their commitment to balance and am no stranger to green smoothies and itchy noses, but it worries me that we lap it up anyway, influencers' seemingly perfect lives far more interesting to watch than our own dysfunctional relationships, boring jobs and weekends spent rescuing wine from a bottle with not a goodie bag in sight.

Someone who knows all about goodie bags is Shelly Horton. She's that vivacious redhead you might have seen on your TV screens, so she has a level of fame herself but she also spent many years interviewing the world's biggest stars, which has given her unique insight. I ask her what it's like being 'a little bit famous'.

'The former host of *Entertainment Tonight* Mark Steines once told me, he was just the right amount of famous—enough to get a good table at a restaurant but not enough for people to interrupt him for photos while he's eating,' she explains. 'I'm what I call micro-famous: I get recognised here and there but I can go to the shops in my trackies and no make-up and not get papped. Of course there are benefits to intense fame, a lot of it is material—money, a bigger house—but the downside is losing your anonymity and your privacy. People expect you to be *on* 100 per cent of the time—and being on is exhausting.'

If you're still angling for a job as an influencer, Horton has some advice.

'Being an influencer isn't a job, it's a by-product of being good at something,' she explains. 'My advice would be to choose an area and become an expert in it. You don't need to go to university, but you need to be well researched and confident in that area. Decide what you want to be influential in, because you need to really love it.'

It's sage advice, because putting yourself out there invites criticism, something Horton knows all too well.

'My job is to offer my opinion, so dealing with trolls comes with the territory,' she says. 'I've had death threats, bashing threats and rape threats simply because a coward behind a keyboard doesn't agree with what I say. At least once a week I get messages saying I'm ugly and fat—it's pretty much constant body shaming. You need to have thick skin and learn to delete and block quickly, but in order to do that you have to read the messages, and they stay with you.'

To prove her point, Horton rattles off a dozen awful trolling comments that have been directed at her over the years, word for word, all of which make me wince and none of which I will reprint here. I ask how she copes, given I would literally run for the hills.

'Lots of the time it's like water off a duck's back, but then you can be having a tough day and it's like someone has winded you,' she says.

On one such day, she called an emergency appointment with her psychologist.

'He gave me some really good advice, which was to make a list ... of the ten people whose opinions matter to you—then ask yourself whether you are happy with what you said that has caused the trolls to attack and if the people on your list are happy with what you said. If the answer is yes, ask yourself if you know the person trolling you. For example, let's say @fuckface69 says you're too fat to be on TV. If @fuckface69 isn't on your list, then they don't get your time or energy.'

Horton works with reality TV stars frequently, so I ask her what the difference is between the ones who leverage their experience into something more and those who end up being a flash in the pan.

'A lot of them go on because they want to get famous but they're also clever business people—they use it as a slingshot to get more eyeballs on what they do,' she explains. 'On the flip side, some reality stars get this instant fame and don't know how to handle it—they do nightclub appearances and hook up with strangers and go on a power trip. They see themselves as more important, so they treat other people badly. But fame isn't a job, it's not a skill—it's just a by-product. The ones that have longevity treat it as one arm of their business.'

No matter how you do it, Horton says, if it's fame you're after you'll need to be patient.

'I don't think anyone is an overnight success, even if they have a viral video or whatever, they've probably put in years of doing videos prior that didn't go viral,' she explains.

'I've been a journalist for 25 years, I've been constantly working and pushing myself. So, when people say anything about anyone being an overnight success the thought exhausts me, like, "God, they've probably put so much work into that."'

Make sure you're 100 per cent up to the job

Cheryl Rixon is the family friend I went to the Playboy mansion with in Lesson 7. She lives a life many will only ever dream of—the type you see on American TV shows with big cars and fancy houses and VIP treatment. Even so, Rixon knows that when it comes to fame, you need to be careful what you wish for.

'If people don't feel they absolutely belong in that world, they shouldn't enter it,' she cautions. 'Obviously the Kardashians felt, starting with Kim, that she belonged there. She used to hang out with Paris Hilton and Lindsay Lohan and she was the third banana, but she had her eye on the prize. Who gets a mother who can pull that stuff together for all the kids? That's a lot of work, a lot of surgery, a lot of things that most people wouldn't want to go through.

'But I greatly admire what Kim and Kris have done. In a time of influencers and reality television they have accomplished so much and while their pursuit of beauty at any cost differs so much from my own, I find the time and effort they put into an entirely new field of fame quite admirable. They retain a closeness despite the challenges their family has faced, attained unimaginable wealth and are living examples of success derived from hard work and commitment to their goals.'

Rixon understands that commitment, and she's had one hell of a ride herself. She started in beauty pageants, modelling and TV in Australia in the 1970s, before picking up and moving to New York City at age nineteen. She rocked up in the Big Apple like an Aussie Daisy Duke: cut-off denim shorts, midriff top, platform shoes and a total knockout. She says people weren't quite sure what to do with her, but she signed with the esteemed Ford modelling agency anyway and kicked off what would become a long and illustrious career.

Famed American photographer and *Penthouse* founder Bob Guccione made her a centrefold and then Penthouse Pet of the Year in 1979. Between high-profile modelling gigs, she travelled the world hanging out with rock stars, Freddie Mercury dubbing her the unofficial fifth member of Queen. It's not hard to understand why, aside from being impossibly beautiful (even and especially now in her mid-sixties), she was a sex icon in *the era* of sex icons—and she's cool to boot. She has understood fame for a long time, so I pick her brain about it.

'Fame is not an imposition, it's a privilege and a responsibility,' she says. 'Success in the entertainment industry is simply about developing an audience or a following—what those people think is of great importance to your professional success. You have to make it truthful and brave, something others can relate to no matter how frivolous it may seem. If you aren't buying it, nobody else will either.

She says being famous before social media was a gift, but there are some lessons that are as true today as they were then, and it reinforces my belief that there are still plenty of people out there who won't just step on your toes to get where they're going, they'll cut them off.

'The perception of centrefolds from that time was of young women chasing exposure and a wealthy man to give them a world of luxury and leisure,' she explains. 'The biggest models of the 1970s and 80s were deadly. I was struck by their power and resourcefulness—men didn't stand a chance against what those chicks were willing to do and what they'd do to you later if they weren't happy. I don't begrudge girls who are willing to trade sex and sexual favours for where they want to get with fame and fortune and lifestyle, because it doesn't matter which way you do it, you earn it—and don't think trading sexual favours is the easy route; it doesn't go very far because there's always someone coming up who looks better.'

Now a successful jewellery designer and business owner, Rixon is married with two sons, both in their twenties and both in the entertainment industry, one an actor and producer and the other a DJ. While they hang with the mega-influencers, Rixon is just like any other mum, teaching her kids about the world and the fact that, regardless of what industry you're in, you need to be adaptable and ready to move fast, not getting too attached to any project or outcome.

'I say to my kids all the time: Follow your dreams and go for it, commit and give it your all. Be considerate but don't be too polite or too timid. If it doesn't feel right, leave. Trust in your instincts and believe in yourself. Anything is possible! People have enormously rewarding careers that have not yet been given a job description. If you've never heard of it, maybe you are the first. And most importantly, remember that opportunities can disappear just as quickly as they arrive, so don't take any of it for granted.'

I'm mindful of the fact that the 'go for it' message is easy coming from someone who has 'made it'. But the entertainment industry is brutal, and most people won't. I asked Maz Compton (remember her from the alcohol chapter?) what she learned from navigating it for so long a little closer to home.

'I have had an amazing career, and I managed to do it by believing in myself and working my arse off,' she says. 'Hard work outlasts talent, you need the talent to start but that alone will not get you to the top or keep you there. Passion, hard work and more hard work are the steel in the spine of the person at the top of the mountain. Also, after leaving the industry I realised no one actually cares that much about what I did on TV or said on the radio for over twelve years, so there's that!'

So, do I still want to be famous? I'd be lying if I said no. What I do know is that I don't want to be famous for famous' sake. I want to be famous for being really, really good at something. Being a great parallel parker isn't really delivering on that for me, yet. But give it time.

Bad-to-better takeaways

- Not being famous is awesome—you can do lots of dumb sh*t and literally no one cares.
- Famous people are people just like you who worked hard and got lucky. They are no more (or less) special than you are, they just get more attention.
- Have something else. If you can find something in the same industry, that's great—one will make you better at the other.
- Be honest: Are you 100 per cent up for the job? You need to be.
- Get ready to work your arse off. Hard work outlasts talent—it's the steel in the spine of every person at the top of the mountain.

Lesson 16
Spend Your Life With Someone Kind

It's the best decision you'll ever make

Remember back in Lesson 10 when I told you I would introduce you to my 'this is it' person? Well, friends, that time has arrived. And he was worth the wait (for me and for you). Even so, when I met my husband, I thought he was too nice for me. He was a teacher—a stand-up citizen and quite literally the last person on Earth I thought I would end up with. I still thought I needed a bad boy to 'keep me on my toes', and this guy wore a man bangle. Luckily future me knew better, and current me was smart enough to listen and do her a major, major solid. We'll call him the teacher.

Let me tell you about the day my life changed forever. One of my many jobs at the time was as a nanny, and I pulled into the school car line in my nanny-family's car, expecting to see my tiny charge jump up and throw himself through the door and onto the front seat—but he was nowhere in sight. Instead, one of the teachers—glasses on, shirt collar popping out of his respectable sweater—stuck his head into the passenger-side window and smiled. I instantly regretted my decision to come straight from a hot-yoga class. I was a mess, and yet there was something about him that made me feel like it didn't matter.

I felt at ease in his presence, like I didn't want to be out of it. We had bigger fish to fry, though (namely—a missing child), and he told me to pull up ahead so he could make a few calls to try to locate my little Houdini. He called the teachers at the bus stops, no child. He called the school secretary, still no child. The teacher suggested he must have hopped a lift home with one of the other parents and said I should head home to see if he was there. (Side note: my charge was aged ten at this stage, so was fairly self-sufficient—i.e. I hadn't lost an infant.) I agreed but offered to leave my number just in case the kid turned up and I needed to come back and get him. *Go, you crafty bitch, go.*

As I pulled out I thought, *I could marry that guy*, which I quickly reasoned away. How ridiculous! As if I would meet my husband-to-be just like that after *years* of disappointment and loneliness.

Driving the short distance home, my phone rang from an unknown number. I answered, hoping it was him.

'Hey Casey, apparently he did get a ride home, so don't stress—I'm sure he'll be at home when you get there,' he said. 'Just wanted to let you know.'

Me: 'Amazing, thank you. I really appreciate the call.'

Him: 'No problem. I'll … uh … talk to you soon.'

Me: 'Okay, thanks again …'

Him: 'No problem.'

Me: 'Cool.'

Him: 'Lovely to meet you.'

Me: 'Likewise.'

It went on like this for a few more torturous seconds, neither of us wanting to hang up.

I got home and found a blissfully unaware child.

'Where've you been?' he said.

'Me! Where've *you* been?' I responded.

Clearly we had miscommunicated about pick-up arrangements that morning. No harm, no foul, though—he was safe, and I had the added bonus of having Mr Handsome Teacher's number. For the next few minutes I had one of those conversations in my head about what to do with it.

I should text him, let him know everything's okay—he could be concerned! No, he'll call if he's concerned, he didn't sound concerned. I'll leave it … But wait, am I missing an opportunity here? What if he did like me? Okay, I'll text him. But wait …

How fun does my head sound? Anyway, bear in mind that at this stage neither of us had a clue if the other person was married, coupled, single or a total psychopath. Any attempt to connect had the possibility of being met with dreaded rejection. Later I would learn that he too felt an instant connection when he stuck his head through my window, but in unknown limbo I spent a few minutes crafting the perfect message—open-ended enough to allow for a little back and forth, but nothing too suggestive. It was something like: *Just letting you know he was at home after all. Thanks for your help today. Do you think my 'babysitter of the year' title will remain intact?*

I'm not sure if emojis were a thing then, but if they were I probably would have put those little prayer hands at the end—because I still feel if I put nothing it's like I'm being rude (so abrupt!) and putting a kiss would have been way too forward. I reserve those little x's for people I know and love, and occasionally my boss or a complete stranger when my fingers work faster than my brain.

I was used to the type of guys who made you wait hours or days for a response even though you know their phone is sutured to their palm. But within seconds, those three little dots appeared. I threw my phone on the kitchen bench, scared something was broken. I rubbed my eyes, watching like I was waiting for the results of a pregnancy test. Putting yourself out there takes guts, man.

His response quickly found its way to my inbox.

All good, but you owe me ...

BOOM. We were on. He was interested and I was blushing.

I guess I do, I casually replied. *What could I possibly do to make it up to you?*

Leave it with me, but it will probably involve food and cocktails we can't pronounce, came his response.

And just like that, he became a permanent fixture in my life. We spent the next month getting to know each other, getting tipsy and enjoying first kisses, first dances (always a good sign when a guy is happy to dance with you on the first date) and asking all the questions. There were no games, no treating them mean to keep them keen and no BS. We were on the same frequency. I would think of him and a message would pop into my inbox asking what I was doing that night, and whether I wanted to hang out. It was easy, and he felt like home.

Life, on steroids

The next few years with him leapfrogged from one milestone to another at a rapid pace.

After eight months we were engaged.

After two years we were married.

After three years we had a baby and a mortgage.

And after six years (of which we've been married for four), we now have two children (and we still have a mortgage, which at this rate we'll have until 2075).

I'll be brutally honest here. While the connection with my now husband was instant, the love was a slow burn. I'd been 'in love' before, and this didn't feel like that. I really liked him, but I was kind of on the fence in terms of him being my 'forever' person. First because I didn't really believe in 'forever', and the one time I did, it ended badly. But also because he wasn't who I had seen myself ending up with. I thought I would end up with the male version of me, but my husband is the opposite. He's just kind of … steady.

The clichéd truth is that he's my very best friend. He's good for me. He calms me down, slows my roll and loves me unconditionally. I am 100 per cent myself with him, there's nothing I can't say or do. He loves me at my best and still adores me at my worst, and that is what we all deserve.

The best decision I ever made

One of my older friends was instrumental in my getting off the fence. She is the mother of the child that brought us together, my former employer, and one night when she came home with a few wines under her belt, she gave me a piece of her mind about how I should do myself a solid and choose to spend my life with someone like him.

'You just want to be with someone who puts your toothpaste on your toothbrush,' she said as I made my way out the front door during the changing of the guard.

'Okay, thanks, nighty-night! See you next time ...' I giggled.

'No, seriously. Do yourself a favour and marry the guy who is kind for no reason, all the time.'

It was the best advice I have ever been given and it encouraged me to make the best decision of my life. Here's the truth about my relationship: my husband is legitimately a better person than I am, on almost every front. He is kinder, calmer, more patient and less judgemental—all things I'm working on but that he finds infinitely more natural than I do. Which is exactly what makes us a good team.

It's not 'settling', it's doing yourself a solid

As you grow up, your needs change. But there is one thing you will always need above anything else, and that is support. Support if or when you decide to have children. Support if you want to have a killer career. And support to let you find your way around friendships, family relationships and those times in your life when things go well, terribly and everything in between, with someone who has your back.

Here's how a friend explained this shift of awareness to me, in the context of her own 'settling':

'After years of bad dating experiences I realised I had my priorities out of order. I was looking for things that seemed impressive to other people, that would make me look good and feel validated, like some sort of achievement, but those things actually aren't conducive to my mental health and growth, or a fulfilling, lasting relationship. When I realised that, I met my partner, who I have been with for five years now. He makes me laugh, he's kind, calm, rational, supportive and ambitious. He's my champion, he loves me fiercely and we make a great team. We give each other space to grow and both put the other person first.'

Sounds like a keeper. Here are some signs to help you identify one.

- They're kinder to you than you are to yourself.
- They know who they are and have their shit together. They don't need fixing.
- They're ready and willing to bring you into the nook, happily introducing you to family and friends.
- They love your people, even if they don't like them.
- They make you laugh, hold you when you cry and everything in between.
- They allow you to be 100 per cent yourself and love you even when you're being an idiot.

In the years since my husband and I chose each other, we've gone from strength to strength. We get on each other's nerves from time to time (show me a couple that doesn't) but 99 per cent of the time we're good, and 100 per cent of the time we're committed. We made a choice to be each other's person for as long as we're both happy, and while we took 'till death do us part' out of our wedding vows, we are both hopeful we'll be each other's happily ever after, and we both work hard to give us the best chance of making that happen.

Muddling through motherhood

One of the best things about meeting your 'this is it' person is that, if you're lucky (and it's what you want), you might get to smush your DNA together and make new tiny people. My daughters are the best thing that have ever happened to me. It's my job to raise them to be smart, savvy, kind women, but more than anything I hope they grow up to be resilient. Because life is hard and shitty things happen, and no matter how much I would like to I can't protect them from that.

One of the things I can do is to warn them (and you) about some of the bullshit we are fed about motherhood. Hear me loud and clear: It is the best thing I have ever done and I wouldn't trade it for the world. I love my girls more than I can put into words, more than I could ever possibly love myself. But motherhood is fucking hard—like, forever—and if it's something you want, it is worth being prepared for that. If we give up our career we lose our capacity to earn our own money and the gift of doing something professionally fulfilling. If we put our babies into care so we can forge a career, we lose precious moments we can never get back, risking them walking, talking and sitting up by themselves for the first time with someone else. And if we try to do both we run the risk of burning out before we learn we can have it all, but not at once.

And yet, having it all is expected of women now: a thriving career, a perfect home and a happy, healthy family. We want picturesque holidays, *Sex and the City*-level friendships and *Fifty Shades of Grey* sex (until you're married, in which case most of us will settle for fifty shades of once a fortnight). We run ourselves ragged trying to get it, and when we inevitably drop the ball at work, home or with our nearest and dearest, we feel like we're failing. But the system is rigged because 'all' is infinite—and that makes it impossible. There simply aren't enough hours in the day or years in a lifetime, for anyone, ever. Which means that to do anything well, something has to give.

So, here's how I do it all: badly. Not terribly, but not well. When it comes to loving my girls I knock it out of the park, but the truth is, outside of that, there's no perfect way to be a parent. Knowing that, and that you will frequently fuck things up, is the only way to survive. Of course, many of us will choose not to go down this path, and live the kinds of lives mums knee-deep in bottles and nappies dream about: the type where you can go to the beach for a swim *on your own*, sleep through the night and head out to a restaurant for dinner just because you feel like it, without organising a babysitter and toddler bribe so you can take one glorious, exhausted hour to reconnect with the person you made the tiny people with.

DIY family

Saying you can't choose your family is BS.

My parents blanked on a few things when I was a kid. One was a middle name, another was any form of immunisation (which I rectified as an adult) and one more was godparents. They weren't being neglectful, we just aren't religious, and given I wasn't baptised it makes sense I didn't get any. But I always felt like I needed some, so when I was 22, I chose my own. *But Casey, do you really NEED godparents at 22?* I did. I still do. I won't ever not need people older, wiser and better at life than me to steer this perpetually-verging-on-sinking ship. And back then, living in Sydney on my own,

I needed even more badly to 'belong' somewhere. The people I chose had been in my life forever. She, a glamorous Perth-born model who had worked for my mum's modelling agency, and he a bass guitarist who'd flexed his entrepreneurial muscles and built an enviable empire in Byron Bay.

But I didn't choose them for their aesthetics or material offerings. I chose them for their unwavering support, guidance and generosity of spirit. And they took it as seriously as I did. From that day forth I was officially their goddaughter. I would frequently disappear from Sydney to their house in Byron Bay, falling apart throughout my twenties and they would carefully and lovingly put me back together again. I got engaged and married at their house, and they stood up to give me away along with my parents. These days I try to play a similar role to their daughters, and their daughters play a similar role to mine. I feel as much a part of their family as I do my own, and the fact we chose each other makes it just as special, in a different way.

In recent years my godmother has been living with a neurodegenerative illness, a disorder of the central nervous system that kind of behaves like multiple sclerosis, characterised by increasing disability and pain. I've watched her traverse the mindfuck that is not knowing when a lesion will strike, and her patience and surrender toward the whole thing has been nothing short of awe-inspiring. I have watched my godfather make peace with the fact that this part of their lives, which was meant to be spent enjoying an empty nest and years of travel and exploration, is now spent holding her hand as she navigates doctors' appointments and stints in hospital, and even simply making the short walk from the couch to the dinner table. I always wanted to be like them, and have probably subconsciously modelled my life (and my relationship) somewhat on theirs. What they probably don't realise is that over the years of affording me the sort of belonging I had craved, they bought me the time and space to do just that. This is what family is all about, and it's an honoured pact for which I am forever grateful.

This is my story. There is no right way to build yours. You might chase down 'the one' or build a kick-arse life on your own. You might be desperate for a family or to pursue a life that's gloriously independent. And you might be building a thriving career, or happy to cruise. Who you love and how you love them is entirely up to you, but given loving someone (and letting them love you) is one of the bravest and most vulnerable things you can do in life, do yourself a solid and choose someone who deserves it.

Bad-to-better takeaways

- It's not 'settling', because you'll never, ever get sick of someone being kind to you. I promise.
- You can have it all, just not at once. Be okay with the different chapters of life, and the change in pace required to navigate them.
- Building a family is not just about your partner and children. Sometimes the most important family are the people we choose.
- It's such a cliché, but when you know, you know. Your 'this is it' person will feel like home and make everything easy. Like it should be.

- You have to believe that you're worthy of someone amazing, drop your expectations of who they 'should' be and build a full, incredible life in the meantime. For yourself.

Conclusion
Build a Life You'll Be Proud Of

I wasted years of my life ashamed of who I was and things I'd done. My estimation of myself was tied up in what I thought other people thought of me, rather than what I thought of myself. I wanted to turn back the clock and start again so I could build the life I wish I'd known I wanted many, many years ago. The truth is, though, that we go through what we need to go through and learn what we need to learn to become who we need to become. And I've become someone I'm really proud of. I've never said that before, and I'm putting it in print so I can't take it back.

We all get there in our own time. My hope is that what you have taken from this book is the confidence and permission to be 100 per cent yourself, while you learn the most important lesson of them all: You are not the things you've done, the people you've been with, the mistakes you've made. You are not your successes or accolades, or your failures or fuck-ups. You are more than all of that. You hold a unique position in the world as yourself, and the world needs you in all your imperfectly perfect glory. There is *nothing* bad about you.

I used to think I needed a label to know who I was. 'Good' girl. 'Bad' girl. But I've come to love that thing you can't put your finger on, and I am slowly but surely making peace with all my contradictions. I can be wild and measured. I can be capable and still learning. I can be sassy and kind. And I can look after myself and still occasionally eat chips for dinner.

You know those pieces of glass you see on the beach, the ones that have been tumbled around in the waves against the sand for years and now their formerly sharp edges are smooth? That is exactly how I feel about life. We get tumbled around, roughed up and smoothed out. We begin as something, shatter into something else and take on another form, in many ways more beautiful and far less likely to hurt anyone than where we started. We are constantly evolving.

Almost everyone I know has been through something they thought would break them. They've lost someone they love, been abused, diagnosed with a serious illness or fired from their seemingly secure job. You probably have too, which means you are already braver and far more resilient than you might give yourself credit for. These storylines seem monumental when they are happening and they absolutely shape our story, but they are also just part of living, and we don't get the reward without the risk.

Our stories make up the patchwork quilt of our lives; some pieces are a bit torn at the edges, some have stains on them, some are missing altogether and some are still perfectly new and in a really bright, exciting fabric. But they're all a part of who we are.

Our story is constantly unfolding—we never know what twists and turns it will take. We're isolated within our own storyline, but the truth is that we're all just tiny cogs in a machine that will continue to turn with or without us, and my question to you is: What will you let take up your time and energy while you're here?

One thing I know is this: emotional baggage is too heavy to carry around for a lifetime. It serves no one (least of all you) and quite simply takes up space that could be far better used for joy, gratitude and love. There's only so much room 'in there', so why fill it with stuff that makes you feel anything less than a hero? And you, my friend, *are* a hero—and let me tell you why. Because showing up every day wanting more for yourself takes guts. Having a go takes guts. Embracing who you are and having a crack at loving yourself takes guts.

Without being morbid, I have always had a strong sense of my mortality. It freaks me out that one day I won't be here anymore, and I'm fearful my time will be cut short now that I finally fully appreciate what an incredible gift it is to be here. I spent so much of my life not understanding this privilege, while grappling with the parts of me other people said were 'bad'. Now I know that the only person who gets to decide what's good and bad for me, is me. And not only that—everyone has a bit of bad in them, no matter who they are or what they tell you. I hope that if this book has taught you anything, it's that a little bad isn't always a bad thing.

One day I will get to the end of my life. And you will get to the end of yours. You don't need me to tell you that when that day comes you're going to give precisely zero fucks about how many followers you have on the 'Gram, how many pairs of shoes you own or how many dollars you have in the bank. You're not going to be pining for that douchelord who kicked you to the kerb or still beating yourself up for calling your mum a c*nt. You're going to be focused on the moments you felt the sun on your skin after an ocean dip, when you held your baby in your arms for the first time and when you laughed until you cried and peed your pants a little. All you will see is how—and who—you loved.

The opportunity is to know what is going to be important to you on that day and go after it now. I spent a long time prioritising calls from my boss over the calls of my babies, and nights at my laptop over nights under the stars. I wanted more out of life, terrified of the mundanity of a 'normal' existence. I wanted fame, fortune and free shit, because for some reason I needed to prove I was special. But for someone who grew up terrified of being ordinary, I have come to a place of immense gratitude for the incredible gift of a sound mind, a healthy body and a few people who love me deeply. Because while we tend to take those things for granted, that is so far from ordinary. It is an *extraordinary* life.

So, cheers to you. We did it. It's time to shrug off the shame, do away with the disappointment, start loving your life and pop that bottle—fill your glass right to the top, and fill mine while you're at it. Because you, my friend, have totally got this.

Acknowledgements

To my husband: Thank you for your extraordinary support throughout this process, there is no way this book would've happened without you. You make my life better in every way and I love you deeply, even when you steal my storm.

My babies: I apologise for the times writing this and other work has taken me away from you. You are my reason for everything and I love you more than I could ever put into words. Also, everything in this book is a lie.

Mum: You are the most remarkable woman I know. I'm in awe of your strength, courage and gumption, and you are hands down my favourite person to sink limitless cups of tea with. I'm only a tiny bit mad at you for passing on an aggressive genetic sugar addiction, but due to the above, I'll let it slide.

Dad: I know how much you love reading, so I hope you enjoy this. You are the smartest, coolest, funniest dad in the universe—and now that's in print, no one can take it away from you. I love you, and am so grateful to have been raised by you.

Kylie: Thank you for being my sounding board through this and for your endless encouragement, always. I'd be as lost without you today as I would've been as a toddler. Also, please stop telling people I used to stick spaghetti in my vagina.

Jo: It makes me so angry you're not here for this. You were always my biggest champion. Your little namesake is you all over, so I feel like you're here, but I still miss you deep in my bones. Also, I'm sorry for getting in bed with you naked that time, but in my defence, I've done some pretty stupid shit while sober, too. Consider it proof of how much I adored you.

Bev: If there was an award for the world's best pseudo-mum, you'd take it out. Your honesty, wisdom and guidance is pure gold. Thank you for *everything*, and especially for making room for me—literally and figuratively—in your lives.

The Murdoch team: I don't quite have the words to thank you for taking a chance on me. Thank you for your foresight, wisdom, guidance and for just 'getting it', every step of the way. Special thanks to Kelly, Julie and Claire—without whom this book wouldn't exist. You made my words infinitely better and I'll never be able to repay you (unless we sell heaps of copies and I take you out for lunch, then we'll be even).

The Lifestyle Suite team: Sim, writing a book while on maternity leave was the best worst idea you've ever had. Thank you for your unwavering faith in me, I am forever grateful to be a part of the stable and, more importantly, a part of the family.

Vonne, Anton, Emma, Charlie and Mase: What a wonderfully fucked-up family tree ours is. I'm grateful you're all in it with me, and love you dearly. My door is always, *always* open to you.

Remi and Lucas: I'm sorry I've been away for so long, but you are in my thoughts and my heart always. You two will take over the world, please don't forget Aunty Cassata on your way up and know my door is always, *always* open to you, too.

Meera, James, Jack, Tilda, Charlotte and Sensei: Thank you for your refuge, your unconditional love and my late-life adoption. Home is where the heart is, and my heart is always with you. Meera—you pulled me through when I couldn't see the way out, and taught me that no matter who you are or what you've done, you are worthy of love, respect, kindness and acceptance. So really, this book is because of you.

Nic, Jack, Arch, Smokes and Moo: My Sydney family, I have so much to thank you for. But the main one is giving me my people in a place in which I had none. I'm forever grateful for our connection and for the trust you placed in me to care for the most important things in the world to you. You having my back is one of the best things to ever happen to me. Thank you.

Nan: There aren't enough good words in the world to describe you, but I hope you know how much I appreciate everything you've done for me. I'm so grateful for our relationship and for your matriarchy—you are the jewel in our crown and the apple of my eye. I love you.

My blood family: You know who you are. I'm so lucky to have grandparents, aunties, uncles, cousins and more who I love but also genuinely like.

My in-law family: I'm so grateful to have been welcomed into your families with open arms. Thank you for accepting me in all my flawed glory and for being the kindest, most down-to-Earth people I could've ever asked to have the pleasure of spending time with.

My girlfriends: You know who you are. You are my sisters and I simply couldn't do life without you. Thank you for your never-ending support and the endless LOLs.

Jenna: I don't know what I did to deserve you, but as far as besties go, I won the lottery with you. Thank you for your sisterhood, your next-level support and for always, always having my back. I love you, even if you fall asleep within three seconds of lying down, which you know makes me furious.

Karen: Thank you for pouring time and energy into helping build me into the woman I am. I'm forever grateful for what we achieved together, but also for our travels and laughs—you taught me more about business and life than I'll ever be able to repay you for. Thank you.

Norman: Thank you for taking a chance on me. I'm forever grateful and will never, ever forget everything you taught me. You gave me a thirst for evidence and a knack for communication that has given me a career I could never have dreamed of. Thank you, thank you, thank you.

To the bad girls who've gone before me: I adore you. Thank you for being the badarses you are, even when you copped flack for it.

To the incredible experts I work with: Thank you for being so smart and letting me ask you all the dumb questions. I'm in awe of you and filled with gratitude to have you in my life, especially those of you who gave me your time to contribute here.

To all of the people who work their butts off and don't get enough credit for it: Our teachers, nurses, aged-care workers, carers, firefighters, cleaners, drivers, waitstaff. I see you. Your time will come.

And lastly—to you, my reader. I hope this book feels like a big warm hug, and if you ever see me in the street, please stop me and ask me for one.

Support services

If you're struggling to cope in ways that are beyond the scope of this book, there are people out there who can help. Please don't hesitate to reach out to any of these free services.

Australia
Alcohol and Drug Foundation: 1300 85 85 84 | adf.org.au
Alcoholics Anonymous Australia: 1300 222 222 | aa.org.au
Beyond Blue: 1300 224 636 | beyondblue.org.au
Counselling Online (free 24/7 drug and alcohol counselling): counsellingonline.org.au
Family Drug Helpline: 1300 660 068
Family Drug Support Australia: 1300 368 186
Kids Helpline: 1800 551 800 | kidshelpline.com.au
Lifeline: 13 11 14 | lifeline.org.au
National Sexual Assault, Domestic Family Violence Counselling Service: 1800 RESPECT (1800 737 732) | 1800respect.org.au
Perinatal Anxiety & Depression Australia (PANDA): 1300 726 306 | panda.org.au
ReachOut.com: au.reachout.com
Sexual Assault and Abuse Helplines: healthdirect.gov.au/sexual-assault-and-abuse-helplines

Canada

Shelter Safe: sheltersafe.ca

Suicide Action Montréal: 1 866 277 3553 (outside Montréal) or 514 723 4000 (Montréal)

International

Better Help: betterhelp.com

New Zealand

Lifeline: 0800 543 354 | lifeline.org.nz

SHINE (Safer Homes in New Zealand Everyday): 0508 744 633 | 2shine.org.nz

United Kingdom

Heads Together: headstogether.org.uk

National Domestic Abuse Helpline: 0808 2000 247 | nationaldahelpline.org.uk

Samaritans: 116 123 | samaritans.org

United States

Lifeline: 1 800 273 8255

National Domestic Violence Hotline: 1 800 799 SAFE (7233) | thehotline.org

Good things to get your eyes and ears around

If you're looking for more inspiration, here are some resources I highly recommend checking out.

Books

The Anti-Cool Girl
Rosie Waterland

The Barefoot Investor
Scott Pape

Becoming
Michelle Obama

Come: A Memoir
Rita Therese

Committed
Elizabeth Gilbert

Daring Greatly and *Rising Strong*
Brené Brown

Everything Is Figureoutable
Marie Forleo

*Everything Is F*cked: A Book About Hope*
Mark Manson

The Girl With The Lower Back Tattoo
Amy Schumer

*The Life-Changing Magic Of Not Giving A F**k*
Sarah Knight

Princesses & Pornstars
Emily Maguire

The Resilience Project
Hugh van Cuylenburg

The Social Rebellion
Maz Compton

Think Like a Monk
Jay Shetty

This Will Only Hurt A Little
Busy Philipps

The Trauma Cleaner
Sarah Krasnostein and Sandra Pankhurst

Untamed
Glennon Doyle

The Women's Brain Book
Sarah McKay

Work Strife Balance
Mia Freedman

Podcasts

Armchair Expert
Dax Shepherd

Conversations
ABC

Dying For Sex
Nikki Boyer

No Filter
Mia Freedman

Well-thy
Casey Beros

Websites

Better Health Channel Vic
betterhealth.vic.gov.au

Brené Brown
brenebrown.com

Harvard Health Publishing
health.harvard.edu

Health Direct
healthdirect.gov.au

Marie Forleo
marieforleo.com

Mayo Clinic
mayoclinic.org

Moneysmart
moneysmart.gov.au

The Butterfly Foundation
butterfly.org.au

The Heart Foundation
heartfoundation.org.au

Women in Super
womeninsuper.com.au

Other

Holly Butcher's letter
facebook.com/hollybutcher90/posts/10213711745460694

TED talk by Brené Brown: 'The Power of Vulnerability'
ted.com/talks/brene_brown_the_power_of_vulnerability

Bibliography

Abramovitz B.A. and Birch, L.L., 'Five-year-old girls' ideas about dieting are predicted by their mothers' dieting', *Journal of the American Dietetic Association*, 2000, 100(10):1157–1163

Ackerman, C., 'What is self worth and how do we increase it?', *Positive Psychology*, positivepsychology.com/self-worth

Alcohol and Drug Foundation, Alcohol, adf.org.au/drug-facts/alcohol

Anik, L., Aknin, L., Norton, M. and Dunn, E., 'Feeling Good About Giving: The Benefits (and Costs) of Self-Interested Charitable Behavior', *Harvard Business School, Harvard Business School Working Papers*, 2009, 10.2139/ssrn.1444831

Australian Broadcasting Corporation (ABC), *How does your income compare to everyone else's?*, abc.net.au/news/2019-05-21/income-calculator-comparison-australia

Australian Government Department of Health, *Overweight and Obesity*, health.gov.au/internet/main/publishing.nsf/Content/Overweight-and-Obesity

Australian Human Rights Commission, *Risk of Homelessness in Older Women*, humanrights.gov.au/our-work/age-discrimination/projects/risk-homelessness-older-women

Australian Institute of Health and Welfare (AIHW), *Behaviours & Risk Factors—Alcohol*, aihw.gov.au/reports-data/behaviours-risk-factors/alcohol/overview

Australian Institute of Health and Welfare (AIHW), *Data tables: Deaths in Australia 2019*, via aihw.gov.au/reports/life-expectancy-death/deaths/data; Source: AIHW National Mortality Database (Table S3.2). via aihw.gov.au/reports/life-expectancy-death/deaths-in-australia/contents/leading-causes-of-death

Australian Institute of Health and Welfare (AIHW), *Family, domestic and sexual violence in Australia, 2018*, aihw.gov.au/reports/domestic-violence/family-domestic-sexual-violence-in-australia-2018/contents/summary

Australian Institute of Health and Welfare (AIHW), *Impact of overweight and obesity as a risk factor for chronic conditions: Australian Burden of Disease Study*, Australian Burden of Disease Study series no.11, 2017, Cat. no. BOD 12. BOD, Canberra: AIHW

Australian Psychological Society, *Australian Loneliness Report*, researchbank. swinburne.edu.au/file/c1d9cd16-ddbe-417f-bbc4-3d499e95bdec/1/2018-australian_loneliness_report.pdf

Australian Psychological Society, *Stress & wellbeing: How Australians are coping with life*, headsup.org.au/docs/default-source/default-document-library/stress-and-wellbeing-in-australia-report.pdf

Bailey, A., 'Here's Lady Gaga's Moving Best Original Song Speech From The Oscars', *Elle*, elle.com/culture/celebrities/a25740522/lady-gaga-oscars-2019-acceptance-speech-transcript

Better Health Channel, *Genes and genetics explained*, betterhealth.vic.gov.au/health/conditionsandtreatments/genes-and-genetics

Beyond Blue, *Anxiety*, beyondblue.org.au/the-facts/anxiety

Black Dog Institute, *Facts about Suicide in Australia*, blackdoginstitute.org.au/resources-support/suicide-self-harm/facts-about-suicide-in-australia

Bonomo Y., et al., 'The Australian drug harms ranking study', *Journal of Psychopharmacology*, 2019, Jul, 33(7):759–768

Breast Cancer Network Australia (BCNA), *Risk Factors*, bcna.org.au/breast-health-awareness/risk-factors

Brown, B., *Rising Strong*, New York: Penguin Random House, 2015

Brown, B., 'What being sober has meant to me', brenebrown.com/blog/2019/05/31/what-being-sober-has-meant-to-me/

Cancer Research UK, *How chemotherapy works*, cancerresearchuk.org/about-cancer/cancer-in-general/treatment/chemotherapy/how-chemotherapy-works

Credit Suisse Research Institute, *Global Wealth Report*, 2019, p. 5, accessed 2 October 2019 via investopedia.com/articles/personal-finance/050615/are-you-top-one-percent-world.asp

Cure Brain Cancer Foundation, *Facts & Stats*, curebraincancer.org.au/page/8/facts-stats

Feldman Barrett, L., *You Aren't at the Mercy of Your Emotions—Your Brain Creates Them*, December 2017, ted.com/talks/lisa_feldman_barrett_you_aren_t_at_the_mercy_of_your_emotions_your_brain_creates_them

Forleo, M., 'Decision Making: 4 simple steps to help you make the right decision every time', marieforleo.com/2017/02/decision-making

Harvard Health, *Exercise is an all-natural treatment to fight depression*, health.harvard.edu/mind-and-mood/exercise-is-an-all-natural-treatment-to-fight-depression

Health Direct, *Dopamine*, healthdirect.gov.au/dopamine

Health Direct, *Drug abuse*, healthdirect.gov.au/drug-abuse

Health Direct, *HIV infection and AIDS*, healthdirect.gov.au/hiv-infection-and-aids

Health Direct, *Sexual abuse*, healthdirect.gov.au/sexual-abuse

Health Direct, *Substance abuse*, healthdirect.gov.au/substance-abuse

Institute For Women's Policy Research, *Employment and earnings*, statusofwomendata.org/explore-the-data/employment-and-earnings/employment-and-earnings

Jantz, G., '8 traits of people with healthy self esteem', *Psychology Today*, psychologytoday.com/au/blog/hope-relationships/201608/eight-traits-people-healthy-self-esteem

Jean Hailes, *Women's Health Survey 2019*, jeanhailes.org.au/research/womens-health-survey/survey2019

Kahneman, D. and Deaton, A., 'High income improves evaluation of life but not emotional well-being', *Proceedings of the National Academy of Sciences*, September 2010, 107(38): 16489–16493

La Trobe University, *Understanding why women have abortions*, latrobe.edu.au/news/articles/2019/opinion/understanding-why-women-have-abortions

Legal Aid Western Australia, *Sex and consent*, legalaid.wa.gov.au/find-legal-answers/young-people/sex-and-law/sex-and-consent

Lowes, J. and Tiggemann, M., 'Body dissatisfaction, dieting awareness and the impact of parental influence in young children', *British Journal of Health Psychology*, 2003, May, 8(Pt 2):135–147

Maguire, E., *Princesses & Pornstars*, Melbourne: The Text Publishing Company, 2008

Mann, M., et al., 'Self-esteem in a broad-spectrum approach for mental health promotion', *Health Education Research*, August 2004, 19(4): 357–372

Mayo Clinic, *Being assertive: Reduce stress, communicate better*, mayoclinic.org/healthy-lifestyle/stress-management/in-depth/assertive/art-20044644

McCrindle, *Fast facts on marriages in Australia*, mccrindle.com.au/insights/blog/fast-facts-marriages-australia

McInerny, N., *We don't 'move on' from grief. We move forward with it*, November 2018, ted.com/talks/nora_mcinerny_we_don_t_move_on_from_grief_we_move_forward_with_it

McKay, S., *The Women's Brain Book*, Sydney: Hachette Australia, 2018

MedlinePlus, *What is epigenetics?*, ghr.nlm.nih.gov/primer/howgeneswork/epigenome

Mineo, L., 'Good genes are nice, but joy is better', *Harvard Gazette*, news.harvard.edu/gazette/story/2017/04/over-nearly-80-years-harvard-study-has-been-showing-how-to-live-a-healthy-and-happy-life

Mollenhorst, G., Völker, B. and Flap, H., 'Social contexts and personal relationships: The effect of meeting opportunities on similarity for relationships of different strength', *Social Networks*, 2008, 30: 60–68

Monash Business School, *How the gender gap hits the superannuation of Australian women early*, monash.edu/impact/articles/superannuation/how-the-gender-gap-hits-australian-womens-superannuation-early

National Eating Disorders Collaboration, *Eating Disorders in Australia*, nedc.com.au/eating-disorders/eating-disorders-explained/something/eating-disorders-in-australia

National Health and Medical Research Council (NHMRC), *Australian guidelines to reduce health risks from drinking alcohol*, nhmrc.gov.au/health-advice/alcohol

National Institutes of Health (NIH), *Osteoporosis and related bone diseases national resource centre*, Exercise for Your Bone Health, bones.nih.gov/health-info/bone/bone-health/exercise/exercise-your-bone-health

Neff, K., *The space between self-esteem and self compassion*, February 2013, youtube.com/watch?v=IvtZBUSplr4

Office for National Statistics, *Gender pay gap in the UK: 2019*, ons.gov.uk/employmentandlabourmarket/peopleinwork/earningsandworkinghours/bulletins/genderpaygapintheuk/2019

Orth, U., Robins, R. and Widaman, K., 'Life-span development of self-esteem and its effects on important life outcomes', *Journal of Personality and Social Psychology*, 2012, 102: 1271–1288

Pape, S., *The Barefoot Investor*, Milton: Wiley, 2017

Robbins, M., *How to Stop Screwing Yourself Over*, June 2011, ted.com/talks/mel_robbins_how_to_stop_screwing_yourself_over

Rowe H., Holton S.H., Kirkman M.M., et al., 'Prevalence and distribution of unintended pregnancy: The understanding fertility management in Australia national survey'. *Australian and New Zealand Journal of Public Health*, 2016, 40(2):104–09

Royal Australian College of General Practitioners (RACGP), *Alcohol tops study ranking drug harms in Australia*, racgp.org.au/newsgp/clinical/alcohol-tops-study-ranking-drug-harms-in-australia

Shaffer, J., 'Neuroplasticity and Clinical Practice: Building Brain Power for Health', *Frontiers in Psychology*, 2016, 7: 1118

Slepian, M., Chun, J. and Mason, M., 'The Experience of Secrecy', *Journal of Personality and Social Psychology*, 2017, 113(1): 1–33

Taft A.J., Shankar M., Black K.I., et al., 'Unintended and unwanted pregnancy in Australia: A cross-sectional, national random telephone survey of prevalence and outcomes'. *The Medical Journal of Australia*, 2018, 209(9):407–08

The Butterfly Foundation, *Myths about eating disorders*, butterfly.org.au/eating-disorders/myths-about-eating-disorders

The Foundation for Young Australians, *The New Work Smarts: Thriving in the New Work order*, fya.org.au/wp-content/uploads/2017/07/FYA_TheNewWorkSmarts_July2017.pdf

The Last Dance, directed by Jason Hehir, performance by Michael Jordan et al., ESPN Films and Netflix, 2020

Victoria State Government, *What is bullying?*, education.vic.gov.au/about/programs/bullystoppers/Pages/what.aspx

Waldinger, R., *What makes a good life? Lessons from the longest study on happiness*, November 2015, ted.com/talks/robert_waldinger_what_makes_a_good_life_lessons_from_the_longest_study_on_happiness

Williams, O.E., Lacasa, L. and Latora, V., 'Quantifying and predicting success in show business', *Nature Communications*, 2019, 10: 2256

'Winfrey's Commencement address', *Harvard Gazette*, news.harvard.edu/gazette/story/2013/05/winfreys-commencement-address/

Workplace Gender Equality Agency, *Australia's Gender Pay Gap Statistics 2020*, wgea.gov.au/data/fact-sheets/australias-gender-pay-gap-statistics

Index

abortions 199–200
Abraham, Keith 228
actors 246–7
addiction 190–5
alcohol 97–110
  addiction to 190
  alternative coping mechanisms 109–10
  choosing to reduce intake 70, 107–8
  consumption guidelines 104
  effect on health 105–6
  reducing intake when anxious 45
  in social situations 30–1, 97–103, 158
  when alcohol becomes a problem 106–9
  why we drink 104, 109
  your relationship with 103, 106–9
Alexander, Preeya 44–5, 46, 105, 147
ambition, and reality 42–3
antidepressants 46, 93
anxiety and worry 27–48
  depression 43–7
  finding the good in 33–4
  prevalence of 32
  things to stop worrying about 40–3
  vulnerability to 32
  ways of managing 38–40, 45–7
  what not to do 30–2
apologising 15–16, 239
apps 45
Aspen 213
assertiveness 236–7, 238
Australian Department of Health, exercise recommendations 93
Australian Human Rights Commission 119
Australian Institute of Health and Welfare 104
Australian Loneliness Survey (2018) 169
Australian Psychological Society 120
awareness 39, 57–8

Baby Boomers 249
bad boys 160–1, 163
bad, how to define 2
Bali 155, 156, 157, 161
The Barefoot Investor (Pape) 121
Barrett, Lisa Feldman 55
belief systems, regarding sex 135–7
belonging 170, 194, 266
Bennett, Vanessa 231
Beyoncé 91
Beyond Blue 32, 47
binge drinking 104, 105
blame 41
blowouts 96

the body 80–96
　acceptance of 41
　effect of alcohol on 105–6
　tuning into 74–5
　weight control 82–96
body image 82, 88
body shaming 251
boundaries, pushing of 2
bowerbirds 69
the brain
　effect of alcohol on 105–6
　emotions and the brain 52–6
　perception of threats by 31–2, 47
　plasticity of 57
brain cancer 177–8, 181
break-ups 195–9
Brown, Brené 9–10, 106
budgeting 120–2
Buffett, Warren 127
business ownership 126
Butcher, Holly 182–4
Byron Bay 266

caffeine 45
career diversity 248
careers *see* professional success
celebrities 244–56
centrefolds 254–5
Chambers, Jaime Rose 94
change 15, 209
charity 69
chemotherapy 182–3
Chicago Bulls 210
child sex abuse 185, 187
childhood 19–20
children 117, 264–5
chlamydia 147
choices
　about food 95–6
　about things that affect well-being 70
　at a micro level 7
　choosing designated times to worry 39–40

choosing friends 70, 173
choosing someone kind 262–3
choosing to reduce alcohol intake 70, 107–8
how to make better decisions 76–8
practising making choices 71
clothes 129–30
comparing oneself, with others 71, 129–30, 249
compassion, for oneself 68, 95
Compton, Maz 107–9, 255–6
condoms 146–7
confidants 16
conflict 234–43
connection, with others 59–60
consent 185–6
consumerism 70
contingency plans 227–8
contraction, versus expansion 75
contradictions, living with 270
control 36–7
conversations, tough 234–43
counsellors 47, 237
Covid-19 228
creativity 127

dancing 215–16
dating 162
de-cluttering 71–2
death and dying 43–4, 176–84, 271–2
decision making 76–8
depression 43–7, 70
Di Lullo, Roni 127
dieting 82, 83, 89–90
Disney, Walt 228–9
Disneyland 228–9
dopamine 143
drug abuse 190–5

eating disorders 80–2
education 72, 219–21
emotional baggage 271

288　THE 'BAD' GIRL'S GUIDE TO ~~GOOD~~ BETTER

emotional intelligence 49–60
emotional literacy 51–3
emotions
  emotional toolkit 57–60
  negative emotions 51, 58
  in personal conversations 242
  physical reactions to 52
  temporary nature of 59
endorphins 70
environment, versus genes 22–5
epigenetics 22
epitaphs 64
Ewing's sarcoma 182
exercise
  benefits of 69–70
  to control weight 90
  guidelines for 93–4
  to manage stress 45
  transforming emotions through 59
  weight-bearing exercise 93
expansion, versus contraction 75

fads, in eating 89–91
failure 28–9, 46, 63, 64, 165, 222, 229, 246
fame 244–56
family 117, 186, 265–7
Farnham, John 142
fasting 94
fault-finding 41
fear, in tough conversations 239–40
fight-or-flight response 31–2
finance *see* money management
first love 152–5, 163
food
  eating healthily 82–4, 90, 91–2
  making choices about 95–6
  mindful eating 94
  positive role of 88
  pretty-good-most-of-the-time approach 84–7
forgiveness
  of one's parents 18–26
  of oneself 13

Forleo, Marie 75
friendships 164–73
  characteristics of good friendships 170–1
  choosing friends 70, 173
  drifting apart 165–6, 172
  going with gut feelings 168, 173
  impermanence of 66, 171
  lowering your expectations about 172–3
  relation to happiness 168–71
  types of friends 166–8, 173

gender inequality, and money 116–19
gender pay gap 116–17
genes, versus environment 22–5, 32
genital warts 147
goals 211–12, 248–9
godparents 265–7
Goldstein, Nikki 13, 134–5, 136, 137, 160
good, how to define 2
gratitude 66, 71, 182, 272
Great Depression 168
grief 176–84
Guccione, Bob 254
gut, learning how to trust 73–5, 79

Hailes, Jean 32
Hall, Leanne 90
happiness
  friendships and 168–71
  money and 114–16, 128
Harvard long-term study 168–9
having a go 221–3, 255, 271
Hefner, Hugh 100
herpes 147
Hilton, Paris 134, 253
HIV 143–6, 147
hormones 55
Horton, Shelly 250–2
house purchases 123–4
hunger, living with 94
hydration 95

identification 57–8
imaginary scenarios 29–30, 37
imperfection, acceptance of 28–9, 68, 91
imposter syndrome 231–2
incest 185
indecent assault 185
infidelity 42, 163
influencers 250, 251
ING 122
intuition 73–5, 79
investing 126–7

job loss 200–1, 205–6
Jordan, Michael 210

Kalgoorlie 156
Kardashian, Kim 134, 253
kindness
  to oneself 68, 95, 221
  in a partner 262–3
Krasnostein, Sarah 226

labiaplasty 147–9
Lady Gaga 229–30
The Last Dance (documentary) 210
Law of Jante 245
libido 140–1
life lessons 4–5
life roadmap 78–9
life-work balance 264–5
Lifeline 47
liking oneself 61–79, 91
listening 168, 170, 235–6, 237
Lohan, Lindsay 253
loneliness 169
Longley, Luc 128–9, 210–11, 212
love
  break-ups 195–9
  first love 152–5, 163
  kindness in a partner 262–3
  the man-meth 160–1, 163
  'the one' 150–63
  the outlier 155–60

the 'this is it' person 161–2, 257–63
Lowinger, Jodie 31, 33–4
luck 42
lust, and sex 137–8

Maguire, Emily 132
'making it' *see* fame
the man-meth 160–1, 163
marriage 261
McInerny, Nora 177–80
McKay, Sarah 38, 52, 54, 57, 105–6
McKibbin, Gemma 186–8
McMillan, Joanna 88
mediators 237
medical abortions 199
medication, for anxiety and depression 46
meditation 45, 109
mental illness *see* anxiety and worry; depression
mentors 224–6
Mercury, Freddie 254
#MeToo movement 185
the mind 54–6
mindful eating 94
mindfulness 68, 142
mistakes, separating from 7–17
money management 111–31
  automating costs 122
  budgeting 120–2
  comparing oneself with others 129–30
  deciding what you want 120
  financial education 117–18
  increasing income 123, 125–7
  living within your means 113
  money and gender inequality 116–19
  money and happiness 114–16, 128
  money as a cause of stress 120
  reducing expenditure 123
  setting goals 123

setting up accounts 122
superannuation 118–19
value distinguished from wealth 115, 130
your relationship with money 127–9
mortality 43–4, 176–84, 271–2
mortgage insurance 124
Moss, Kate 84
motherhood 264–5
motivation 87–8, 230–1
movement *see* exercise
Musk, Elon 26

National Health and Medical Research Council 104
negative emotions 51, 58
negative thoughts 12, 37–8
negativity bias 31–2, 58
networks 66
neuroscience 52–5
New York City 214–16
Nietzsche, Friedrich 12
'no', learning how to say 236, 237
nutrition *see* food

obesity 85
Olympic Games 212
'the one' 150–63
opinions 40–2
the outlier 155–60
OWN (TV network) 229

Pankhurst, Sandra 226
Pape, Scott 121
parent–teacher days 203
parental leave 117
parents, forgiveness of 18–26
pay rises, asking for 240–2
Penthouse 99–100, 254
personal conversations, how to have 242
physical reactions, to emotions 52
planning 77–8, 207, 227–8

Playboy mansion party 99–103
pornography 142–3, 187
Princesses & Pornstars (Maguire) 132
Princeton University 114
privilege 112–13
problem solving 235
processed food 91–2
professional success 203–33
  dealing with self-doubt 231–2
  deciding what you want 217–18
  defining success 207–8, 212–13, 227
  developing a work ethic 209–12
  hunger for success 224–6
  learning from failure 229–30
  the non-linear road to success 204–7
  randomness of 216–17
  role of hard work 125, 208–12, 229–30, 255–6
  in show business 247
  ways of achieving 218–28
promiscuity 132–3, 138
pros-and-cons lists 76–7
psychologists 47
public speaking 223

Queen Mary University 247

rape 185
Ratajkowski, Emily 134
reality TV 252
rejection 197–9, 200–1
relationships, and happiness 168–70
religion, and sex 135
respect 170
right and wrong 12
ringworm 49–50
risk-taking 125
Rixon, Cheryl 99–100, 253–6
roadmap, for life 78–9
Robbins, Mel 209
Rumi 175

safe sex 146–7
secrets and secrecy 10–12, 13
self-acceptance 4, 39
self-awareness 39, 57–8
self-compassion 68, 95, 221
self-doubt 231–2
self-education 72, 219–21
self-esteem 62–6, 221
self-forgiveness 13
self-loathing 70, 246
self-love 61–79, 91
self-punishment 14, 15
self-worth 62–6, 133–5, 149, 160–1
sex 132–49
   attitudes towards 134–5
   belief systems regarding 135–7
   libido 140–1
   lust and sex 137–8
   safe sex 146–7
   sex education 138–40
   sexual self-worth 133–5, 149
   tips on enjoying sex 141–3
Sex and the City 165
sexual abuse 184–90
sexual desirability 134–5, 137
sexually transmitted diseases 143–7
shame 4, 9–10, 50
shares 127
Sharp, Tim 51, 52, 223–4
show business, success in 247
skinniness 84
sluts 132
social media 169, 249–52
The Social Rebellion (Compton) 107
social situations, feeling nervous in 30–1, 158
Stamp, Nikki 28–9, 231–2
Steines, Mark 250
stock market 127
stress 45, 120
substance abuse 190–5
success *see* professional success
suicide 43–4
superannuation 118–19

support, in a relationship 262–3
surgical abortions 199–200
survivors, of sexual abuse 188
Swinburne University 169
syphilis 147

tall poppy syndrome 216, 245
tattoos 150–2
therapy, for sexual abuse 189
the 'this is it' person 161–2, 257–63
thoughts
   negative thoughts 12, 37–8
   observing 72
time capsules 26
tough conversations, how to have 234–43
The Trauma Cleaner (Krasnostein) 226
traumatic events 174–202
   abortions 199–200
   addiction 190–5
   as anxiety triggers 32
   break-ups 195–9
   grief 176–84
   losing your job 200–1
   sexual abuse 184–90
trolls 251–2
trust 42, 73–4

uncertainty 34–5, 47
United States 213–14

vaginas 147–9
vegetables 92
victims, of sexual abuse 188
Virago, Zenith 175
volunteering 69

water 95
weight-bearing exercise 93
weight control 80–96
   eating disorders 80–2
   guidelines for 88–96
   measured approach to 84

motivation and 87–8
pretty-good-most-of-the-time
   approach 84–7
your relationship with food 82–4
weight loss industry 90
Winfrey, Oprah 229
women, causes of death 43–4
The Women's Brain Book (McKay)
   38, 57
Women's Health Survey (Hailes) 32

work *see* professional success
work ethic 209–12
work experience 220
work-life balance 264–5
work style 218
Workplace Gender Equality Agency
   118
worry *see* anxiety and worry
the worry bully 34–6
worst-case scenarios 37